GW01086814

The Murder of the
Whitechapel Mistress

The Murder of the Whitechapel Mistress

Victorian London's Sensational Murder Mystery

Neil Watson

PEN & SWORD
TRUE CRIME

First published in Great Britain in 2023 by
Pen & Sword True Crime
An imprint of Pen & Sword Books Limited
Yorkshire – Philadelphia

Copyright © Neil Watson 2023

ISBN 978 1 39904 974 0

The right of Neil Watson to be identified as
Author of this Work has been asserted by him in accordance
with the Copyright, Designs and Patents Act 1988.

A CIP catalogue record for this book is
available from the British Library

All rights reserved. No part of this book may be reproduced or
transmitted in any form or by any means, electronic or mechanical
including photocopying, recording or by any information storage and
retrieval system, without permission from the Publisher in writing.

Typeset by Mac Style
Printed in the UK by CPI Group (UK) Ltd, Croydon, CR0 4YY.

Pen & Sword Books Limited incorporates the imprints of After
the Battle, Atlas, Archaeology, Aviation, Discovery, Family History,
Fiction, History, Maritime, Military, Military Classics, Politics,
Select, Transport, True Crime, Air World, Frontline Publishing, Leo
Cooper, Remember When, Seaforth Publishing, The Praetorian Press,
Wharncliffe Local History, Wharncliffe Transport, Wharncliffe True
Crime and White Owl.

For a complete list of Pen & Sword titles please contact

PEN & SWORD BOOKS LIMITED
47 Church Street, Barnsley, South Yorkshire, S70 2AS, England
E-mail: enquiries@pen-and-sword.co.uk
Website: www.pen-and-sword.co.uk
or
PEN AND SWORD BOOKS
1950 Lawrence Rd, Havertown, PA 19083, USA
E-mail: uspen-and-sword@casematepublishers.com
Website: www.penandswordbooks.com

For my family – Gillian, Samantha & Mike, Thomas & Hannah, and especially my Granddaughter Emily, who I hope one day, will love history as much as I do.

++++

I also dedicate this book to all my old colleagues, some of whom have become lifelong friends:

(**Cannon Row**) 'Big Al' (A.K), 'Ginger' (G.A.), 'Anj' (P.A.), 'Slog' (M.D.), 'Smudger' (K.S.), 'Just' (J.C.), 'Squillet' (M.S), 'The Horses K' (K.W), 'Mick from NYC' (M.S.), 'The Guvnor' (Insp A.B.):

(**Wembley**) Jelly Belly (W.D.), Gazza (G.H.), Tommo (A.T.), Nina (N.S.):

(**Harrow**) Terry (T.T.), Hammy (H.B.), Monty (T.M.) Boys & Girls: You know who you are!

Contents

Dedication

I dedicate this book to the pursuit of justice and all the people that strive to see that criminals don't get away with murder. The Wainwright's very nearly got away with it 'Scot free' following the murder of Harriet Lane. It was a year to the day of the killing that a simple missing person case became a murder investigation.

Criminals should always have to look over their shoulders. They should never be able to relax. Too many lesser 'routine' crimes go unpunished these days. This is due to the drastic cuts in police numbers and increasing demands on the service. However, the police still have an excellent record on homicide investigations, which is a good thing for all of us.

The advent of DNA was a game changer in the world of crime detection. Its development has easily been the best new weapon for law enforcers for a century since the arrival of fingerprinting. Oh, how the Victorian detectives could have done with DNA; It would have made solving this case so much easier.

It is the pursuit of the truth and the great dedication of the police in finding the killer that should make all potential murderers consider their options. Have I thought of everything? Is my alibi sound? Have I destroyed 100% of all particles of blood and other DNA material? Was I seen on CCTV? Has my computer or mobile phone placed me at the scene or incriminated me?

The police go to extraordinary lengths when a major crime occurs. The police teams swing into action to maximize the *golden hour* which is then followed by weeks and months of hard work. Long tours of painstaking and often laborious work then follow, with the hope of getting a breakthrough. Some investigations take years; cold case reviews 20 years after a crime can sometimes catch a criminal who thought he had got away with it. We take it for granted that the police will try everything to bring the killer to justice.

I dedicate this book to the men and women of the British police service, the scientists, police civilians, and the Crown Prosecution Service who go the extra mile to strive for justice and to obtain a conviction. Murders are never '*solved*' in the space of a one-hour TV broadcast. It's to all those unsung heroes doing the leg work, unseen by the public, *and* all the paperwork!

Finally, I also dedicate this book to all the victims of crime and their loved ones. Sometimes people only remember the murderer when thinking back about an old crime. Everyone knows the name of Fred and Rosemary West, but can you name *any* of their victims? They should always be at the forefront of any investigation. We should *never* forget the victims. The tragic murder of Harriet Lane left many broken lives in its wake. She was a living, breathing, loving mother whose life was cruelly cut short. This book brings her memory back to life and tells her heartbreaking story.

About the Author

Neil Watson was a Metropolitan Policeman for 30 years during the turbulent times of the mid 1970s, ending his career in 2005. He served in central and north west London. Neil retired for a second time from his 'other' job as an anti-social behaviour officer in 2017.

He has written several articles about police history including the History of Pinner Police Station, as well as a chapter of the book *Discovering More Behind the Blue Lamp, Policing Central, North and South West London* by Peter Kennison, David Swinden and Alan Moss. The chapter covers the history of all five police stations in the London Borough of Harrow.

In 2018 his first solo book, *The Denham Massacre – 19th Century Britain's Most Shocking House of Horrors Murders*, was published. A second edition followed in 2019.

Neil is currently the Copy Editor for the *Whitechapel Society Journal* where he also writes historical articles on a wide range of unusual Victorian London topics. These have included:

Magnificent Seven: Kensal Green Cemetery (History of this huge London cemetery);

Newgate Prison's Auction of 'Creepy Lots' (The closure of Newgate Prison and the sale of items);

The Wormwood Scrubs Tragedy – 'Lucky' George and the Three P's (Murder by Pc Cooke of his 'girlfriend' on Wormwood Scrubs);

Whitechapel Vigilance Committee - Don't put your daughter on the stage Mrs Worthington! (The story of actress, Ada Reeve);

'You were only supposed to blow the bloody wall down' – The Clerkenwell Outrage of 1867 (Blowing up of the Clerkenwell House of Detention);

Whitechapel's David v Goliath – 'We shall not, we shall not be moved!' (The battle between Wickham's Department store and Spiegelhalters Jewellers shop);

Roll up, Roll up for the Greatest Show on Earth – (Jamrach's Whitechapel Menagerie);

Not saved by the bell – The Whitechapel Bell Foundry – (History of the Foundry);

Rota, the Pinner Garden Lion – (The WWII Lion who lived in a suburban garden which was gifted to Winston Churchill);

Oliver Twist – The Whitechapel Workhouse – Half a bed and breakfast! Can I have some more? (History of the Whitechapel Workhouse).

The Power of Historical Photography; Meeting John Hearn; Flash, Bang, Wallop – The life of a 12-year-old London criminal from his prison record and photo;

Florence Maybrick – Victim of Circumstance? Her life in prison, the Appeal Court and Defendants giving evidence.

Neil has a passion for all things history, including researching his, and friends' family histories for more than 25 years. He has also written historical articles for the Proud of Pinner Magazine.

Acknowledgements

Ancestry.com – Genealogical information regarding the characters mentioned in this book has been obtained using the wonderful Ancestry website: www. ancestry.co.uk

Bickley, Paul (Curator) – The Crime Museum, New Scotland Yard.

Bishopsgate Institute – Archive and Special Collection staff.

Blomer, Steve – Map expert who helped me finally track down the precise location of 215 Whitechapel Road, the murder scene.

British Newspaper Archive – Authority to reproduce images from the BNA with the kind permission of The British Newspaper Archive: www.britishnewspaperarchive. co.uk. This book would simply not have been possible without the help of the newspaper archive which finds amazing history at the touch of a button. Long lost items of historical interest are now available again due to this wonderful resource. I cannot recommend the B.N.A. highly enough to all budding historians. I'd also like to thank the BNS's, Data & Copyright Executive, Eddie Bundy at the BNA for his great assistance regarding copyright for the treasure trove of newspaper drawings.

Burgess, Sarah & Richard – For their unfailing encouragement in my historical writing over the last 5 years since we met at the Police Rehabilitation Centre, Goring in 2017.

Barnett, Gary & Isabel Couffot – Provided the information about Thomas Wainwright in prison, which kick started the idea of this book.

Dennett, Sandra – Friend and budding writer with a good eye for detail and advice for improving the text.

Eames, Ian (Bereavement Services Assistant) – City of London Cemetery and Crematorium Service.

Field, Duncan – Owner of 54 Borough High Street (originally the Hen and Chickens).

Hodges, Beverley – Waltham Abbey Town Council – For help in finding out details of Harriet Lane's burial at Waltham Holy Cross Cemetery.

Jordan, Amy – What can I say about Amy? She has been a complete joy to work with. She is forever positive, helpful and enthusiastic, with a cheerful Yorkshire charm. I'm in awe of her publishing and editing skills while she has calmly guided the book from its raw original state to this highly polished finished article. Like me, she is passionate about history and her work, and I'm delighted that I was lucky enough to to have gone through this project with her. Thank you Amy for all your many, many hours of hard work. Your input improved the book immeasurably!

London Metropolitan Archives – To the helpful staff who assisted me navigate the Archives amazing document collection.

National Archives, Kew – For assistance in researching the criminal case files for the matter of the Crown v Henry and Thomas Wainwright. The amazing N.A. at Kew is my favourite archive.

Parry, Sue – Writer and Historian. Without whom, this book would never have been written. In 2019, Sue suggested I take a look at this murder, which I had never heard of. I was immediately hooked, and we both visited the National Archives together where I read the case files. Sue has constantly encouraged and supported me during this project which has been a joy to do. Sue is an amazing historian and we work as a great team. She also rekindled my interest in history when she invited me to join the Whitechapel Society in 2017. I always refer to Sue as the Whitechapel Society, '*Big Cheese*'.

Pelling, Chris – My longest standing history pal of 35 years who was the first person to read the initial draft of the book. His input to the book was critical. The first draft is *never* good enough. Chris pointed out how the text could be improved and especially on how to improve the flow of the story. Chris also challenged me to make the story better. After Chris' critique, I completely rewrote quite a number of chapters, making it a far more exciting read, and his editing skills were crucial.

Severn, Oliver (London Cabbie) – Who drove me from the exact spot that Henry picked up Alice Day in his cab with the body of Harriet Lane and then drove to the Hen and Chickens.

Sivitar, Lindsay (Historian) – For help with details of some of the murder exhibits.

Slack, Claire (Tower Hamlets Cemetery Park) – She discovered the location of the Wainwright family grave and was so helpful when I visited to see the headstone for myself.

Skinner, Keith (Crime Historian and Author) – For help re the Hen and Chickens.

Smith, Dr Clare and Edward Smith (Curators) **Metropolitan Police Heritage Centre** – For assistance in discovering historical information on the policemen involved in the case.

Tower Hamlets Cemetery Park – Where the Wainwright Family grave is located. Manager, Kenneth Greenway was very helpful during my visit.

Watson, Gillian (My wife) – For allowing me once again, the time to go exploring the Victorian 1870's in search of another amazing murder case. She is my sternest critic when reading my work, but her support and editorial expertise have helped me make this a better book than it would otherwise have been. She is my handiest sounding board. Thank you darling!

Watson family – To all my family who I'm sure are tired of hearing me drone on about this case, but are secretly looking forward to reading the book?

Whitechapel Society – It was only because I am a member of the society that the idea for this book was born. I have been a member since 2017 and the Copy Editor for the WS Journal since 2019.

Introduction

D o you like jigsaw puzzles with a bit of mystery added? The thrill of opening an old chest; the anticipation of not knowing what you are going to find; shining a torch on a long-forgotten story of infidelity, cunning, family feuding and murder. It's a bit like the ingredients of a recipe. Then add some spice of Victorian London into the melting pot of Whitechapel, the bustle of Borough High Street and London Bridge and the efforts of the Metropolitan Police in trying to catch a calculating killer. Well, I love all of the above, and I suspect the fact that you have picked up this book and are reading this, means you do as well.

I have been writing about history and genealogy in my spare time on and off over the last 20 years. I've found it to be a wonderful and intriguing hobby and one that I *never* grow tired of. I have been very lucky with all my research and writing, and fortunately people seem to enjoy what I have written.

When I am deciding what to write about next, it's often a suggestion from a friend or an accidental discovery when I trip over a new case. What I always insist on however, is that the subject matter immediately draws you in and that it has elements of mystery, plus a story that makes you sit up and take notice. Going back to my school days, my English and History teacher, 'Billy' Bishop used to read us the adventures of Sherlock Holmes and Dr Watson. Mr Bishop ignited my fascination in history, but particularly the London of Queen Victoria.

Ever since those far off school days, history generally, and that of Victorian London, has been my passion, so that's what I predominantly write about. In 2014, I 'tripped' over the story of the Denham Murders of 1870 and because it was such a unique and infamous crime, I decided that I needed to write its history. I loved every minute of researching and writing that book. I didn't think I would ever write another one as the last one took so long to compile.

The story of the Wainwright Murder of 1875 has literally taken over my life. When I am researching and writing, I'm transported to another time and place, usually it's 1870's Whitechapel. In 2019, my 'history buddy' Sue Parry, suggested that I have a look at the 'Wainwright Murder' case. I had never heard of it, but I set off with the intention of writing a short article on it for the Whitechapel Society.

This crime really has everything you want in a Victorian 'whodunnit'. There are still some mysteries about the murder itself. It was a case of the attractive Harriet Lane ruthlessly being lured to her death and being killed by a devious set of brothers, Henry and Thomas Wainwright who so nearly got away with it, but for some schoolboy errors. As captivating as this story is, so many lives were ruined by the tragic events and poor Harriet Lane lay undiscovered for a year. This is her story. It's one you shouldn't miss.

Once I had written the three-page article about the case, a key development occurred. Sue Parry, who is my go-to history guru, then pointed me in the direction in finding a previously undiscovered prison record for one of the brothers, Thomas Wainwright. This amazing document contained some very revealing facts about the case and it was at that moment the book was conceived. Soon after this revelation, I found a huge archive of drawings about the case in the *Police Illustrated News*.

That discovery was a jaw-dropping moment when, one after another, the murder was featured on the front pages, week after week. All the characters and places that I had a vision of inside my head were now in front of me on paper. It was literally a *light bulb* moment as the ninety-two drawings appeared. It was the best discovery that I had made in 20 years of research.

What this is really about is the fact that history always has the power to both educate and excite us. The police arrest of Henry Wainwright is one of high drama, but with a, 'you couldn't make it up' quality. This Whitechapel Murder, unlike the other slightly more famous ones that came 13 years later, was rather more of a success for the police.

I have meticulously researched every facet of this case. I dread to think of all the hundreds of stolen hours of research I have done at 6.00am when I couldn't sleep, or at midnight when I was in a seam of history gold, not wanting to go to bed.

I love the amount of detail that I have been able to discover about this case; it has been a joy to investigate as more and more information kept coming to light. I have done a lot of the research online, but the best part has been visiting all the various archives where you can get your hands on actual items from the murder. Perhaps the best moment was finding, in the National Archives, a letter and envelope written by poor Harriet Lane to her parents. The same visit also produced a large plan of the murder scene. The handwritten prison statements of both Henry and Thomas Wainwright were also an amazing find and their contents allow us to hear both suspects speak.

I absolutely commend you to read this unusual story; I have tried to write in a very readable way as well as with the occasional wry smile. The details of the case are not for the fainthearted. It's a story that rattles along. It's a drama that will transport you to the London of horse drawn hackney cabs, of scenes where everyone seemed to wear a moustache and a flat or bowler hat, and where having enough money for your next bed and meal was the primary concern. It's also a story keeps you guessing whodunnit! Prepare to be transported to 1875. I have been!

Neil Watson

Chapter One

The Main Players

Background to the case

Picture the scene. You are a pair of police constables on an unremarkable foot patrol when a breathless man shouts at you, 'Officer, stop that cab, there's a dead body inside.' What do you do? Do you; A. Ignore the man who is obviously mad, and is trying to play a trick on you? Or B; stop the cab and investigate if there is a parcel containing a sliced-up young woman?

It was precisely this unlikely scenario that faced two sets of officers, one pair in the City of London, who chose answer A, while a pair of Metropolitan policemen decided to give plan B a try. What happened next was to hit the headlines the following day with a sensational discovery of the body of a young mistress in two large bags.

The year is 1875 in Victorian London. Without the aid of fog and dark alleyways, or a plethora of knife wielding suspects, the 'Whitechapel Murder' of that year caused a sensation in the capital which kept the newspapers engaged for several months. The hacks chased a juicy story of a wealthy and respectable Henry Wainwright living a double life which ended in the brutal murder of a young, attractive mother.

Unlike the more sordid events of 1888 when all the victims of a certain 'Mr J. Ripper' were the flotsam and jetsam of East End slum dwellings, our earlier outrage was of an altogether more upmarket variety. It was also a more successful investigation for the hard-pressed officers of the Metropolitan Police who nabbed their suspect literally, red handed.

This was a remarkable story of wickedness, deception, lust, conspiracy, tragedy, and a man who was prepared to gamble with his life. Henry Wainwright was an unsuccessful card player who left many lives ruined in his wake. His life, which had started so brightly, went seriously off the rails in 1874, leading to his appearance in the dock of the Old Bailey a year later.

We need to set the scene on this incredible case which involved the weakness of an outwardly respectable Henry Wainwright. He turned into a devious and dangerous liar as he tried to cling onto his respectable and comfortable life and reputation, as all of his 'affairs' flew out of control.

The 1871 Census[1] gives us clues about the success of Henry Wainwright and his business at that time, before it was all to go horribly wrong. Henry had married Elizabeth Fanny Minshull in 1862. He and Elizabeth were then living at 40 Tredegar Square, Mile End, a beautiful terraced house of 3 floors and a basement looking out onto the attractive Tredegar Square Gardens.[2] His occupation was listed as a 'Brush maker, employing 103 men, women and boys', so business must have been flourishing.

Henry was a successful man, enjoying a good living from his brush manufacturing business. He was popular in the district, his business premises were nearby the local Pavilion Theatre, where he enjoyed the company of several of the actresses and dancing girls[3] rather more than was good for his reputation. Henry's father had died a year after Henry's wedding on 27 October 1863,[4] leaving him without a guiding hand for the rest of his life. Significantly however, he did leave him some of his money.[5]

The Hobart Mercury[6] painted a picture of Wainwright as something of a split personality; he was outwardly respectable as a pew holder at Trinity Church, Bow, and was involved in a local debating society as well as the Union Book Club. It went on to say that he was addicted to 'billiards and betting' leading to debts piling up, and that he was often to be found in the 'company of girls at the Pavilion Theatre' as well as 'girls of loose character'.

WAINWRIGHT BEHIND THE SCENES.

'Wainwright behind the scenes'. A drawing of Wainwright with Pavilion dancing girls. (*Courtesy of Bishopsgate Institute*)

In the late autumn of 1870, Mrs Elizabeth Wainwright found herself pregnant for the 5th time. Meanwhile her distinguished-looking husband was doing well at business and in life, and as a well-educated man with fingers in a number of pies, he had become well known in the district and had a swagger about him. His wife had fallen pregnant almost like clockwork every 2 years since the year after their marriage, and it's easy to imagine that the over confident Henry may have decided to look elsewhere for his home comforts.

The first three years of the early 1870s was going to prove to be a huge turning point for the fortunes of Henry Wainwright. His marriage, love of his children, financial stability, home and good name were about to come under threat like never before.

He was a man driven by the good life, money and the company of women especially. Mrs Wainwright was blissfully unaware of his East End adventures. Henry was very happy flirting with and receiving the attention of the show girls, especially when he was paying for their drinks. He was skating on thin ice for now, but he was soon to meet an attractive young woman with whom he would soon become completely and dangerously entwined.

From the day that Harriet Lane walked into his life, Henry was to gamble everything he held dear. He was embarking on a relationship which was akin to making a tightrope walk while carrying two large suitcases. It was a gamble of a lifetime that would not end well.

Henry Wainwright – The Good Times

As the main character of this East End tragedy, Henry Wainwright is arguably the most interesting of the Wainwright family. A man of many talents, not least in the use of language in which to entertain the local Whitechapelians as well as some of the female thespians of the Pavilion Theatre.

He was born in 1838[7] and his father, Henry William Wainwright, was a respected local businessman in the manufacturing of brushes at 84 Whitechapel Road. Henry had two sisters and five brothers. Two of his brothers, Charles and Alfred, had died young, so he was the second eldest male, and namesake of his father. He had the potential to go far. His elder brother, James, died in 1872, leaving him to compete for family supremacy with his brothers, William and Thomas.

Henry married Elizabeth Fanny Minshull on 7 August 1862,[8] at Stepney Parish Church. The nuptials had been mentioned in the *Birmingham Gazette*[9] and was the start of an initially successful partnership. Henry was described on the wedding certificate as, 'gentleman' and a rosy future for the well-educated and affluent couple beckoned. Five children then followed between October 1863 and June 1871.[10]

Henry's father died in 1863, but on a positive note, his father's death did mean that Henry would benefit from a slice of his father's fortune. The Probate Register[11] stated that the estate was worth 'under £4,000', around £397,759 in 2023* The will[12] made several points: His mother got all the household goods while the house at 7 Cambridge Terrace, Bromley-by-Bow, was to go to the son, James Wainwright; Number 84 Whitechapel Road was to go to Henry and William.

They were also to receive their father's shares in the 'Commercial Gas Company'. Henry and William were to have £50 each for expenses to perform their role as executors. James was to receive a gift of £150, Thomas and Alfred (Alfred was deceased by this point) were to get £100. The residue of the estate was to go to Henry and William.

It can be seen therefore that Henry and William were to receive the lion's share of the estate. Thomas Wainwright received a mere £100,[13] only a fraction of what his elder brother received. Could this have later affected his relationship with Henry?

Fourteen months into their marriage, the Wainwrights became parents to a son, Henry.[14] While Mrs Wainwright had her hands full at home with a new baby and more children to follow, Henry worked hard and played hard as he sought to take advantage of his near perfect station in life.

By 1860 Henry was a prominent member of the Christ Church Institute, St George's in the East, and was a supporter of both its musical as well as elocution classes. He could be found in an East End school giving a talk entitled 'An Evening with Thomas Moore'. His talents also stretched to taking part in private theatricals as well as giving readings from Dickens.[15]

A glimpse of what Henry's home life and personality was like before he got caught up in scandal is explained by a chance meeting Henry had with a new neighbour in Tredegar Square. A piece appeared in the book, *The Cosmopolitan Actor: His adventures all over the world*,[16] by J.B. Howe. Mr Howe, who was described as an 'East End tragedian of the day', happened to bump into Wainwright as he was passing Henry's house in Tredegar Square and was invited inside. Mr Howe took up the story;

> I was led to an elegantly furnished parlour. A pretty, dark lady entered with two lovely children. I elicited from him the fact that he was in some sense an actor himself that is, said he, "I play for charitable purposes sometimes, and also give lectures at the Bow and Bromley Institute and other places.

The two men then left in a cab together heading towards Whitechapel, Mr Howe enjoying his new friend's company along the way. He continued his observation of his neighbour: He jumped up saying, 'good-bye my dears' then kissing the children and his wife', he then joined Mr Howe in the cab:

As we drove along, I thought I had never encountered a nicer man. A fine head of hair, firmly balanced on square shoulders; raven locks, and large penetrating blue eyes and a really wonderful power of conversation.

The Penny Illustrated Paper[17] gave some further detail about Henry's after work activities in an article entitled, 'THE STORY OF WAINWRIGHT's LIFE'. The article stated that he had been educated at Stepney School, and was a member of the Sheridan Club where he performed entertainments such as 'an evening with Charles Dickens' and 'The Charge of the Light Brigade'.

Henry was a very active member of the United Book Society and was a pew holder at the Trinity Church in Bow where he would support any worthy causes. Henry's name regularly appeared in the Tower Hamlets Independent including on 17 April 1869 when he attended The Lyric Glee Union meeting where he read Tennyson's Balaclava Charge.

It was sad, to see the end of the *Penny Illustrated* article that the halo which had previously been floating just above his head, seemed to be slipping. Worryingly, the paper reported the following:

He became addicted to billiards and betting, and eventually found himself £300 or £400 in debt to a bookmaker for betting debts unpaid. He was frequently seen with the girls employed at the Pavilion Theatre and women of loose character.

Another report[18] described the appearance of Wainwright, with tell-tale hints about his allure to women:

In appearance Henry Wainwright is described as moderately tall, thick, and broad shouldered in build. There was a Jewish cast in his countenance, accentuated by a large nose and his dark brown hair and beard, waved and curly. His beard and moustache concealed a heavy and sensual mouth. His blue eyes were full and prominent, but with the curious dusky, sleepy look associated with those of Orientals. The whole effect of the face was by no means displeasing, and to women Mr Henry Wainwright was anything but unattractive.

If you look at a photo of Henry Wainwright, you can imagine him looking in the mirror in the morning, stroking his beard and feeling rather pleased with the image that was looking back at him.

The report continued:

> Among no class of people in the Whitechapel Road at that time was Wainwright more popular than with the actors at the Pavilion Theatre. The theatre was next door to Wainwright's shop at No. 84. Wainwright supplied them with brushes and mats, evinced great interest in all things connected with the drama, and enjoyed practically the free run of the theatre. He was always lavish in entertaining, and to actors getting very humble salaries it was a much-desired privilege to be asked out to sup with Mr Wainwright. Vanity played no small part in Wainwright's character.

He was spending too much of his time and money on the young actresses next door. It's hard to avoid the suspicion that Henry thought that his bohemian life, out of sight of Elizabeth, was of no consequence. His love of women and of himself was setting him on a course for disaster, but he couldn't see it coming.

Harriet Louisa Lane

The other main player in this case was a young woman from a working class family who grew up being blessed with beautiful hair and good looks. Harriet Lane was the daughter of John Lane and his wife Elizabeth Evans. The couple produced 9 children at regular intervals, all of them being born in Weymouth, Dorset. Elizabeth was blessed with twin girls on 3 November 1842. Sophia Ann Lane and Harriet Louisa Lane had arrived in the world. Sadly, Harriet died the following year in 1843. She was therefore the 'original' Harriet.

The last of the Lane children, Harriet was christened on 15 February 1852 in Holy Trinity Church,[19] Weymouth, and was named Harriet Louisa Lane, and so becoming the second child to bare that title. It was not uncommon in those days for parents to give the same name to another child after one had died earlier. The family later moved east, arriving in Ponders End at the end of the 1850s.

The Lane family were living at the newly built 'Ponders End Gas Works', where John was working as a 'manager of gas-works'. By 1871, 19-year-old Harriet was a milliner living with her parents at Alexandra Road, Waltham Abbey. Harriet had been learning her trade as a dressmaker and a milliner (making hats). The census[20] revealed that in 1871, Harriet was one of 300,000 dressmakers and milliners living in England and Wales.

Details of Harriet's apprenticeship[21] were provided by her friend, Ellen Wilmore, from the witness box at the Old Bailey. Ellen and Harriet had both been apprenticed together with Mrs Ann Bray[22] in Waltham Cross in 1866. Harriet had two, 2-year periods with her. *The Illustrated Police News* on 11 December 1875 provided a drawing of a shop premises with clothes and materials in the window. The sign above the door shows the shop to be called 'Walk Late', and the title of the image is 'Where Miss Lane was apprenticed'.

Thomas Wainwright

Many families have a designated 'black sheep' within their relations. In the Wainwright clan there were two, with Thomas being the younger 'sheep' alongside his brother Henry.

Thomas was the seventh of eight children, and the fifth boy to be born. His place in the pecking order of favourite children was always below brothers William and Henry. While his older brothers made a name for themselves, Thomas was always lagging behind in the race for sibling superiority.

The Wolverhampton Express & Star[23] gave us some details about his life in an article entitled, 'ANTECEDENTS OF THOMAS WAINWRIGHT.' The piece painted his working life as a series of highs and lows, and business failures. It stated that he had inherited money from his father and that later he had deserted his wife and children in order to live with another woman[24]. He then became an ironmonger in Westminster which eventually failed before taking on another venture in the Mile End Road which also went under. After these disappointments he travelled on commission, sometimes working for Henry before becoming a manager at an Oxford Street firm.

The South London Press[25] published details of another failed business in 1866. The brief notice read as follows; 'Partnerships Dissolved – George Smith Mells and Thomas George Wainwright furnishing ironmongers, 146 High Street, Borough, March 26.'

Thomas' life had been anything but plain sailing for a man who had come into a tidy inheritance from his father's estate. His many failed business ventures had left his finances in a perilous state, which, coupled with his dalliance with a married woman, made his life rather too complicated. After the problems he had faced in previous years, the last thing he needed as he approached his 30th birthday was to become embroiled in an infamous murder!

Chapter Two

The Affair

Henry meets Harriet – The Affair Begins

Our story begins in 1871, when 32-year-old Henry Wainwright met the very attractive and golden haired 19-year-old, Harriet Lane. Their eyes met and the affair began. She would easily have caught the eye of Henry, who was a secret 'ladies-man'[1]. The story of their affair was soon going to capture the attention of the British public like no other, as well as commanding thousands of column inches in *all* the newspapers. The Victorian public, not unlike today, liked a scandalous and saucy case to get their teeth into, and this story was going to run and run.

Harriet was apprenticed as a milliner in Waltham, where one of her fellow apprentices was a lady called Ellen Wilmore who features later on in the story. At the end of 1870 Harriet moved south to London. She was said to be

Harriet Lane, 'Supposed to have been murdered'. *Illustrated Police News* supplement, 27 November 1875. (*Copyright The British Library Board. All Rights Reserved*)

of 'superior education' with good writing skills, she had also been a nursery governess.[2] Harriet and Henry met at Broxbourne Gardens, a favourite pleasure resort for Londoners on the banks of the River Lea.[3]

Henry Wainwright, actually tells us in detail how he got to know Harriet in his own words later in this book. (*See chapter 27; Prison Statement by Henry Wainwright.*) Harriet and Miss Wilmore used to walk out together and they would pass Henry's shop and buy brushes from him. Polite conversation then followed between them until they later met on the platform of Broxbourne Station.

Although we don't have a proper record of that *Brief Encounter* moment, this is how it could have taken place. We do know that Henry bought flowers. (*This short fictional account is purely speculation, but is based on educated guesswork*). Henry tells us what might have happened:

I made my way towards Broxbourne Station, for my train to London. The day was sunny and warm, and everything seemed well with the world. As I approached the entrance to the southbound platform, I decided that I would buy some flowers from old Charlie Rochester from his little stall. I knew Miss Lane came this way by train, so I bought 2 small bunches of tulips on a whim, perhaps on the off chance of seeing her. Charlie had given me a knowing look and a little wink after he had asked me who the lucky lady was.

I bought my ticket and then strolled onto the platform waiting for the 20 past, Great Eastern train to arrive. There were few passengers about. As I checked my pocket watch and compared it to the large station clock on Platform 1, my attention was drawn to the figure of a young woman coming through from the entrance. She was neatly dressed and recognising her blonde hair immediately, it caused my heart to skip a beat. This woman was the attractive girl I had seen near my shop whom I knew came from this area.

What luck. She wasn't with her usual travelling companion, Miss Wilmore. What could be better? As she looked down the line, I could see my train approaching in the far distance. Miss Lane was by now in the near distance, only 30 yards away, and there were no other travellers between us. I took my chance and started to walk towards her. With the train slowing down but still not at the platform, she turned in my direction and our eyes met. 'Oh Mr Wainwright, what a surprise meeting you here, are you going to London'? I assured her that I was, and that I would be delighted to share a compartment with her.

As the steaming and smoking London train pulled in, it looked sparsely filled. I pulled open a door to an empty compartment and bade Miss Lane to enter. She sat facing towards London while I positioned myself opposite her. Suddenly the guards whistle blew and our door was slammed shut, we were off. As I sat looking at this beautiful young specimen of womanhood, I suddenly came under her spell. Her eyes sparkled and her warm smile melted my heart. She had a sweet voice, and as she spoke, I held onto her every word. At first, we spoke politely to one another, pleasantries really, then it happened. Alone in that train compartment, I picked up the tulips that I had placed on the seat.

Looking at her I told her how much I had enjoyed seeing and chatting to her before. I had only ever seen her with Miss Wilmore, but this was different. Her countenance dazzled me. I had never seen anyone so attractive. I was consumed with the excitement of that feeling of new love. When we had met previously, she had always smiled at me and given me a look as if she reciprocated my warmth towards her. Her body language and smiling face assured me that she was also attracted to me, as I was to her.

Without thinking of the consequences for a married man, the red and yellow tulips were thrust towards her to take. 'I got these for you'. She gushed with surprise, as I don't think she had ever had flowers given to her before. She was very grateful for the flowers, never for a moment refusing the offer of them.

In passing the flowers over we had both shuffled forwards on our seats. Our shoes were touching and her perfect, pink cheeks reddened slightly as we came withing touching distance of one another. Our eyes were locked together. Seeing her right up close for the very first time, I was thinking to myself, 'Harriet, you are simply divine'. I said something to her but I cannot recall what, but it was something complimentary.

She took hold of the tulips and put them to her nose, sniffing gently, then she whispered, 'They are beautiful Mr Wainwright'. As she placed them down, we remained close to one another across the carriage. She hadn't moved back in her seat. The wall behind her contained pictures of places of interest in England such as Norwich and Canterbury, but at that moment I wanted to be nowhere else but here, inches away from the astonishingly beautiful, Miss Lane.

I was trembling inside, as I had just taken a step I had never taken before, showing interest in a romantic way to another woman who wasn't my wife. I couldn't help myself. I was carried along by the fact that she seemed to be encouraging me and not moving away towards the window in distain. As we looked at one another for a moment, she took my hand in hers. As the train steamed southwards towards the first station and no one being able to see us, I lifted her small ungloved hand towards my mouth. I planted a soft kiss on the back of her hand.

Young Harriet may have been swept away in the excitement of her first love as well as the prospect of catching a well-heeled older man who might provide for her. The motivation for Henry was probably rather different. He was a married pillar of the community, with status, a wife and five children. His predatory attitude to attractive woman was more likely to have been his motivation. He was old enough to know better, and he was willing to risk everything on this pretty young lady. He had started the relationship for one reason: sex.

There then began a secretive and intensive relationship between the couple. She must have known that he was married. During this period, Henry was abroad on business a lot and the couple used to send letters to one another, using aliases to disguise the goings on.

The Trial of the Wainwrights gives a flavour of the new-found relationship, and described Harriet as 'a lively little woman with pleasing manners and a love of finery'.[4]

The Crown's 'brief' papers gave details of dozens of letters that had been received by Harriet from Henry, which had then been kept by Miss Wilmore in one of Harriet's boxes. (The original letters have not survived, only small transcripts from a few of them.)

The letters began in 1871. He always wrote using one of three aliases to avoid his love affair being discovered. The letters were written in assumed names between 'Miss L. Varco' or 'Mrs King' and 'George Williams', 'Mr George Varco' or 'Percy King'. The letters expose his feeling for her as he writes from abroad, by sending her, 'oceans of love.' His nervousness of being discovered is also evident. Some of the letters are reproduced below. The earliest letter is from the summer of 1871.

On 24 July 1871, George Williams writes:

Darling creature, off to Paris – for God's sake don't write etc drop me a line in about a fortnight, (if you don't in that time thoroughly forget me) to P.O., Whitechapel Road. Oceans of love. Believe me yours.

On 25 August 1871 he makes an appointment to meet 'Miss Varco' in the first-class waiting room at Bishopsgate Station. On 24 September 1871 he writes to her from Wiesbaden, this time signing himself 'George Varco'. He complained of having been travelling for fourteen hours on a train:

It is very uncertain how long I shall stay away from England, perhaps for ever, God knows, so think no more of me, and quite forget you ever saw me. Yours most affectionately, Geo. VARCO.

A letter from Strasburg follows this: 'My little Beauty, drop me a line to P.O. by Dec. 1st, if you don't forget me, as in all probability you will. George Williams.' It seems likely that as soon as he returned to England late in 1871, Harriet became pregnant by Henry.

In November 1872, he writes to her at 26 Alfred Place, asking to meet her at Temple Bar. Between January 1873 and August 1873, twenty-five letters from Henry were received at her abode at 20 Cecil Street, The Strand. The nature of their secret assignations is evident in a letter dated 20 May 1873. It reads; 'My Dear Child, I will be with you tonight about 8pm, open the door for me yourself. Yours for ever, Percy'.

A further seventeen letters and telegrams were sent to Harriet at 17 St Peter Street. The intimacy between the couple had ripened quickly after his return from Germany. It's a shame that all these love letters have been lost, even though they were obviously important to Harriet.

Inevitably, the affair, which had ripened quickly after Henry's return from Germany, led to Harriet giving birth on 7 August 1872 to a daughter, Beatrice,[5] fourteen months after the birth of the Wainwrights' fifth and last child, Lillian Flora, born on 4 June 1871.[6] Harriet's pregnancy is hardly surprising, but faced with the prospect of a huge scandal, it may have been advisable for Henry to have cut his losses at this point. He could have paid her off or financed a move away from London for her. It would have been the sensible course of action. Henry was going to have his work cut out, running a business, being a husband to a wife and five young children and then having enough energy to keep Harriet and their child happy. This was not to mention all his other commitments in and around Whitechapel.

Henry did set his lover up with a place to stay as well and an allowance, which saved her from the disgrace of a return to her family or a sojourn at the workhouse. It also meant that Harriet would remain as Henry's 'bit on the side' so that he could happily retain his afternoons of passion. Neither partner wishing to finish the relationship, they decided that deception was the best way forward. Both assumed aliases. Henry gave himself the name 'Percy King', while his again pregnant partner became, 'Harriet Lillian King'.

Their deception made them appear married. If a wedding between them had taken place, it would have been a bigamous union rendering them both liable for arrest. It was interesting to note then that a local newspaper announced that an actual wedding had apparently taken place

In the February of 1872 there appeared in the *Waltham Abbey and Cheshunt Weekly Telegraph* an advertisement, sent to the newspaper in a woman's handwriting, to the effect that 'Percy King' had been married to Harriet.[7]

A check of the Essex marriage records has unsurprisingly failed to uncover any such event having taken place. It can be surmised that the newspaper advert had been a ruse by the couple to try and show that Harriet and 'Mr King' had tied the knot.

Authors Note: I visited the British Library and discovered that a small notification entitled 'Married' had been made in the *Waltham Abbey and Cheshunt Weekly Telegraph* in the Saturday, 10 February 1872 edition. It read thus: 'On the 22nd ult., at St. Marys, Percy King Esq, of Chelsea, to Harriet, ninth daughter of John Lane of Waltham Cross.'

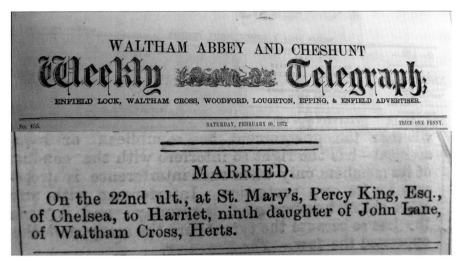

WALTHAM ABBEY AND CHESHUNT

𝕿𝖑𝖊𝖊𝖐𝖑𝖞 — 𝕿𝖊𝖑𝖊𝖌𝖗𝖆𝖕𝖍;

ENFIELD LOCK, WALTHAM CROSS, WOODFORD, LOUGHTON, EPPING, & ENFIELD ADVERTISER.

No. 455.   SATURDAY, FEBRUARY 10, 1872.   PRICE ONE PENNY.

MARRIED.

On the 22nd ult., at St. Mary's, Percy King, Esq., of Chelsea, to Harriet, ninth daughter of John Lane, of Waltham Cross, Herts.

Announcement of the wedding of 'Percy King' and Harriet Lane in the *Waltham Abbey and Cheshnut Weekly Telegraph*, 10 February 1872. (*Copyright The British Library Board. All Rights Reserved*)

When Harriet had Beatrice on 7 August 1872, she had been accommodated by Henry at 22 St Peter Street, Mile End, less than two miles[8] away from his marital home at Tredegar Square. This was close enough for Henry to be able to visit, though hopefully not so close as to cause them to be discovered.

The baby's birth had to be registered, and entry number 394 of the Mile End Old Town Register of Births makes for interesting reading. The child was named 'Beatrice Wainwright King'. The father was named as 'Percy King, a traveller'. The mother's name was recorded as 'Harriet Lilian King, formerly Lane'. The whole document was full of untruths. The name Percy King was of course a fictitious one while Harriet's name was actually Harriet Louisa but for some reason here she gives her middle name as Lillian. She also gives her fictitious 'married name' as King. The registrar would not have questioned the details furnished by Harriet. The true identity of the father is, however, given away by baby Beatrice's middle name: 'Wainwright'. Harriet later became pregnant for a second time, giving birth to 'Miriam Wainwright King' on 3 December 1873.[9]

What is clear by this point is that Henry's personal life was not cheap to run. With many mouths to feed and bills to pay, plus the loss of a good income from the factory, where problems had begun in 1873, was squeezing Henry Wainwright to such an extent that his mind was wandering to other 'risky' methods of economising. None of these alternative actions could be found in the 'How to Succeed at Business' manuals.

In addition, gambling debts were exacerbating Henry's financial situation. His savings and inheritance money[10] were starting to look perilously low. And the 'keep gambling till I get lucky at the tables' policy was also doomed to failure.

Henry failed to see that his high-risk lifestyle was unsustainable, and was rushing headlong for disaster but in order to keep himself afloat there was still the possibility of an insurance fraud against his failing business or even murder?

One of the first outward signs of uncertainty came in January 1873, when the *Lloyds List* newspaper[11] reported that the partnership between Henry and William Wainwright, 'brush and matting manufacturers' was being dissolved. A year later on 6 March 1874, the *Morning Post* reported that a meeting of creditors had decided to liquidate the company and appoint trustees. Liabilities were assessed at £6,643, and assets at only £5,505 (£57,651 and £47,775 in 2023).

Proceedings finally ended at the Bankruptcy Court, which was reported in the *Shipping and Mercantile Gazette*.[12] At the hearing, Mr Registrar Pepys, acting on an application from Joseph Barrett, ordered that the creditors should be paid at a rate of 12 shillings in the pound.

The early 1870s may have initially been an exciting time for both Harriet and Henry, but Harriet's father later discovered that his daughter was living as the mistress of Henry Wainwright when she confessed to him about the relationship. He urged her to return home, but her response did not produce a desire in her to make an emotional homecoming. Her reply said everything you needed to know about her infatuation with Henry and his money. She told him, 'Wainwright keeps me like a lady'.[13]

While money continued every week, Harriet was a comfortable, 'kept woman'. She was being looked after very generously by Henry on her £5 a month allowance (around £456 today). What changed the dynamics between the two and, in addition, Harriet's behaviour, was her unwelcome loss of income, which was starting to bite into her standard of living. Though she moaned at Henry and demanded her allowance, he was no longer in a position to be nearly so generous; some weeks he couldn't afford to pay her at all.

It was as if someone had removed the plug from the bottom of Harriet's boat and, suddenly, she was taking on water. Cries of help to her captain were falling on deaf ears. As the good ship Harriet Lane slowly began to list to port, there didn't appear to be many spare life jackets with which to save herself, and in so doing, save herself and her babes from the workhouse. The honeymoon period of their relationship had well and truly hit the rocks. It was not clear who, if anyone, could be saved from the wreckage as their love affair finally began to sink below the waves.

While Harriet struggled to manage, she may not have been fully aware of the financial crisis that Henry was in. His upper-middle-class world was falling around his ears. His options of a way out were reducing by the day as his cash dwindled. The money he paid to Harriet was proving to be the straw that broke the camel's back, and Henry Wainwright was now a desperate man.

Henry needed cash soon, but his options were limited. A long-term project could be to burn down his 84 Whitechapel Road shop for the insurance money. In the short term, he had to eliminate the money he gave Harriet in order to be able to feed his family, who were now living in hugely reduced circumstances.

With no other options available, cornered Henry Wainwright, seeking a miracle, decided on murder. The further advantage of killing Harriet was that she would no longer be a risk to his good name by telling his wife about their affair. It was a win-win situation for him but lose-lose for Harriet and her 2 girls. Henry now needed a plan.

The Deception of Mr Frieake: Preparation for murder

Henry devised a plan to make people think that Harriet had met another suitor and was going abroad with him. It was not going to be a quick solution, but this stealthy plan might allow him to get away with murder. The plan involved deceiving not only Harriet's friends and relations, but also Harriet herself.

'Mrs King and her mysterious visitor'. *Illustrated Police News* supplement, 16 October 1875. (*Copyright The British Library Board. All Rights Reserved*)

The plan was for Henry to introduce another man, who might want to take her on both emotionally and financially. The man introduced to her was a stranger, but someone Harriet seems to have a been attracted to. His name was Edward (Teddy) Frieake. He made an appearance at her lodgings and was seen by the landlady, so the man definitely existed, but the question of his identity was the key one. Was this man really called Edward Frieake?

The introduction of Frieake was simply to convince people that Harriet would be leaving London with him. The details of the actual murder still had to be worked out. But the plans for the elimination of Miss Lane were now in motion. One thing that seemed a certainty was that the plan to introduce a new suitor for Harriet could not have been done by Henry alone. He would need an accomplice. That man would need to be cunning, fearless and ruthless. He would also have to be someone that Henry could trust. A family member might just fit the bill?

Harriet Leaves Sidney Square

By May 1874, Harriet had arrived at her final abode, Jemima Foster's house at 3 Sidney Square, Whitechapel. Things had begun well, but following an unpleasant incident where Harriet had drunk too much and had made a scene in the street outside, Mrs Foster decided to think of her own reputation. She decided that Harriet was now too risky a tenant, and so she was given nine-days-notice to leave, with her departure day being set for 11 September 1874.

Harriet was to leave her digs, not knowing what was to befall her. Mrs Foster[14] described Harriet's relationship with the children on the day of her leaving: 'She seemed very fond indeed of her children; She left on Friday, 11th September. I bade her good bye, I never saw her again alive.'

Close friend, Miss Wilmore,[15] gave further details about her time at Sidney Square and Harriet's seemingly happy departure. She stated that she had gone to stay with Harriet from 3 August until 11 September 1874 but that Harriet had left at 4pm on the 11th, carrying only a night dress and an umbrella. She added that Harriet had been in good spirits, saying goodbye affectionately to the children. Meanwhile, Miss Wilmore left later, taking the children to new digs at 6 The Grove, Stratford. She also took Harriet's luggage and love letters.

Due to lack of funds, Harriet had pawned her 'wedding ring and keeper' which had been in pledge at Mr Dickers pawnbrokers[16] in the Commercial Road, but Miss Wilmore had taken them out for her on 11 September.

Ellen Wilmore was later asked in court about Harriet's relationship with her children.[17] 'She was very fond of them, more especially of the younger one,

Henry shooting Harriet Lane, *Famous Crimes Magazine*. (*Courtesy of Bishopsgate Institute*)

He owned a small revolver and enough bullets to fill all the chambers. What if the gun jammed? Would his hand be steady enough to enable him to shoot her dead? As he awaited her arrival, he took a small tot of brandy to steady his nerves. The brandy in the glass shook slightly. After checking the gun, he slipped it into his trouser pocket and out of sight. For insurance reasons he also had a small knife which he placed in his other pocket, just in case something went wrong with the gun. If it failed, he could always stab her to death.

As he paced up and down at the rear of the shop, time seemed to stand still. Every few minutes he checked his watch to see if the appointed time for Harriet's date with destiny had arrived. As the clock ticked closer to her arrival time, the more foreboding he felt. Suddenly she was here. Two knocks on the door nearly made Henry jump out of his skin. It must be her. Worse if it were some tradesman or other friend calling at just the wrong time.

Nervously, Henry approached the back door and saw the petit figure of Harriet. Neatly attired, she was still an attractive young woman. Her optimistic appearance on the other side of the glass was unnerving. Harriet was arriving in a good mood, expecting news of her move. Her normality was off putting to Henry who felt anything but normal and just wanted the next 10 minutes to be over.

"Hello Henry, I hope you have everything sorted for me? Everything went well at Sidney Square and Ellen has taken the girls and my things, so what happens next?" Henry did not reply. Harriet then said, "I hope you have a little money for me. I got my rings out of pawn today and I could do with a few shillings to keep me going".

Henry was not usually short of words, but tonight he was nervous and could not say much as his tongue seemed to be tied in knots. "Of course, everything is fine, and I'll see you all right with half a crown for tonight". He then invited her to sit down and offered her a drink. As she sat on the low backed chair, he drew her attention to the East London Observer newspaper on the table. While she had her interest elsewhere, he knew that this was the moment to act while she studied the headlines.

Henry shoved his sweaty hand in his pocket and slowly drew out his revolver. He mustn't fumble it or drop it on the floor. He then raised the gun from five feet away and pointed it in the direction of the back of Harriet's head. She was oblivious to the presence of a deadly weapon. Now Henry was seized by power and determination. The woman who in his mind had been causing him so many of his problems, both financially, and socially, threatening to expose him, was there for the taking. She deserved what was coming to her, and she would never embarrass him again. He could put an end to their affair here and now.

Feeling justified and empowered, the surge of adrenaline rushed through his body like electricity. He took aim and squeezed the trigger. As the hammer snapped forward, the shock of the loud bang and the recoil of the gun surprised him. Harriet let out a yelp, but she remained fairly upright. He immediately pulled the trigger again, firing towards the rear of her skull. This shot may have lodged in the pins and the hairpiece she regularly wore. He had assumed that 2 shots would have killed her, but she was moaning but wasn't dead and was still in the upright position with her head now leaning over to one side.

Fearing he had missed, or that the small bullets were not deadly enough, he again pulled the trigger. It felt a relief when she suddenly slumped off the chair and onto the wooden floor. He wanted her dead but she had not yet expired. She was making the sounds of a person dying, but the noise continued. He needed to shut her up. He had only planned on one gun shot. He had fired 3 times but she was groaning. Would any of the neighbours be listening and come rushing in? Would at any moment, a policeman of 'H' Division be banging on his door?

He had to end things now, so put down the gun and took out the knife from his pocket to finish the job. Rushing over to her as she lay dying and with her eyes spinning upwards, she was still a living, breathing woman. Firing at her from 5 feet away was one thing, but ending her life with a knife was not what he had planned. But he had to stop her noises, he couldn't bear to hear them. He grabbed her hair with his left hand and pulling back her head, he sliced across her beautiful neck with a single and powerful slash. Harriet immediately became silent and still. The deed had been done.

Poor Harriet was mortally wounded. What Henry had not anticipated was the spurting of blood from her carotid artery. It splattered him as the knife cut into her. It was warm on his face and clothing. It was not a nice feeling. As the assault ended, Henry slumped to his knees. He dropped the knife onto the floor. It was covered in blood, as was Harriet's neck, face and clothing. He took a moment to try and compose himself. His breathing was rapid and his heart felt like it was going to jump out of his chest.

As he contemplated Harriet's bloodied corpse, his emotions were mixed. He had actually completed the task he thought he might not be able to bring himself to perform. He had done it. Harriet was now history. But he also regarded the enormity of what he had just done. He studied her face for a few moments, comparing the pretty and carefree look that she possessed just a few minutes previously, to what now lay before him. A woman in a bloodbath, dishevelled and unworldly. Was this the woman he had once so coveted?

Henry had instantly become a new person. He was now a murderer and a fugitive, but he had to try and carry on his life as if nothing had happened. All he needed to do was to dispose of the body. His actions had also just changed a lot of other people's lives as well. Her girls had just become orphans. Her parents had lost a daughter and her siblings a sister.

After killing Harriet in a premeditated attack, the second part of the night was now to begin. He had a long job on as he had to hide her body under the floorboards. He was still full of fear. Anyone now entering the premises would discover the body and the game would be up!

Chapter Four

In Search of Harriet

Part one of Henry's plan had been achieved. Harriet's body was safe enough for now under the floorboards of 215 Whitechapel Road, but he could not feel secure until her friends and relations had accepted that she had left London with Edward Frieake and gone to France. Though most of her family did not see her that often, the main person who would enquire as to her wellbeing was Ellen Wilmore. After all, she had taken the children to her new digs in Stratford, east London, on Friday 11 September 1874, and she was expecting Harriet to follow her on later. At no time did Harriet mention to her that she would be going away with a new man and/or leaving the country.

After a few days, when Harriet had still not appeared, alarm bells started ringing. Troubled, Miss Wilmore travelled to Whitechapel to confront Henry about what was going on, being the only person she could think of to question regarding Harriet's whereabouts. Here, Henry fobbed her off, telling her that he had sent Harriet to Brighton with money for clothes, and that she would soon be in touch.

Miss Wilmore[1] told Harriet's family that she had taken the children with her to their new lodgings at Stratford, together with Harriet's luggage, but she never saw or heard from Harriet on the Saturday, Sunday, or Monday. She then went to Wainwright's premises to confront him, but he fobbed her off, telling her that he had sent Harriet to Brighton and that he had given her money for clothes, and that she would soon be in touch.

After a further four days of no news, on Tuesday, 15 September, and now greatly concerned, Miss Wilmore wrote to Harriet's sister, Elizabeth Taylor. Mrs Taylor and Ellen visited Henry on Monday, 21 September 1874, asking for news of Harriet. In typical Wainwright style he sidestepped their questions. He added that he had heard nothing, but would 'get the address as soon as he possibly could.' He needed a plan B to stop the continual dangerous visits from Harriet's loved ones.

A few days later, Miss Wilmore and Mrs. Taylor visited Henry again. This time, he moved forwards with the second part of his plan and told them that he had heard from Harriet, and that she had gone off with his friend, a man called Frieake, an auctioneer who had come into property, though he did not

'Searching for the missing woman', *Illustrated Police News*, 16 October 1875. (*Copyright The British Library Board. All Rights Reserved*)

specify where Frieake lived. About three weeks after Harriet disappeared on 11 September 1874, Miss Wilmore received a letter at her lodgings in Stratford from the Charing Cross Hotel.

LETTER 'E': Charing Cross Hotel, Wednesday:

Dear Miss Wilmore, I am very much surprised at not receiving a reply to my last letter in which I gave you all the particulars as to our arrangements. She is now quite content, and has solemnly promised never to see or speak to King, or any of her old friends and family again, as if she did, I told her we should have to part. If her promise is kept, I intend to marry her in a few weeks. I distinctly tell you I will never allow her to see any of her old acquaintances as it will only cause unpleasantness. With kind regards, I remain, yours truly, E. Frieke. We are off to Dover.[2]

The following morning, Miss Wilmore rushed back to Wainwright with her letter. She gave it to him and he read it. The wind was taken out of her sails, however, when he stated that he had received a similar communication. He showed her the letter which appeared to be in similar handwriting, also from E. Frieke, and containing the same information.

This letter was written in a way to try avert any further enquiries being made about Harriet. The unequivocal claim of never being able to see any of her family or friends again was an outrageous request for a partner to make. Why did the letter make things sound as if they had been so unpleasant? There was no justification for this. Unless you were a murderer trying to avoid further enquiries being made. It was a bold statement, though it did seem to work.

Wainwright succeeded again when Miss Wilmore received a telegram from 'Frieake' from Dover. The Dover idea planted in the receiver's head that the runaways were just about to step on a steamer to Calais.

Around the start of November, Mrs. Taylor again visited Wainwright, who told her that Harriet was alright enjoying herself and would doubtless return. It was at this point she decided that she would have to take further steps to find her sister as she was getting nowhere with Wainwright.

As the months passed with no further word, Miss Wilmore kept the children and was still being paid Harriet's £5 a month allowance by Henry Wainwright up until June 1875, when the payments suddenly dropped to 3 or 5 shillings, which was not enough to live on.

When she saw Wainwright regarding the payments, she always asked about Harriet but he consistently dismissed any concerns, saying he had seen her somewhere in town, or that someone else had seen her. She received no money for the 6 weeks prior to 11 September 1875.

Meanwhile, Harriet's father, John Lane, became involved in the case. The explanation that Harriet had gone abroad with Mr Frieake had stalled the enquiries for several months. By January 1875, and still not being happy with the explanation of the circumstances of her going away, Mrs. Taylor had employed enquiry officer Ernest Eeles to try and discover Harriet's whereabouts. There had been no contact from Harriet for 4 months to any of her family or friends by this point, and her children were still with Miss Wilmore.

Eeles and John Lane visited Wainwright in Whitechapel on 16 January 1875 and, seeing him outside number 215, Eeles approached Henry from behind and placed a hand on his shoulder. The unexpected hand must have been something Henry had been dreading. Henry admitted to him that he had had two children by Harriet, but all he knew was that she had gone off with a man who had recently inherited a fortune by the name of Freddy Frieake. Lane made it clear that if he failed to find his daughter, he would be calling in the police.

After discovering the address of an Edward Frieake on a handbill, Eeles and John Lane visited 11 Coleman Street in the City of London two weeks later to discuss the missing mother with the mysterious-sounding Mr Frieake. Eeles must have done a good job of alarming the genuine Mr Frieake, who also had his reputation to think of. After explaining the allegation of the missing woman, Frieake immediately accompanied Eeles and Mr Lane down to Whitechapel Road. He wanted to know what Wainwright was playing at, putting about such a story about him.

As the three men arrived at Wainwright's, they located him in the street outside, with Eeles announcing his discovery of Mr Frieake. Henry calmly replied 'Oh, this is not *the* Mr Frieake; You have made a mistake'. Frieake then told Henry, 'You are getting me into a mess that I know nothing about, and may do me a serious injury.'

The explanation given by Wainwright was likely the first thing to have popped into his head: 'You are not the Teddy Frieake I mean; The Teddy I mean is a billiard player; I have seen him frequently at Purcell's, the Philharmonic[3] and the Nell Gwynne'.

The genuine Teddy replied with incredulity. 'You mean to say you have ever known another Teddy Frieake, and not inquired who he was? I do not believe there is another Teddy Frieake, with the name spelt the same as mine in the 'London Directory.[4] I saw you with a fair-haired girl a short time ago. Is that the one?' Henry said, 'No, I can produce her in five-minutes'. It is not recorded whether his offer to produce her in five minutes was taken up, though he could certainly have achieved this feat, but would have needed to take the floorboards up first!

Edward William Frieake[5] had known Henry for around fourteen years and he used to call him 'Teddy' or 'Frieaky' and, until September 1874, they had always been on friendly terms. Teddy did not know the brother, Thomas Wainwright. Mr Frieake first became involved in the case when he received letter 'A' on or about 29–31 August 1874 from 'L. King', in reality, Harriet Lane. He stated that he had been astonished to receive the letter, but then put it away and forgot about it.

The letter purports to be from L. King, AKA, Harriet Lane. Considering the number of false letters and telegrams that were being circulated at around this time, it might be assumed that this letter was a forgery. The letter exists only as a prosecutors copy of the original in the case file' and so cannot be compared to the hand writing to letters in the case file known to have been written by Harriet Lane. It seems unlikely however that this correspondence was anything other than genuine. Harriet Lane certainly had reason to apologise for her behaviour in the street in Sidney Square. Most importantly, why would Henry Wainwright have written a letter of this sort to his friend Mr Frieake?

LETTER 'A' – dated, 'Sunday night'

'My Dear Mr Frieake, I trust you will pardon me writing to you but I feel I ought to apologise for my rude behaviour to you last evening after the kindness I have received from you. I felt very sorry you left me so cross. I have well considered the subject we spoke of and think if Harry and yourself could see me tomorrow evening, we may be able to arrange matters satisfactory as the time is now very short. Please write by return, and let me know if you will call. For the future I promise to behave more ladylike. Should I not hear from you, I shall conclude I am not forgiven. I remain, very truly yours, L. King[6]

During this late January 1875 swoop on Henry Wainwright, the 3 visitors were intent on getting more information out of their suspect. Mr Frieake was by now armed with the letters marked 'E' and 'A'. The letter 'E' had been signed '*FRIEKE*'. (The wrong spelling), as he stated that he always signed as 'E.W. Frieake' so that he could not have written the letter. Mr Frieake was unhappy about his visit from Mr Eeles asking him impertinent questions and accused him of taking Harriet Lane away. Mr Eeles' had advised Frieake that his informant had been Henry Wainwright, so he now demanded some answers from the apparently cornered Henry Wainwright. Henry of course had denied any impropriety on his behalf, by his old friend was not to be put off.

Frieake added, 'It is a very serious imputation to cast upon my character, and should it get to the ears of my lady's friends I am engaged to be married to, it will very likely ruin my happiness.' Henry stated that the Teddy Frieake he was talking about was a young man of 23, with a black moustache. Teddy then asked a very logical question of his old friend; 'It is strange you should have known another Teddy Frieake without asking him if he had any relations, as mine is not an ordinary Brown, Jones, or Robinson name.' To that he replied it was another person entirely.

Henry had ignored the question that was far too difficult for him to answer, simply giving a bland reply. It was inconceivable that he would not have asked the other Teddy Frieake if he was related in any way to the real one of that name who was personally known to this Frieake. After Eeles had left, the auctioneer said to Henry; 'Harry, old man, if you know anything about this girl why don't you ease their minds and let them know.' He replied, 'Teddy, old man, this is only a get up to extort money from me. The girl's all right'.

Mr Frieake's next involvement was several months later when he attended the police station in September 1875 after the body had been discovered. He handed in his business card[7] in order to tell the police what he knew about Henry Wainwright. The ornate business card[8] can still be seen in the file at the National Archives.

The search for Harriet Lane had ground to a halt due to the procrastination of Henry Wainwright's frankly implausible excuses. The enquirers had tried but failed to make any impression by disproving any of his monstrous lies, but while they may have been thinking of any further lines of enquiry, by September 1875, Henry was very definitely feeling the pressure. Ellen Wilmore met with Henry about money on 10 September 1875, but he could only promise her 5 shillings till November. His note to her that day was not of the polite variety; 'if you give me all this annoyance by calling and leaving letters I shall then do nothing for you: your stupid threats are quite absurd'.

It was obvious that Henry Wainwright was the key to unlocking the whole mystery. He wasn't giving anything away with his bland responses. It is a shame that Mr Lane had not followed up on his threat to get the police involved. If they had called in the determined detectives of 'H' Division, the case may well have been solved earlier? Police officers are generally sceptical souls with built in lie detectors, and would hopefully have seen through his outrageous deceits.

Chapter Five

Henry's Arrest

Follow that Cab: The Chase, 11 September 1875

Turn the clock forward by exactly one year and it was a routine Saturday late shift for PCs Turner and Cox as they paraded for duty at Stones End Police Station in Southwark. Saturday nights could prove tricky down the Borough High Street, especially when the many pubs got going. Fights, drunken sailors, and domestic violence was likely to be waiting for them. Every police officer goes on duty hoping for the best but fearing the worst. Would the policing Gods be kind and allow them an easy day walking 10 miles on their beat without any fisticuffs?

Three miles away in Whitechapel, Henry Wainwright was about to make the most important journey of his life. Henry's only goal for the day was to safely move Harriet Lane's body from

'A.P. Stokes', *Illustrated Police News*, 25 September 1875. (*Copyright The British Library Board. All Rights Reserved*)

Whitechapel to the Borough, and he certainly didn't want to be anywhere near the boys in blue.

So far, it seemed Henry Wainwright had succeeded in getting away with murder, but his financial situation would force him to vacate 215 Whitechapel Road very soon. Any new tenant would have wanted an empty building – not one with a corpse under the floorboards – so a suitable new hiding place for the body was needed. It was decided to move Harriet's body to the Hen and Chickens[1] in Borough High Street near London Bridge, where Thomas had once started a hardware business, but the premises were now standing empty and he, rather conveniently, had a key!

It's likely that Thomas knew the building well and was aware that it had a cellar where a body could easily be concealed. Moving the body was risky, but the removal of two parcels with half of Harriet's body inside each might just work. Wainwright was a tradesman, so it was unlikely two largish parcels being removed from his premises would raise suspicion.

Thomas wasn't involved with the plan to move the body, so Henry had to enlist the help of someone who could be relied on. The man he chose was Alfred Philip Stokes, a former employee. Using someone who could identify Henry was a questionable decision, and one that would ultimately cost him his life. Wainwright asked him to help by carrying a parcel for him. On being asked, his reply was, 'Yes sir, with the greatest of pleasure'.[2] They went together to 215 Whitechapel Road, and entered the premises at the rear through Vine Court.[3]

Alf had arrived in the afternoon of 11 September 1875 to perform an 'unremarkable little job'. On arriving at the warehouse, Stokes said that the two bags were too heavy for him. His complaints also observed that the axe that was there smelt terrible. As Stokes struggled with the bags, Wainwright told him he would take one of them from him at the bottom of Vine Court and that he was watching to see if their neighbour, Mr Johnson, was watching.

As they turned left into Whitechapel Road, Wainwright took the lightest of the bags as they walked down to Whitechapel Church. Stokes, meanwhile, was

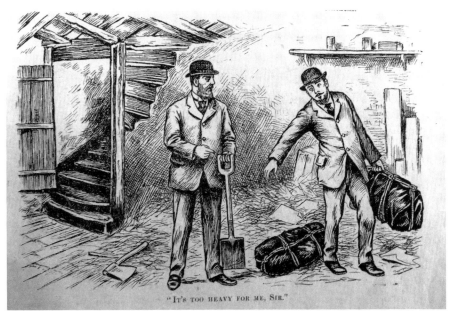

"IT's TOO HEAVY FOR ME, SIR."

'It's too heavy for me, sir'. An illustration showing Henry Wainwright and Alfred Stokes, as Henry directs Stokes to move Harriet's body. (*Courtesy of Bishopsgate Institute*)

really struggling with the weight. Henry told him, 'For God's sake don't drop them or else you will break them'. When they reached the church, Wainwright told Stoke to wait with the bags while he fetched a cab. Stokes then took up the story;

> 'I felt as if I must do it. I opened it, and the first thing I saw was a human head, and then proceeding further I saw a hand which had been cut off at the wrist, and then I had the presence of mind to cover it up again quick and wait till Mr Wainwright returned with a four-wheeled cab'.

He realised that he had stumbled across a murder, and that the suspect had just arrived back in front of him. With no time to think, Stokes remained silent while he pondered his next move. Wainwright got him to help put the bags into the cab and he then drove off down Church Street. Stokes decided to follow the cab on foot as it reached the chemist's shop in Commercial Road, opposite the Plumbers Arms[4] where it stopped and Wainwright got out. Here he saw him meet with Alice Day. They both got in the cab and Wainwright told the driver, 'Drive on as fast as you can over London Bridge to the Borough'.

Alice Day was later to give her version of events of 11 September.[5] She stated that she had gone into the Duke of Clarence pub on the corner of Greenfield Street with a friend. At about ten to five she left the pub when she saw Henry Wainwright, 'unexpectedly' approaching her on foot.

She added that the meeting on her part was completely by chance. Wainwright then asked her to go in the cab with him to London Bridge. She did see the two bags in the cab, but paid them no heed.

Having made a snap decision not to confront Wainwright about his horrific discovery, Stokes decided that the next best course of action was to follow the cab in the hope of finding a policeman who could nab Wainwright red-handed.

In the 1870s, London had the same problem of traffic hold ups as it does now, but with streets full of horse-drawn carts and buses. The traffic couldn't move very quickly, giving Stokes the chance to run along after the cab on foot[6]. Stokes takes up the story; 'I ran after the cab until I saw two (City of London)[7] constables by Leadenhall Street. I called their attention to the cab as I was then exhausted, but they laughed at me and said "Man, you must be mad" I called to them to stop the cab. I did not tell them why. I could not speak at the time'.

Stokes must have been getting desperate by this stage, seeing the cab speeding on and the policemen disappearing out of sight behind him. Seeing the constables in Borough High Street, Stokes told them, 'For God's sake run

'The Murder of Harriet Lane'. An illutstration depicting Alfred Stokes speaking to the police and the cab with Henry Wainwright in the back. (*Courtesy of Bishopsgate Institute*)

after the man with the high hat with the parcels in his hand, there is something wrong. PC Cox spoke to Alice Day. I saw PC Turner follow Wainwright to the Hen and Chickens'.

Stokes had somehow managed to keep up with the horse-drawn cab all the way from Whitechapel to the Borough, never losing sight of his quarry. Suddenly, help was at hand in the form of PCs Cox and Turner. The out of breath informant, Alfred Stokes, had pulled off a feat of endurance. Wainwright was blissfully unaware of any danger, and the policemen would soon be feeling his considerable collar. For now, Stokes had done his job and he left the scene rushing off to tell Mr Martin before later attending Stones

End Police Station. This was a life changing moment for Alfred, but it was to be even more life changing for Henry Wainwright, who was about to start 'helping' the police with their enquiries!

Caught Red Handed: Henry Wainwright's Arrest

Police officers soon get to know when an informant is being serious, or is trying urgently to get their attention to do something very important. That particular afternoon's beat had been passing by without incident when highly excited Alfred Stokes ran up to officers PCs Cox and Turner.

Transcripts of the Old Bailey trial[8] gave details of the evidence of PC 48M Henry Turner, who stated that at 5.04pm on Saturday, 11 September he had been on patrol at Borough High Street on the corner of St. Thomas Street.

> The witness, Stokes, spoke to me; he seemed very much exhausted, he had his hat in his hand and perspired very much in the face; he made a communication to me, in consequence of which I went up to a cab which was just drawing up; the cabman was just commencing to rein up at the corner of Southwark Street. I went up to the cab, I saw Henry Wainwright get out of the cab before it had stopped, he was carrying a parcel. I walked a little way down on the other side of the road to see where he went.
>
> I saw him go into an empty house called the Hen and Chickens; he took a key from his pocket, unlocked the padlock, and went in. I then went back to the cab, which was then about 45 yards from the Hen and Chickens.[9]
>
> PC Cox 290M came up. There was a female in the cab who I now know to be Alice Day, and there was a parcel on the front seat tied up in American cloth with a large string, it was about 18 inches long and about 9 or ten inches wide.

Alice Day had been picked up in the cab by Henry, and, as far as she knew, she was simply coming along for a joy ride. She had been asked to come with him to keep him company. They clearly hadn't discussed the contents of the bags. PC Turner continued his account;

> I waited till Henry Wainwright came out, he walked straight on towards the cab. He did not lock the door, he had the padlock in his pocket, he was smoking a very large cigar; He went to the cab, and opened the door and took out the parcel. I said 'What have you got there, sir?' He said

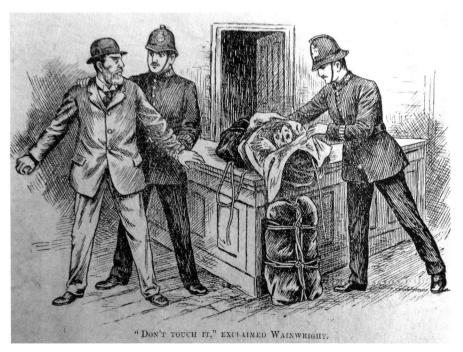

"Don't touch it," exclaimed Wainwright.

'"Don't touch it", exclaimed Wainwright'. Having been apprehended by police, Henry asks them not to open the package. (*Courtesy of Bishopsgate Institute*)

'Why do you interfere with me, I am only going down to an old friend of mine'

I walked alongside of him until we got to the Hen and Chickens, the door was shut, but the padlock was off. He seemed to want to pass by it. I caught hold of him and we stopped. I said 'Do you live here?' He said 'No.' I said 'Have you any business here?' He said 'Yes, and you have not'. I said 'Go inside'. He seemed very reluctant to go in, Cox then joined me and we pushed him inside'.

Turner and Cox meant business, and the fact that they pushed Wainwright inside indicated their haste to have him somewhere from where he couldn't escape or be rescued. The officers, having secured Wainwright, needed to see what was in the mysterious parcels and ask him some searching questions about their contents. Turner went on;

When we got inside, I said 'How came you in possession of this place, I thought it belonged to Mr Lewis?' He said 'So it does, now say nothing and ask no questions and there is £50. each for you'. Cox barred the door. He had the parcel in his left hand all the time. I said to him 'What did you do with the first parcel that you brought in here.' He said it is only on the first floor. I told Cox to go up and see if he could see it. I saw the parcel on the cellar steps. I then called Cox down and said 'Get hold of this man and I will see what is in the parcel'

Cox took hold of him and I went and put the parcel on an old counter in the shop; I then perceived what a dreadful stench it was. Before opening the parcel, Henry Wainwright said, 'Don't open it, policeman, pray don't look at it, whatever you do don't touch it'. I then pulled the cloth over, and my fingers came across the scalp of a head, across the ear; I found that it contained part of the remains of a human body. I then got hold of the prisoner and Cox went to get the cab. The prisoner said, 'I will give you £100. I will give you £200 and produce the money in twenty minutes if you will let me go.'

PC Turner continued. 'He said nothing more. The cab was then brought up to the door, the parcels were put inside. They were put into the cab and the prisoner also; the woman was still in the cab. We were then all driven to the station.' The journey to the station must have been cosy, with two policemen, two suspects and two bags containing a corpse squeezed inside. It must have been an awkward silence as well, apart from Alice Day scolding Wainwright.

'Policeman', 48-year-old PC Henry Turner, arresting officer. *Illustrated Police News*, 16 October 1875. (*Copyright The British Library Board. All Rights Reserved*)

Wainwright was in huge trouble. PC Turner continued with details of the journey and their arrival at the station;

On the way to the station, the female said to the prisoner, Mr Wainwright, you have done a fine thing for me, or words to that effect, to which he made no reply. The parcels were put down in the yard at the station, they were found to contain portions of a female body much decomposed; the features were not recognisable, the hair on the head was very much clotted with blood, lime, and dirt.

'Mr Larkin, the surgeon saw them and they were taken to St. Saviour's dead-house the same evening. At the station, Henry Wainwright and Alice Day were charged with having in their possession a human body, supposed to be murdered. They both made a statement which was taken down by Inspector Fox in writing.

PC Cox[10] gave a very similar account of the arrests. He added that he had left the cab and Miss Day in the charge of another officer, PC 310M,[11] while he

THE ARREST OF WAINRIGHT

Front Page of *Illustrated Police News*, 25 September 1875, featuring Henry Wainwright's arrest. (*Copyright The British Library Board. All Rights Reserved*)

was at the Hen and Chickens. Concerned about the security of this potentially important prisoner, Cox called out to his colleague,

> 'Wait Turner, while I fasten the door,' as there was a crowd outside. I picked up an iron bar that was lying on the floor and placed against the door as there was no proper fastening on the inside.

PC Turner's statement didn't exactly go overboard on detail in his version of the arrest. There was no mention of the arrest being communicated to the prisoners, or the immortal lines, 'Mr Wainwright I'd like you to accompany me to the station.' No detail was given in the way of any comments made by the suspects which is frustrating, but the actions of PC Turner[12] and Cox[13] were decisive enough to ensure that Wainwright could not fob them off, or dispose of the body. Henry Wainwright entered Stone's End in police custody. He would never need the services of a hansom cab again.

Chapter Six

The Investigation

Stones End Police Station

Central London police stations in the 1870, just like today, were very busy places, and the Southwark based Stones End Police Station was no different. Stones End was run on strict codes of discipline with the constables and sergeants patrolling the area. These men were supervised by the duty officer inspectors who, on 11 September 1875, was the efficient Irishman, Inspector Matthew Fox.[1] The station was commanded by Superintendent Thomas Garforth.[2]

On Saturdays, the station was normally full of prisoners clogging the charge room, who had been drinking and still wanted to fight. That Saturday late shift, without warning, the charge room door burst open and in walked the well-dressed 'gent' in the shape of Henry Wainwright and a young lady, Alice Day. The station sergeant must have wondered what he had here? This didn't look like a run of the mill case.

PCs Turner and Cox had already removed the two large bags from the cab and placed them in the yard, not wishing to stink the station out. It was at this point that the constables would have stated the reason for the arrest. The custody officer may still have been up to his eyes in drunks to take much notice of yet another new arrival in the custody area.

The station sergeant may hardly have looked up as the unlikely pairing of Wainwright and Day came in and sat on the bench awaiting their turn. But the moment that PC Turner mentioned the word murder would have had the sergeant choking on his half-drunk cup of tea.

The newspaper hacks would be scurrying about Stones End as well as Leman Street nick looking for updates. Everyone in the press wanted a piece of the action, as newspapers from the *John O'Groats Journal* to the *Cornish Times* wanted to read more revelations over their breakfast tables. The story, like the bags in the yard, was going to run and run.

Call the Fox – Inspector – 'M' Division

Inspector Matthew Fox had likely seen it all in his fifteen years of policing. Murders, especially the domestic variety, were not unusual in Victorian

Britain. Assaults and larceny were common place, so Inspector Fox would have been ready for anything on that Saturday, 11 September 1875. That is until PC Turner marched into the station holding onto the well-dressed Henry Wainwright and the actress Alice Day. They probably looked a bit out of place on the charge room bench that they may have shared with a scruffy 13-year-old bread thief and a slowly sobering up drunk.

Inspector Fox, *Penny Illustrated Paper,* 25 September 1875. (*Copyright The British Library Board. All Rights Reserved*)

PC Turner seemed not to be a man who called a 'spade a spade,' though later enquiries *would* discover a spade at the murder scene. On reaching the charge room, instead of announcing he had arrested two suspected murderers, he simply explained that the prisoners had been found in possession of two bags which he had discovered were 'wrong.' On checking the contents of the bags in the station yard, Inspector Fox soon discovered exactly how wrong they were.

After licking the top of his pencil with his pocket book open, Fox was ready to take down Wainwright's vital statement. His story amounted to a less than convincing explanation. Inspector Fox tells us his question and Wainwright's response.[3]

What are in those parcels and where did you get them? He said 'I do not know what they contain, a gentleman gave them to me to carry.' I took them into the yard, and saw that they contained portions of a body. I sent for Mr Larkin,[4] and he examined them. I said to Wainwright and Miss Day, 'I will charge you with having the remains of a female in your possession believed to have been murdered.'

The best defence Wainwright could come up with was the old, 'it was a man in the pub' routine. This is an old ruse used by criminals when asked how they came to be in possession of something incriminating. They put the blame on a mysterious person who has no identity and no forwarding address. Fox went on:

Henry Wainwright made a statement which I took down in writing: Yesterday week, a gentleman known to me by meeting him in public houses, said 'I can put a sovereign or two your way, by taking two parcels over to the Borough. I said it was a big price for so small a job. He said, take them over, ask no questions, and here is a couple of sovereigns for you. He gave me the key and told me to take them to the Hen and Chickens, an empty house in the Borough. He brought them to me, and I brought them over.

Wainwright could just have admitted the whole thing there and then. His game was up and he must have known that he could surely only look forward to incarceration or worse in the coming months. The story would unravel and he would be disgraced. But he clung to the hope of freedom like a man holding onto the lifeboat of a sinking ship in choppy waters. It would prove only to be a delaying tactic.

The explanation of the man in the pub giving him a 'no questions asked' job of moving the parcels to the Borough was unconvincing. Not surprisingly, this thinly veiled lie was not put forward as a defence by his barristers at any of the various court hearings. No record of a police search for this mysterious man in the pub exists in the police files.

With the minimum of fuss, Wainwright and Day were charged with murder of an unknown female and were kept in custody to appear at Southwark Police Court on Monday, 13 September 1875.

Inspector Fox visits the crime scene

The Metropolitan Police will celebrate its 200th birthday in 2029, and during those years the service has seen continual development and radical change. The first Met Commissioner, Sir Richard Mayne laid out the 'Primary Objects'.[5]

'The primary object of an efficient police is the prevention of crime: the next that of detection and punishment of offenders if crime is committed. To these ends all the efforts of police must be directed. The protection of life and property, the preservation of public tranquillity, and the absence of crime, will alone prove whether those efforts have been successful and whether the objects for which the police were appointed have been attained'.

The primary object of this investigation was to detect who was responsible for Harriet Lane's brutal murder. It was a case of old-fashioned police work and teamwork that would hopefully lead to the detection of the offenders.

This murder enquiry was shared by two Met Divisions, 'H' Division (Whitechapel), and 'M' Division (Southwark). The crime actually occurred on 'H' but the arrest was affected on 'M'. Inspector Matthew Fox (M), was the main investigating officer, though he was ably assisted by Chief Inspector McDonald and 2 detectives from Whitechapel in the shape of DS Forster and DC Newman.

Unmarried Irishman, Inspector Fox had 15 years police experience. He could almost have been described as being married to 'The Job'[6] itself. It was a big case to be in charge of, but it was one in which he could make a name for himself.

Inspector Fox probably did not get much, if any, sleep that night. The adrenaline rush that one gets when involved in a murder case was probably in his head for several of the following days. Having to carefully prise open the bags containing Harriet Lane's rotting body would not have been a moment that he would ever forget. Being the first person to set eyes on the face of Harriet Lane for a year would certainly linger in his memory.

Fox's head would have been spinning, but he would have been calm enough to start putting a plan in place. The coroner and the medical examiners needed informing. Station commander, Superintendent Garforth, would need to be consulted, along with Scotland Yard. But the next most important job would be to examine the crime scene. Though where that was exactly still had to be determined. Henry Wainwright's premises at 215 Whitechapel Road was top of the list, and the Hen and Chickens would also need to be checked.

The most important statement that needed to be obtained was from Alfred Stokes. After that, urgent enquiries into the character and background of Henry Wainwright, as well as Alice Day, needed actioning. Opening the lid to Henry Wainwright's double life was going to be very enlightening. The one thing Fox was desperate to know, however, was, who was the person in the bags? Finding this out was, of course, not crucial on the first day of the investigation, but it was going to be pivotal in moving the case along and providing a motive for murder.

A search of Wainwright's person was the starting point, but it was only the beginning of a case that would keep Fox busy for the next three months. The evidence of Inspector Fox[7] continued: He stated that he searched Henry Wainwright, who was in possession of twenty-seven keys, two cigars and other items. He also found two yards of American cloth and seven yards of rope. That evening he went to 215 Whitechapel Road with Stokes. He found a small axe, a spade, a hammer and a pocket knife. The spade smelt similar to the body and it had lime, clay and hair on it.

The spade, axe and pick. An illustration of the murder weapons, *Illustrated Police News*, 23 October 1875. (*Copyright The British Library Board. All Rights Reserved*)

The search had brought immediate results, and very good evidence of somewhere that could have hosted the dismemberment of a body. The account from Fox continued; He arrived at 8pm on 11 September, bringing police lanterns with him. They found three loose floor boards and four cut joists. He could also detect that smell again. Below this site he found earth mixed with chloride of lime.

The following day, on the 12 September, he returned to number 215, where the search continued in daylight. He discovered a grave, five feet long, two feet wide, and two feet deep. The earth was mixed with the lime, and he removed one lump of it as an exhibit. Hair that was discovered in the grave appeared to him to be a similar light colour to that on the skull of the body.

Wainwright's premises proved undoubtedly to be the place in which the body had been concealed and later dissected. Fox said he discovered what looked like blood spots on the stone floor, which also appeared to have fresh indentations in it, as if being made by a small axe.

Exhibits for a later prosecution were accumulating fast. Whoever had been in the premises at 215 had not had time to tidy up after themselves, leaving many vital clues behind. Fox, who was acting as exhibits officer, was also being given the finds made by his colleagues. He continued, describing some of the items: 'I have two rings which I received from the detective Newman, also two jet buttons which I received from Inspector McDonald, and two earrings.' These were significant finds, as later this evidence would help to prove that this was the body of Harriet Lane.

Another job which needed completing quickly was to search[8] Henry's house in Chingford, a place that was then a rural part of Essex, north of London. Two officers, one of whom was Inspector Fox, made the trip to the country, away from grimy Whitechapel on 12 September, to see if anything of evidential value could be found. *The Penny Illustrated*[9] newspaper took up the story of the long and fruitless day that they spent looking for the Wainwright abode. The paper stated that the officers 'got out at the wrong station on the forest',[10] so had a very long walk to find Wainwright's cottage. His wife showed them Henry's clothing.

Henry's coat may have contained incriminating evidence. Mr Martin had possession of the coat[11] that Henry had apparently been wearing on or around the date of 11 September. The coat had stains on it but, following Dr Bond's chemical examination, he found only grease and no blood.

Cellar of the Hen and Chickens during a search by police, *Penny Illustrated Paper*, 25 September 1875. (*Copyright The British Library Board. All Rights Reserved*)

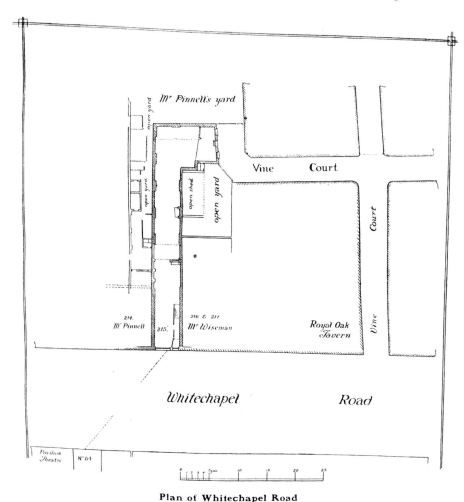

Plan of Whitechapel Road
(Showing the premises at Nos. 84 and 215 occupied by Henry Wainwright).

Plan of Whitechapel Road. (The Trial of the Wainwrights, *1920*)

Proving the identity of the body became the main objective, to allow the case to move forward, as well as establishing a motive for murder against Henry Wainwright, which might be clearer once the body had been identified. The prosecution had to prove murder at the inquest, then successfully have the criminal case pass the test of there being a 'case to answer' at the Police Court, before the matter ever reached the Old Bailey. Matters moved quickly however and, following an arrest in mid-September, the police had the case ready at the Central Criminal Court in late November.

Inspector Fox had been in the right place at the right time when Henry Wainwright arrived at the station. His methodical approach to evidence gathering stood the case in good stead. The whole country would be watching developments, so he had to get things right. His efforts later earned him a well-earned commendation.

Another place where police needed to search was the unoccupied Hen and Chickens. The body parts had been on their way there when their journey was interrupted by Turner and Cox. Inspector Fox made another incriminating discovery: He stated that on checking the cellar there he found three cartloads of loose earth which he found after he had crept through a hole.

These discoveries were hugely important. The key found by PC Turner on Henry Wainwright fitted the door to the Hen and Chickens. Henry had no business being there. What was effectively a grave in the cellar was obviously the intended final resting place for Harriet. Three cartloads of earth meant that a lot of time and effort had been taken to prepare it. Who had dug the hole? There was much more to be done, but the case was strengthening all the time.

Chapter Seven

Criminal Hearings

The Police Court Hearings

The First Appearance – Monday, 13 September 1875

Henry Wainwright would not have spent an enjoyable weekend, incarcerated for the first time in his life in a grubby little cell at Stones End. The Monday morning brought a new experience for Henry, travelling to court, not in a smart London cab, but in a police van.

The first appearance at Southwark Police Court would see both prisoners being remanded in custody. However, there was a large amount of detective work that was still required for a case to be put together, including the key element of identifying the deceased. The police van entered the court via the rear yard. The *Police Illustrated News*[1] helpfully provided a drawing of the back of the court, showing the gates being guarded by policemen as well as a mounted officer.

Borough Police Court, *Illustrated Police News* supplement, 11 December 1875. (*Copyright The British Library Board. All Rights Reserved*)

The prosecution only needed to buy some time by presenting enough evidence to the court for the magistrates to adjourn the case to allow further enquiries to be made.

The prosecution presented the evidence of Alfred Stokes, PC Turner and Cox and Dr Larkin. The evidence of this group of key witnesses was more than enough to convince the magistrate to grant a remand. The case was duly adjourned by Mr Ralph Augustus Benson till the following week on the 21 September 1875. The case was too serious to consider bail, so

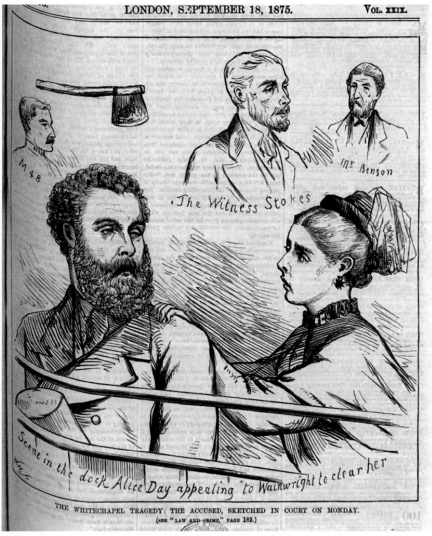

LONDON, SEPTEMBER 18, 1875.   VOL. XXIX.

The Witness Stokes

M 48

Mr Benson

Scene in the dock Alice Day appealing to Wainwright to clear her

THE WHITECHAPEL TRAGEDY: THE ACCUSED, SKETCHED IN COURT ON MONDAY.
(SEE "LAW AND CRIME" PAGE 182.)

Wainwright and Alice Day in the dock (below), the murder weapon (top left), Stokes (top middle) and Mr Benson (top right). Sketched in court, Penny Illustrated Paper, 18 September 1875. (*Copyright The British Library Board. All Rights Reserved*)

both defendants were sent to Horsemonger Lane Gaol[2] to sit out the next seven days. The *London Evening Standard* commented on the effect on poor Mrs Wainwright following the first hearing, stating that she was unable to believe that her husband had been implicated in such a charge as he was so uniformly kind. The report added that thousands of 'curious spectators' had visited Wainwright's premises in Whitechapel.

The same edition of the *Standard*[3] continued with some basic information about the first hearing;

> At the Southwark Police Court yesterday. Henry Wainwright aged 36, School House Lane, Chingford, and Alice Day, aged 20, a dress-maker, of 2 Queen's Court, Commercial Road East, were placed in the dock charged with having in their possession the mutilated body of an adult female.

The Second Hearing – Tuesday, 21 September 1875
The following week, the case returned to Southwark Police Court. One important breakthrough that had been in the interim was that the identity of the victim having been discovered. This enabled the Crown to bring a more specific charge, as mentioned in the *Weekly Dispatch* newspaper.[4] 'Mr Poland in opening the case, said he now charged Henry Wainwright with the murder of Harriet Lane.'

Medical evidence together with information from Harriet Lane's father had helped in identifying the corpse, so the fog of intrigue and mystery surrounding the events of the case was slowly beginning to clear.

The Buckingham Express[5] gave more detail about the prisoners and proceedings at a packed courthouse, stating that; 'Alice Day's release from custody was received with applause in court, and on leaving the building was cheered on all sides. She would never meet Henry again.'

Mr Poland had told the court that the Crown was offering no evidence against her as no incriminating evidence had been discovered. Alice Day's representative, Mr Louis Lewis, commended her release adding that some newspaper reports had published some detrimental comments about her character. Mr Benson told her, 'As the Crown withdraws every charge against you, you are at present discharged'.[6]

It was reported in the *Weekly Dispatch*[7] that the departure from the building of both Alice Day and Alfred Stokes was effected despite the crowd rushing forwards to see them. At the end of proceedings that day, the case was adjourned till 28 September.

The Third Hearing – Tuesday, 28 September 1875

The third court appearance was a short affair, being heard by magistrate Mr Partridge in the absence of Mr Benson. No new witnesses or evidence was heard. Superintendent Garforth asked for a remand till 5 October as enquiries were still ongoing. According to the *London Evening Standard*,[8] a vast crowd awaited Wainwright's arrival at court. At the end of proceedings, as he left court, Wainwright was hissed at by the mob waiting outside.

The Fourth Hearing – Thomas Wainwright joins the case – Saturday, 2 October

On the morning of Saturday, 2 October 1875, Thomas Wainwright's luck finally ran out, and having been picked up on a warrant for desertion of his wife, he appeared at Clerkenwell Police Court. That case against him was discharged, but Chief Inspector McDonald was waiting to feel his collar on the more serious matter of having assisted his brother Henry in murder. *The York Herald*,[9] reported that there 'was a scene' when he was taken. He was then conveyed to Stones End Police Station and then onto Southwark Police Court by the afternoon.

At court, Thomas was charged with being an accessory after the fact in the wilful murder of Harriet Lane, on or about 11 September 1874, at 215 High Street, Whitechapel.

Mr Poland was at court to represent the Crown in prosecuting, while Mr Moody appeared for Thomas. Poland told the court that evidence existed that suggested Thomas' involvement by impersonating Edward Frieake and to being responsible for purchasing the chopper and the shovel which were used for mutilating Harriet Lane's body.

Chief Inspector McDonald, Inspector Fox, Detective Sergeant Forster and the genuine Mr Frieake all gave evidence which was more than sufficient to have Thomas remanded in custody until 5 October to tie in with his co-accused, Henry Wainwright. The application for bail from Mr Moody was, not surprisingly, refused, but he did say on behalf of his client that Thomas denied all knowledge of any connection to the murder, though he did admit to the purchase of the shovel and the axe.

With Henry's brother now implicated, a murderous conspiracy had been uncovered and the police were getting closer to discovering the truth of the Whitechapel Mystery.

The Fifth Hearing – Tuesday, 5 October 1875

An immense crowd jostled to get a look at the most infamous brothers in England, while 200 people[10] queued to get a ticket outside the court. The brothers entered the dock surrounded by policemen.

The hearing heard further live evidence from several witnesses including Ellen Wilmore and Edward Frieake. The whole investigation would become something of a three act play with so many court proceedings going over the same evidence. This police court case was simply to establish whether there was sufficient evidence to decide whether there was a 'case to answer' against the brothers. The court would pass no opinion on the brothers' guilt, so long as they decided that the matter warranted a full judge and jury trial. The case would simply be committed to the Old Bailey. The court adjourned at 5.35pm till the following morning.

The Sixth Hearing – Wednesday, 6 October
The case resumed at Southwark Police Court with a new group of the less significant witnesses. Mr Moody again asked for bail for Thomas. *The Evening Standard*[11] described the magistrate's decision, stating that there was a peculiar chain of evidence, though not a strong one, against Thomas, but that bail was out of the question. The case was adjourned again till 12 October.

The Seventh Hearing – Tuesday, 12 October
The hearing began at 1.25pm and another long list of witnesses appeared in the shape of Dr Larkin and some other lesser witnesses. The case was finally adjourned at 6.15pm.[12] The court would reassemble for its final act on the following morning. Henry must have known that his case would be committed to the Old Bailey, but Thomas was still clinging to the hope that the case against him was not compelling enough. He would spend the night pondering his fate.

The Eighth Hearing – Wednesday, 13 October – Decision Day
The final hearing at Southwark Police Court began at 12.20pm. It was a final push from the prosecution to get the case over the line and see it safely through to the Old Bailey at some time in late autumn. Superintendent Garforth and Inspector Fox looked on with fingers crossed that they had done enough.

Mr Benson dealt first with Henry. *The Globe*,[13] gave the details; 'I shall commit you to take your trials, you, Henry Wainwright, for feloniously and with malice aforethought wilfully killing and murdering Harriet Louisa Lane'. Mr Pelham reserved Henry's defence and called no witnesses.

The magistrate then turned to the charge against Thomas. As he began his summing up, Thomas' heart must have been pounding out of his chest. He was praying to be released from the torture he was now suffering.

Prior to his judgement, Mr Moody addressed the bench on Thomas' situation. He told the court that Thomas denied all the charges. He added that any letters written by Thomas were made without any guilty knowledge and that the witnesses who had attended an identity parade to pick him out, had failed to make a positive choice with any degree of certainty. *The Globe* reported Benson's final decision. It was short and sweet; 'I do not feel it to be my duty to otherwise than to send Thomas to take his trial us an accessory after the fact'.

Moody[14] again broached the subject of bail, promising a substantial surety for Thomas' release. Benson thought the idea of bail preposterous, saying, 'You are asking me to take a step which is utterly without precedent. There is no precedent for admission to bail under these circumstances.'

The risk of flight was more than a concern for Mr Benson.[15] Who would have risked putting up what would have been a huge sum of surety cash? Perhaps his brother William could have offered his money? After all he was already paying for the lawyers. As the court clock struck 7pm, the long committal trial was finally over.

It was not the end of the road yet for the brothers. They had lost the police court round, but the final match of the series was now awaiting them at the highest criminal court in the land. They were down, rather than out, and the final inquiry was to set the score back to even. The case would have to be proved beyond a reasonable doubt, surely this would give them a chance? The trial at the 'Big House'[16] was going to involve another 6 weeks of waiting and hoping.

The Inquest

On the day before the Inquest began, the criminal proceedings had begun at Southwark Police Court. That process would be the start of hearing evidence to justify committing the case to the Old Bailey for a criminal trial. While that process was going on, the Inquest was running in parallel hearing evidence from the same witnesses. There would later be a full blown nine day trial at the Central Criminal Court.

The inquest was a vital part of the legal process and was held in the vestry of what is now referred to as Southwark Cathedral, but was known in 1875 as 'St. Saviours'. The all-male panel of thirteen jurors[17] all lived close to the magnificent building. Jury Foreman, George Riley, lived in Borough High Street, as did 8 of the others.

An inquest was held by the coroner to determine four main points following a death;

'Viewing the body', *Illustrated Police News*, 25 September 1875. (*Copyright The British Library Board. All Rights Reserved*)

- Who the deceased was
- When and where they died
- The medical cause of death
- How they came by their death

In most 'routine' inquests, the answers to these questions will be straightforward, but following the discovery of an 'unknown' corpse which had been hidden undiscovered for a year, all of the questions were going to be much harder to establish. The court had to establish for certain, who the body was.

The inquest began on 15 September 1875. Inquests in those days were often held in places like pubs, and usually lasted just a few hours. This case was going to be far lengthier than the average, and required 4 separate hearings, including 3 additional dates on 24 September, 1 October and 14 October.

The first job of the day was to be the most unedifying. *The Globe Newspaper*[18] on 15 September described what happened; 'The jurymen proceeded to view the remains, which were deposited in the mortuary adjoining St Saviours'. It was customary in those days for the jury to physically see the body. It was not a job for those with weak stomachs.

As there were to be three court cases, the Police Court, the Inquest and the Old Bailey, the main evidence of the witnesses is described in the later chapters concerning the main Central Criminal Court trial.

On the first day of the Inquest there was a lot more for the police to discover in the matter, and no conclusion could be arrived at, at that stage. The police and medical men needed time to complete their enquiries. At the first hearing, there was still no absolute certainty who the corpse actually was, but Alfred Stokes' evidence gave everyone a pretty good idea who it might be.

The medical men got to work on the post mortem. *The Illustrated Police News*[19] gave a graphic account of the procedure in the mortuary. The smell of death consumed the location. The smell was so bad that only the doctors seemed to be able to cope with it; 'In a narrow passage, lay fragments of a human being. When I entered, Mr Larkin, a surgeon, was poising a saw in his hand, and about to cut the sternum: the trunk, from the shriveled neck to the pelvis, being, as is commonly the case, the 3 most perfect parts of the divided and rudely slaughtered body'.

The coffin contained twelve pieces of remains. The viscera had been taken from the stomach and placed in jars for future examination. There was hair still on the head, clotted with earth and dirty lime. The body was placed in an elm coffin with a lid, which contained an inserted pane of glass measuring 1 foot by 6 inches, so that any potential witness who was trying to identify the body would be spared the overpowering stench.

The inquest was presided over by the coroner for Southwark and the City of London, Mr William John Payne.[20] On the last day of the Inquest on 14 October, the jury had to decide who, if anyone, was responsible for the death of the body who had been proved to be Harriet Lane. The Inquest record in the National Archives gave the answer quite simply. The record stated: 'Wilful murder against Henry Wainwright.[21]

By the end of proceedings, all four points of the inquest had been established by the coroner's jury. It wasn't quite so much a 'Professor Plumb in the ball room with the lead piping,' verdict, but they established that the body was that of Harriet Lane, killed on 11 September 1874 at 215 Whitechapel Road, death being due to two bullets into her brain, by the hands of Henry Wainwright.

'Henry and Tom in the police van', *Illustrated Police News*, 30 October 1875. (*Copyright The British Library Board. All Rights Reserved*)

Chapter Eight

Harriet Lane's Funeral

A drawing of the funeral of Harriet Lane on Tuesday 19 October was featured on the front page of the *Illustrated Police News* in their 30 October 1875 edition. It was a large affair with crowds of people attending to gawp or to pay their respects. Horse drawn funeral carriages are shown entering the large gates of the Waltham Cemetery. Several policemen on horseback and on foot are on the scene to control the crowds.

Newspaper reports[1] noted that the funeral of poor Harriet Lane had attracted a large crowd of 2,000 mourners. A polished elm coffin contained the mutilated remains which were transported by hearse from London to Waltham Abbey Cemetery. Details of the 11am funeral had been kept secret in order to avoid large crowds attending the event, but with onlookers forming near the cemetery, the service was put back till 3pm.

Miss Ellen Wilmore was in attendance with Beatrice before a large and mainly female crowd had gathered. The concluding act of the afternoon was

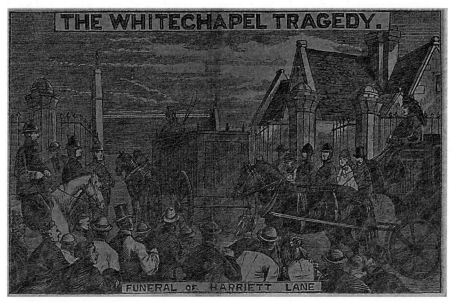

Funeral of Harriet Lane, *Illustrated Police News*, 30 October 1875. (*Copyright The British Library Board. All Rights Reserved*)

when Miss Wilmore 'held up the little child Beatrice who dropped some flowers onto the coffin.'[2]

The Burial Board for the Parish of Waltham Holy Cross, 'Notice of Interment' showed that Harriet Louisa Lane, 'an unmarried woman', aged 23 years, was buried on 18 October 1875 in an 'unbricked', but consecrated grave.

The record was signed by William Gardener and was endorsed, 'by Coroner's warrant'. Harriet was buried in Plot 1167, and is on the end of a row not far from the main entrance to the west side of the Cemetery in Sewardstone Road, not far from the rear of the chapel.

Authors Note; I visited the Old Cemetery myself in January 2022 on a beautiful, frosty morning. The entrance gate, gatehouse and chapel were remarkably unchanged from the 1875 drawing from the *Illustrated Police News*. The plot number could not be pinpointed exactly and there were very few actual headstones in this section. It was a shame that Harriet's final resting place didn't have a suitable memorial.

Tuesday, 19 October 1875 had seen the final act in the life of the unfortunate Harriet Lane. Having been heartlessly executed with pistol shots to the back of the head, the poor girl at least may not have suffered for long after being silenced by Henry Wainwright. No one had been able to mourn her loss for over a year, with family and friends being perplexed as to her sudden 'supposed' departure from London. At least now, her body had been given a decent Christian burial and she could finally rest in peace.

Chapter Nine

Alice Day

As we know, Henry Wainwright liked the company of young and attractive women. It was one of several of his failings in life. He had married Elizabeth Fanny Minshull in August 1862, when she was just about to celebrate her 22nd birthday. The following year, in October 1863, they were blessed with the arrival of a son, Henry Minshull Wainwright. Further children arrived at regular intervals, and finally, Lillian Flora Wainwright arrived on 4 June 1871.

When Wainwright first met Harriet Lane in 1871, Mrs Wainwright would just be recovering from baby number five and was then 31 years old. She may not, in Henry's eyes, have been looking quite as attractive as she did in 1862 when they had got married, and his eyes had started to wander towards a younger, more attractive model?

The Policeman and Alice Day (in cab), *Illustrated Police News*, 25 September 1875. (*Copyright The British Library Board. All Rights Reserved*)

Enter stage left, the 'young and attractive' Harriet Lane. Enter stage right, the young and relatively attractive actress, Alice Day. I have seen an original photograph of Alice at the National Archives (Ref Copy 1/30/356.) The picture was registered under the Copyright (Works of Art) Act on 23 September 1875. It was taken by Alfred Bowes of 86 Whitechapel Road. Her hair was tied back in plaits and she wore a dark Victorian dress. Beauty is in the eye of the beholder of course. I will let you decide where she rates on the scale of attractiveness. The date of Mr Bowes' application is significant. It's only 4 days after Alice's release from custody at Southwark Police Court. I think she holds a worn expression and her eyes appear somewhat sunken; hardly surprising when you consider what had just happened to her.

Henry Wainwright's premises at 84 Whitechapel Road was right next door to the Pavilion Theatre. It was a hugely popular venue for the East enders to flock to, to enable them to forget their troubles for an hour or two. One thing that such a theatre always had in good supply was good looking young ladies to attract the punters. Alice Day was one such entertainer. She also attracted Henry Wainwright.

The life of Alice Day has been difficult to follow after the Old Bailey trial. It seems that she had become a regular at the Pavilion Theatre, and though she got good reviews, she had not got near the top of the bill in any of her shows, and appears to have been a girl well suited to playing supporting rolls.

Alice was, whether by bad luck or Henry Wainwright's judgement, in the wrong place at absolutely the worst possible time. Was it an accidental meeting between the pair on 11 September 1875, or had Henry maneuvered the meeting in order to make him look less of a murderer should he be stopped by the police? Why else would he have invited her on such a cab ride?

Being found in the cab with half of Harriet Lane's body, her arrest had been justified in the circumstances. Alice and Henry made their first appearance at Southwark Police Court on 13 September. She told the magistrate, Mr Benson, that she had met Wainwright in Commercial Road and he had asked her to go with him, but she had had no idea what was contained in the bags. She was merely going for a ride with him to pass the time.

At this stage, although there was no actual evidence of her involvement in a murder, police enquiries were ongoing and a remand in custody was the certain outcome of the hearing, but Alice Day was innocent of any crime, other than associating with a man like Henry Wainwright. The *Penny Illustrated Paper* of 18 September 1875 stated that as Mr Benson informed the couple of their remand in custody, Alice made an impassioned plea. 'Alice Day clutched the male prisoner and piously exclaimed; 'For God's sake, tell them what I know of this matter. I know nothing'

Wainwright told the court he agreed with her assertion, but Benson's hands were tied. He told Miss Day the following;

> It is quite possible that this statement may be true; but, in the presence of such details as I have before me, it is impossible that the female prisoner can be discharged. All I can recommend her to do is to get up as much favourable evidence as possible before the next examination.

Alice Day spent 10 days in custody at Horsemonger Lane Gaol following her initial court appearance on 13 September. The Crown later dropped all charges against her and she was released on 21 September. Although the experience must have given her sleepless nights, it did at least give her a chance of a business opportunity. She would not have been a highly paid performer, and the infamy of her incarceration and association with a murderer would, for the time being, have rendered her as unemployed, with little prospect of work.

She then did what a lot of people in similar circumstances would have done, she wrote a pamphlet on her experiences to be sold to the masses. Her story, entitled *From the Footlights to the Prison Cell* was available at all good newsagents priced at one penny.[1] To tempt prospective customers, the booklet contained a 'facsimile of handwriting' as well as a 'portrait of the authoress.'

One can only hope that Alice got a good cut of the profits of this publication. Not being one to rest on her laurels, another Wainwright Murder related publication hit the bookshops around the same time.[2] This second offering proclaimed news of, 'Startling disclosures of the lives of Harriet Lane and Alice Day', with the promise of 'highly interesting and facts never before printed'; 'private secrets exposed'.

'Don't believe everything you read in the papers', is a commonly known true expression, and the newshounds in 1875 (as well as in 2023) printed the truth, the whole truth and nothing like the truth? Reporters are driven by editors to get bigger, better stories, to titillate and entertain readers who would be ready to part with another hard earned penny[3] so as to keep abreast of the latest news. Perhaps there was no such thing as bad publicity for Alice Day, as each new report would generate more interest in her story.

We don't know what became of Alice, but anyone looking at her character in this case could feel a modicum of pity for her. She had met Wainwright due the proximity of their respective workplaces. He already had a wife with five children, and a second 'wife' with their two children, but he could not resist the company of a pretty face, especially one unencumbered by children, and she was conveniently right on his doorstep.

Alice always maintained that she and Henry shared a strictly platonic relationship. She was someone who may have seen the brush maker as a man who would stand her food and drink and generally treat her nicely. A working girl could always do with any little help that she could get, but she would never have expected to have been drawn into Henry's dangerous high stakes double life.

She claimed in court that her meeting with Henry on 11 September was by accident. Was she taken aboard the cab as a cover for his moving of the body? Who would suspect a well-to-do man and woman in a cab to be transporting a corpse? He certainly wasn't bringing her along for her witty conversation as he told her not to talk to her on the journey, which suggests that she was part of his plan.

It would be helpful to hear what Alice had to say for herself following her release from custody. In fact, in order to try and protect her reputation, she released a statement to the press regarding her acquaintance with Henry as well as how she came to be in a cab with him and the incriminating dead body. This is what she told the *IPN* in its 2 October edition:

> I have been on the stage nine years altogether, first at the Pavilion. I made the acquaintance of Wainwright several years ago, he was a constant visitor behind the scenes at the theatre. It was his habit to converse with everybody, but not more with me than any of the other ladies of the ballet. At times he showed me more special attention, and occasionally I must admit, thoughtlessly – I accompanied him, when not engaged at the Pavilion, to the West End theatres.
>
> He never saw me home in my life on any occasion, but I have in the company of others, partaken of refreshments with him at various public houses in the neighbourhood of the theatre. I have been in one or other of his shops many times, but it was always when his shopmen have been there, or I have been accompanied by some female friend. Lately his visits seemed to fall off as his money got short. Before that time, he would send for champagne and sandwiches for the members of the ballet corps, and as he was such a favourite with all, nobody felt any reason for declining his kindness.

Alice was saying that Henry Wainwright was a friend to all at the theatre, loved by all, not just her. She may not have been aware of his predatory character? Wainwright's bonhomie good nature seems to have tailed off dramatically when his creditors started closing in. But essentially, we are asked to believe that Henry's intentions were perfectly honourable, and that Alice only saw him as a generous neighbour who could show the girls a good but innocent time. It's hard to know whether he actually had designs on Alice. One thing we should question is, did Henry tell his wife that he was taking show girls to the theatre and the pubs? I think we probably know the answer to that. As for Alice, perhaps she merely saw Henry as a bit of fun and a provider of a free lunch?

Alice's statement about meeting Wainwright on 11 September 1875 expresses that she encountered Wainwright that day by chance coming towards her near the pub. She was only killing time. While for Henry, placing her in her cab was a chance to give him a more innocent appearance if he had been stopped by the police. This chance meeting was to change Alice's life.

Wainwright showed her into cab that was standing nearby. She was aware it was heading for the city. She saw two parcels packed in American Cloth on the front seat, side by side, but she took no notice of them. She stated that she had accompanied him with similar parcels to the city previously, and so was not the slightest bit curious about these bundles. Wainwright did not mention anything about the parcels, but he gave her a newspaper, saying to her, 'Read that, I have something to think about'. He certainly did. There was no further conversation on the journey.

As Wainwright was smoking a cigar, she had not noticed any smell, but as the journey wore on, she did notice something smelling very unpleasantly, which she put down to the sunshine on the American leather. Alice then continued her story:

> We stopped at some place like a bank on the other side of London Bridge. Then he said' I'm going to take these parcels to a warehouse round the corner here. I'll take one first, and if the warehouse is open, I'll leave it and come back for the other.

As Wainwright exited the cab, Alice could have been forgiven for thinking she was out for a pleasant afternoon drive through the city, and that she would soon be back in Whitechapel in time for her evening performance at the Pavilion. A few moments later as she sat in the cab waiting for Henry's return, the door was opened not by her fellow traveller, but a uniformed policeman with a serious expression on his face. This shocking turn of events put Alice into a fluster. She admitted that she may have, in her agitated state, have told the officer that she was waiting for 'her husband'.

Alice then went on to describe what she knew about Wainwright:

I never heard Wainwright speak of Mrs King – Never. I never saw her. I never knew he had illegitimate children – not even a whisper about it – till now. There is no truth in the assertion that Mrs King has seen me and Wainwright together, or that she ever threatened me. It's said that I received money from Wainwright. – Ten shillings a week. To that assertion I give the most emphatic denial. If I had ten shillings from him, which would have been a considerable amount to me, I should not have killed myself by working all the day at dressmaking and going on the stage at night. I am not particularly fond of the stage, though I was one of the front row ladies in the ballet.

There were lots of rumours and speculation flying in all directions about Wainwright's association with Alice Day, though actual evidence of any impropriety is markedly lacking. But mud sticks, and Alice was trying her best to distance herself from scandal and her former friend. Her statement had the ring of truth about it.

Alice then went on to describe her experience in prison. On being asked, 'How were you treated in prison'? This was her surprising response:

Very kindly indeed by everybody from the Governor of the prison downwards. I did not hear one unkind word from either the warders of the gaol or the police at the station. All were very kind to me indeed and I never felt afraid, I knew I had a clear conscience. I have got somewhat thinner from the confinement. So confident did I feel of being discharged on Tuesday that I promised to see a particular lady friend next Saturday.

The 2 October 1875 edition of the *Illustrated Police News* carried a drawing of Miss Day, this time showing her being released from custody. As she emerges through a group of policemen, she escapes to freedom to the cheers of the waiting crowd. Men wave their hats in celebration of her liberty being granted, even a small black dog looks excited at the news. This may have been Alice's last cheering audience for a while, or maybe even forever?

Alice was born[4] in Whitechapel on 23 December 1854 to parents, George, a mariner and dressmaker, Eliza Day, at 14 Moss Buildings, Whitechapel. Alice's parents lived on into the 1890s but no trace of Alice can currently be found in any official document after the murder. Her release from custody had lifted the worry of execution from her mind, but it hadn't helped her employment prospects. It's a shame that she disappeared as it would be nice to think that her life improved after becoming an unwilling cast member of the Whitechapel Mystery.

Chapter Ten

The Old Bailey Trial

The Trial Approaches

E ntering the Old Bailey is a sobering experience. The current Edwardian Old Bailey,[1] with its later modern court additions, is a mixture of stunning architecture[2] with some cramped and old-fashioned courtrooms where the public have to queue up outside to gain admission. The 22-ton golden Statue of Justice on top of the dome reminds visitors of the purpose of the most important criminal court in the land.

The Old Bailey of 1875 was a different structure to the present one, but the building known as the Old Bailey[3] had been trying London's criminals on the site since 1674. In 1875, it would still have provoked fear in the hearts of the two Wainwright brothers as they entered the courtroom for the first time. Contemporary drawings[4] of the trial show a crammed court, with the judge at the highest level in the room on the right, looking directly across to the dock, where the brothers were flanked by two warders.

Arrival of the Wainwrights at Newgate. *Illustrated Police News* supplement, 13 November 1875. (*Copyright The British Library Board. All Rights Reserved*)

To the right of the judge, with their backs to the windows, was the jury box where the twelve member all male panel sat in two rows watching the proceedings. Between the judge and the jury was the witness box, almost in touching distance of the jurors. Below and in front of the judge was the clerk of the court who looked out on the well of the court where the numerous lawyers all sat.

The case was to be heard by the Lord Chief Justice himself at 10am on the morning of Monday, 22 November 1875. Proceedings eventually got under way at 11am with Henry being charged with the murder of Harriet Lane as well as an alternative charge of 'murder of an unknown woman'.[5]

The Old Bailey Trial begins

Some weeks prior to the trial commencing, the London correspondent of the *Glasgow News* had been invited on a tour of inspection of Newgate Prison where, by happy coincidence, he had had the chance to see both prisoners. He began by reporting on a sighting of Thomas. This is the article from the Stroud News;[6]

> The prisoner Thomas Wainwright, was seen pacing rapidly round the exercise yard. The party were taken to the Henry Wainwright's cell. He sat at a small table. He looked pale, and he sat at a three-legged stool, and on a similar seat beside him sat a warder. He is not left alone day or night.

The public don't normally get to hear from the witnesses and about their experiences of the trial, but one of the minor witnesses in the case did write down something about the case in a 1916 book that appeared 40 years after the trial, called *Survivors Tales of Famous Crimes*, edited by Walter Wood. The pages devoted to the Wainwright case came from an interview with one of the cases', minor witnesses, John Matthew Steel,[7] who was a pawnbroker who worked in Mr W. Dicker's business in the Commercial Road. He gave evidence to prove that a wedding ring had been pawned by Harriet Lane in the name of King.

Steel described that he was on speaking terms with Henry Wainwright and sometimes spent time with him and that he was 'always very good company, full of cheerful conversation and always ready with a laugh and a joke'.

Mr Steel described the boredom of being involved in a long, drawn-out court case with lots of waiting around. He described the court attenders as well as how he passed the time.

Day after day that horrible court was packed by people who ranged in rank from a duchess downwards, for the case had aroused intense and universal interest. We passed a good deal of our time while waiting to be called, by playing cards, draughts, and dominoes.

The case ran for 9 days, beginning at the Bailey on Monday, 22 November 1875, and took place every day except Sunday, 28 November, until the verdicts were delivered on 1 December. The trial was registered as case number one in the Surrey list.[8] Sitting in the best seat in the house for the trial was the Lord Chief Justice, Sir Alexander James Edmund Cockburn, (1802–1880).

Henry and Thomas were both provided with chairs and were sat down in the dock to endure the following nine days. The Clerk, Mr Avory, then read out the arraignments. The charge against Henry was simple. The 'wilful murder in the county of Middlesex of one Harriet Louisa Lane'. Thomas' indictment was rather longer in that;

'The said Thomas Wainwright did aid and abet, counsel and procure, the said Henry Wainwright to do and commit the said felony; and that he did also, well knowing the said felony to have been committed, feloniously receive, harbour, and maintain the said Henry Wainwright'.

Both prisoners pleaded 'not guilty' and the trial commenced.[9] This big case required the services of two prosecuting barristers, Sir John Holker (1828–1882) and Sir Harry Bodkin Poland, (1829–1928). It was a formidable team. Taking centre stage that morning for the prosecution was the Attorney General, Sir John Holker QC. It was his job to set out to the jury the Crown's case against both prisoners. He rose to his feet to begin nine dramatic days of witness testimony and legal arguments.

John Hamilton described Holker in the *Dictionary of National Biography*, praising his power in the courtroom, stating; 'Persuasiveness, shrewdness, and tact made him extraordinarily successful in winning verdicts'. In his opening address, Holker pointed out that whilst the cases against both brothers were linked, they had to be examined by the jury completely separately. He then laid out the history of Henry's financial problems, as well as his intimate relationship with his mistress, Harriet Lane, leading on to the decline in the relationship between the two and adding that he was in possession of a revolver. He continued that Henry Wainwright had formed a plan to enable him to get rid of his inconvenient woman, with an 'Edward Frieake' being introduced into his scheme.

Thomas and Henry Wainwright in the dock, *Illustrated Police News*, 23 October 1875. (*Copyright The British Library Board. All Rights Reserved*)

Sir John made mention of the letters and telegrams apparently sent from Mr Frieake which was all part of a deception, and also the attempt to bribe the arresting officers when caught red handed with Harriet's body. The identity evidence to prove who the body was outlined, but the opening speech concluded with details of the evidence against Thomas. His final point being that if there was an innocent explanation from Thomas as to his involvement in the murder conspiracy then he would be glad to hear it, 'but if no such explanation could be given, they would be entitled, in the face of the proof of guilt, to act upon them'. It had been a sobering start for the Wainwright brothers. Their own barristers were going to have an uphill task trying to throw doubt on the Crown case.

After lunch the first witness called was John Butler[10] of the Metropolitan Police's Surveyors Department. He had constructed models of the site of the discovery of Harriet's remains in Whitechapel Road as well as the prepared grave in the Hen and Chickens. He also produced a scale map of both locations which are now in the National Archives. He was led through his evidence by

Mr Harry Bodkin Poland, who used a white wand to point out particular points of interest about the model.

Witness of the day however was the eagerly awaited hero of the hour, Alfred Stokes. After giving his evidence of chasing Wainwright's cab, the defence had its first real opportunity at cross examination and trying to cast doubt on a primary prosecution witness. Defence barrister, Edward T.E. Besley (1826–1901), took to his feet to interview east ender, Mr Stokes. *The Worcester Chronicle*[11] report stated that the grim evidence of Stokes was no cause for laughter;

> Though the naivete of the speaker and his intense cockneyisms were frequently the cause of a suppressed titter in the court'. The witness was also severely questioned by the learned Judge.

Stokes was followed by PCs Turner and Cox who successfully gave their evidence as mentioned earlier in this book in Chapter Five.

Constables Turner and Cox completed the day's witnesses as they told of the horrific find in the two parcels. It had been a dramatic day with these vital witnesses having got in body blows to the defence. The jury, not being allowed out, were then escorted by an officer of the court to spend the night at the Cannon Street Hotel.

The Dundee Courier[12] reported that the William Wainwright was footing the bill for the defence of his brothers. The trial of the decade had finally begun. With a huge witness list to get through, it was going to be a trial that required stamina on the part of the defendants, legal teams, officials, not forgetting the friends and relations of Harriet Lane. News of each day's events would be eagerly read over the breakfast tables of Britain.

Chapter Eleven

Day 2 of the Trial

After a dramatic first day where possibly the most exciting witnesses involved in the case had opened for the prosecution, day two was another big draw for spectators. Stokes and the arresting officer's evidence would have made a huge impression on the jury. Interest was such that the second day in court was going to be even more packed that the first.

The Daily Telegraph,[1] described the crammed nature of the main show court;

> More crowded even than on the first day, if that was possible, the chief court at the Old Bailey. There seemed, a greater number of ladies, of counsel, visitors on the bench, and of the general public. Seats that had then been filled by four spectators were now packed with five. Where fifty wigs and gowns had covered an allotted space, there might now have been counted sixty.

First witness of the day was the cabman William Andrews who had unintentionally become the 'getaway driver' for Henry and the body to Borough High Street.

After the cab driver's short appearance, everyone in the court was eagerly awaiting the witness box being filled by the now infamous Alice Day. A young lady who was very close to Henry Wainwright and had begun as a suspect for murder, was now appearing as a witness for the prosecution. *The Evening Standard*[2] noted her improved appearance.

We have already heard from Alice in the chapter, 'Alice Day', so we knew that she appears to have innocently taken a ride in Henry's cab at precisely the worst possible moment to do so, resulting in her unfortunate arrest on suspicion of murder.

The next witness was 'M' Division Inspector, Matthew Fox who repeated his evidence as was mentioned in earlier chapters. He was followed into the witness box by Detective Constable Newman who discovered the loose floorboards at 215 Whitechapel Road and was also the finder of the keeper ring and wedding ring belonging to Harriet Lane, along with teeth, bone, and hair of the victim.

The last of that day's police officers was Chief Inspector James Constantine McDonald from 'H' Division who gave evidence of the search of the crime scene as well as the cutting of the joists and floorboards.

The next witness on the second day who was going to give crucial evidence was Ellen Wilmore. Her evidence, apart from being long, was going to test the barristers and the onlookers of the case because she was partially deaf. *The Evening Standard*[3] gave details of the difficulties this presented to the court;

> Ellen Wilmore, dressed in mourning, appeared to be so deaf that she could not hear the questions of the Attorney General. Mr Poland consequently had to go round to the witness box and bawl his questions into her ears.

Miss Wilmore told the court that she and Harriet Lane had been apprentice milliners together at Waltham Cross in 1866 and that she first met the prisoner with Harriet in 1872, though he then went by the name of 'Percy King'. She later discovered his real name was Henry Wainwright, a brush maker. Harriet was then going by the name of 'Mrs King' and had had a child by him in August 1872. When the baby was about 3 months old, Henry had given Miss Wilmore money for the child's keep for her to look after her. She continued to care for the child until December 1873 when baby number two had arrived, after which time Harriet took on both children.

Ellen told the court that Harriet later moved to 3 Sidney Square where she used to go and visit her on Sundays. She later moved in with Harriet there between 3 August and 11 September 1874. During that period, she never saw Henry Wainwright visit. The only person that did visit however was a Mr Edward Frieake. She recalled that he visited at the end of August or start of September. She did however only see him once, and then '*only for half a moment*'. She had never seen him previously. She was asked whether she recognized the prisoner in the dock, Thomas Wainwright? She stated that she had seen him before but could not recall where.

She said that it had been arranged for her to take the two children into lodgings at 6 The Grove,[4] Stratford and look after them for 25 shillings a week. She was aware of Harriet's financial difficulties as she had been pawning items. Ellen had taken Harriet's wedding ring and keeper ring out of pawn at Dickers pawnbrokers in the Commercial Road on 11 September 1874. She had had to lend Harriet £2 in order to get her rings back. Miss Wilmore was shown the wedding and keeper ring found on the body, and stated that although she could not be certain, they resembled the rings that she had last seen Harriet wearing.

The reason that she gave for Harriet leaving Sidney Square was regarding a disturbance that had taken place one evening when her friend had been 'intoxicated' and 'excited'. She had not seen anyone else, but she had taken Harriet indoors. Following the incident, she stated that she 'had been up all night' with Harriet. Harriet was to leave the house on 11 September at 4pm.

She described Harriet as looking very neat, wearing a grey dress with jet black buttons that Harriet had sewn on herself on the morning that she was to leave. The buttons had been obtained from a shop in Commercial Road. The buttons were significant, as jet buttons had been found on the body. Some extra buttons which were fixed to a card had been retained and were shown in court to Miss Wilmore. She recognised them as she had put the extra buttons in a box. This evidence helped the prosecution to establish that the body was that of Harriet Lane.

Ellen was also able to describe the method Harriet used in doing her hair. She stated that she was accustomed to wearing a large pad at the back of her head. She had worn it every day for the last year. The pad, which was bought in the Hackney Road was fixed to her hair by a 'great many hairpins'. Her hair was fastened with a black velvet band. A black velvet band was handed to Ellen in the witness box to examine. This must have been a poignant moment for her, holding it in her hands, the band that she had worn when she had been gunned down. She was unable to positively identify it, but stated that it was similar to what Harriet wore.

Miss Wilmore then gave details to the court about her several meetings with Henry Wainwright following Harriet's disappearance (See Chapter, 'In Search of Harriet').

On 11 September 1875 Wainwright was arrested by the police. Det. Sgt. Forster came to see Miss Wilmore and her next job was visiting the St. Saviour's Dead House for the purpose of viewing the body.

The visit to visit the mortuary would not have been one to take the children to. It must have been a chilling experience for poor Ellen. As she saw the remains, she noted that the 'light auburn hair' was the same as Harriet's. Other similarities existed, as with the size and height of the body as well as the similarities in the hands and feet. Ellen also gave evidence to confirm that Harriet had a burn mark on her right leg, 4 inches below the knee which she had seen many times.

The defence took their turn in cross examining Miss Wilmore. They made great play on her reporting that the fact that she had seen a woman near the Bank of England around 6 weeks *after* 11 September 1875 in a handsome cab in the traffic while she was with one of the children. She thought the woman *might* have been Harriet, but she was unable to follow the cab due to having the child with her. The final question of Miss Wilmore's examination was a poignant one from the Lord Chief Justice. 'From the time she disappeared, has anyone directly or indirectly made enquiries after those children of yours?' – 'No Sir, except the aunt'.

After the very lengthy cross examination of Ellen Wilmore, Harriet's sister, Elizabeth Taylor, was the next occupant of the witness box. She gave evidence of her visit to Henry Wainwright to establish what had become of Harriet. He told her that he did not know Harriet's whereabouts, and that he had last seen her at Sidney Square. He had given Harriet £15 the day before leaving Sidney Square and then gave her a further £10 to go to Brighton. Mrs Taylor stated that a letter had been received from Harriet and so she and Miss Wilmore had gone to see Henry.

Mrs. Taylor was told that although he hadn't seen Harriet himself, his foreman had spotted her in a cab. She was shown a letter which stated, 'I have a lady under my protection, and I dare you or anyone else to annoy her in any way. We are now off to Paris, and mean to have a jolly spree'. Henry added that he had also received a telegram from Dover, but that he expected her to return home once she had finished 'their frolic out.' Henry continued the suggestion that Harriet was now romantically involved with 'Mr Frieake'.

Harriet's sister then gave evidence about an accident that her youngest sister had suffered with a poker. She stated that the scar on her leg was the size of a 2-shilling piece. She stated that she had visited the St Saviour's Dead House where she viewed the body, but that she had not thought about the burn mark at the time so had not looked for it. However, the remains had the same colour hair as Harriet, and the same sized hands and feet.

George William Rogers was the last witness of the day. He was called to give evidence of the handwriting of some of the letters that had been in the possession of Mrs Taylor. He was familiar with the handwriting style of both Wainwright brothers. He identified that some of the letters marked 'B', 'I' and 'F' were in the hand of Henry, while letter 'E' was in the hand of Thomas Wainwright. Letter 'G' with the signature, 'Percy King' was not in Henry's handwriting.

After a long and intriguing day, proceedings were halted at 4.50pm.

Chapter Twelve

Day 3 of the Trial

On day three, the Crown rolled out sixteen prosecution witnesses against the Wainwrights. The first group called that morning were relatives of Harriet Lane;[1] William Taylor, her brother-in-law; Sophia Allen, her sister; and her father John Lane; who all gave evidence regarding the identity of the remains as being Harriet's. Their evidence was a vital link in the chain of the evidence against Henry.

William Taylor was first in at 10am. After viewing the body, he concluded it was Harriet due to the small hands and feet, and the colour of the hair. He also noticed that two of the upper teeth projected a little, like those of Harriet. He knew about her teeth as she had previously complained about toothache to him.

Sophia Allen, said Harriet Lane was her sister. She had not viewed the body herself, but she recalled seeing an accident happen to Harriet when she was about ten years old. Harriet had been sitting on a little stool by the fire, 'when a hot poker fell out and burned her right leg', which left a scar 3 or 4 inches below the knee. Mrs Allen had last seen the scar six years previously. The scar evidence was quite crucial, more of which can be seen in the chapter regarding the evidence of the doctors who performed the post mortem.

Mrs Allen stated that Harriet was well educated, and at one time had been a governess for a family. She then identified a photograph[2] which was shown to her as one of herself and her sister taken together at a shop in Shoreditch, six years previously. She described Harriet's hair as having a 'golden tinge' in it.

The Globe then described the next witness. Harriet's father, John Lane, struggled to give his evidence of seeing his daughter's body in the dead house. 'On viewing the remains, he faltered, and almost broke down, his voice sinking to a whisper, and his distress becoming too obvious, that murmurs of sympathy arose from all parts the court'.

Mr Lane told the court that he was shown the body by Inspector Fox on 15 September. *The Hour*[3] newspaper gave details of his evidence; He said that as soon as he saw the body, he felt it was his daughter based on her hair, the hands, and feet. He also recognised the body due to the scar on the leg which he hadn't seen for 9 or 10 years.

The ID evidence from the relatives could not be described as 100 per cent conclusive, but with several unique features all being present, it was perhaps too much of a coincidence to not to have been Harriet? John Lane was sure who the body belonged to, and the jury must have been similarly convinced, but the scar was surely the clincher.

John Lane then gave some background detail about Harriet. He stated that she often used to visit her parents in Waltham, but strangely he seemed unsure of whether she was married. She last visited him in August 1874 when she was in good health. He had never met 'Mr King' by this point.

He then discovered that she had gone missing in September 1874. Around this time, he had employed Mr Eeles to make enquiries on his behalf into Harriet's whereabouts. He then gave evidence of meetings with Henry Wainwright as well as Mr Edward Frieake. (See Chapter Four, In Search of Harriet).

Ernest George Eeles then gave his evidence of dealing with both Henry Wainwright and Mr Frieake. (See details of that evidence in Chapter Four.

Edward William Frieake was the next witness who furnished the court with damaging evidence against Henry. (See details in Chapter Four).

The jury must surely have been questioning the behaviour of Henry Wainwright in relation to the Frieake business. It smacked of a cover up. As Teddy departed the witness box, the next 6 witnesses were employees of the Post Office who had dealt with the sending of telegrams from the 'other', unknown Mr Frieake. Peter Crofts had come to court from Kent, where he was a telegraph clerk at the Admiralty Pier, Dover. He stated that on 17 October 1874, three telegraphic messages in the name of Frieake were telegraphed to London. Four other GPO officials gave evidence of the telegrams.

After the GPO officials had been examined, it was the turn of Harriet Lane's landladies to appear. First to enter the witness box was widow, Mrs Susan Wells. She told the court that in 1873 she had lived at 14 St Peter Street, Hackney Road, where she rented out apartments. Between October 1873 and April 1874, she had let her rooms to 'Mr Percy King', whom she identified as Henry Wainwright. He rented the rooms for 'Mrs King', who he said was his 'sister-in-law'. Percy only visited occasionally and Mrs King then had a baby, after which time Mr King visited sometimes with another man called 'Edward'. She saw this man a few times letting him in and out of the house. She was later taken to the Southwark Station House[4] where she saw the other prisoner, Thomas Wainwright. She believed that Edward and Thomas were one and the same person, though her identification evidence was weak. She stated, 'I am not positive, but to the best of my belief, he is the party'.

The next landlady to be called was Mrs Jemima Foster, who had rooms to let at 3 Sidney Square, Commercial Road. Henry Wainwright called and asked her to take a lady, her nurse and two children. The lady was Mrs King and she charged £1 a week in rent. She wasn't sure if she was Wainwright's wife, but 'supposed' that she was. She had asked him for a reference, but not surprisingly he paid a deposit instead, and never supplied the promised reference. Mrs King lived there between May 1874 and 11 September 1874. Henry occasionally visited, but only ever came to the front door.

Someone who did come across the threshold to visit Harriet was a man called Frieake who called on three separate occasions. On the second visit, Mr Frieake brought champagne with him but no glasses. This had necessitated Mrs Foster going to the nearby Princess Royal Public House, 1–2 Sidney Square, to get some. The third visit was rather more worrying than the last one as, at 9pm, Mr King, Mr Frieake and Mrs King arrived at the front door as a disturbance was taking place. Mrs King was worse for drink and was quarrelling with Mr King, as well as telling her landlady that she had no business interfering with her and her 'husband'. It was following this unpleasantness that Mrs Foster gave her notice to leave.

Mrs Foster described that Mrs King conducted herself as a lady normally and that she was very fond of her children, who slept in her bed when the nurse, Miss Wilmore, wasn't there. Mrs King left on Friday 11 September 1874.

Mrs Foster's identification evidence as to Mr Frieake being Thomas Wainwright was also on the weak side. She had seen Thomas in an identity parade in the yard at Leman Street Police Station where she had been unable to recognise him. She then saw him again for a second time in the dock at Southwark Police Court where her memory suddenly recalled him. She stated rather unemphatically, 'I believed very possibly that he was the man.' It was hardly a conclusive identification.

A rather more persuasive identification of Mr Frieake as being Thomas Wainwright was provided by the pub landlord, James Humphries. He owned pubs in The Strand, Long Acre and Whitechapel Road, as well as the Princess Royal in Sidney Square, next door to Mrs King's lodgings. Mr Humphries knew both of the Wainwright brothers personally, having known Henry for 6–7 years, and Thomas for 4–5.

He gave evidence to say that he had seen the brothers in the private bar of his Sidney Square pub on 5 September 1874 as well as one previous occasion about a week earlier. His knowledge of their visit on 5th was detailed. The men had stayed from 4pm to between 6 and 7pm and had smoked two cigars and drank brandy and soda. Crucially, they had ordered two bottles of champagne. Mrs Foster had borrowed some glasses, while an hour later Thomas had taken away a bottle of champagne. Later that evening he saw the disturbance outside the pub as had been described by Mrs Foster.

A letter was then read to the court which tied in the date to 5 September. The letter was as follows;

LETTER 'I' 5 September 1874[5]

Dear Pet,
E.F. is coming down at 7 tonight, he will give you a call with a message from me.

Yours, P.K.
(Envelope addressed to, 'Mrs King, 3 Sidney Square, Mile End').

The important evidence linking Thomas into being Edward Frieake had been somewhat lacking from the two landladies, but the evidence from Humphries appears fairly conclusive. The two women had only seen Frieake on a few fleeting occasions, and considering the passage of time, it was no surprise that their recollections were unconvincing. The publican knew Thomas and Henry as friends for a number of years, so could 100 per cent positively identify them, and he was able to place both men in the bar next to Harriet's lodgings on the same day that Henry had written to Harriet to say that Frieake would be calling on her that evening. The pieces of the jigsaw fitted perfectly. Thomas had to be the other Teddy Frieake. In the case against Thomas Wainwright, this was very damning evidence.

Mrs Amelie Stanley was next in the witness box. She was a relation of Mrs Foster of 3 Sidney Square. She gave evidence that on a single occasion that she had been visiting Foster in September 1874, she briefly saw Teddy Frieake in the hallway of the house standing under the gas light. She attended Southwark Police Court a year later when she saw Thomas Wainwright in the dock. Asked whether he was one and the same as Mr Frieake, she said; 'He is the man I saw, to the best of my knowledge.'

It was another identification of sorts, though the fleeting aspect of her view of Frieake over 12 long months of not seeing him again brought into question whether her evidence could be relied on. It was however the 4th person to 'identify' Thomas. Could they all be wrong?

As the day neared its end, the final witness took his oath on the bible. It was Oil and Colour man, John Baylis from 149 Whitechapel Road. His business, not far from Henry Wainwright's premises, sold various goods including chloride of lime. He knew Henry Wainwright, though not intimately. He recorded in his ledger book that on 10 September 1874 (the day before the murder), he had an order for half a hundred-weight of chloride of lime from Henry Wainwright. The lime, which cost 7 shilling and sixpence and was never paid for, was delivered to 84 Whitechapel Road, but he could not be sure whether Henry or his manager Mr Rogers had ordered it. Wainwright had never ordered this substance before.

This witness gave only a small piece of evidence, but fixing the date as the day immediately before the murder showed premeditation on the part of Henry Wainwright. Why else would he want a substance like chloride of lime? He had never needed any before. The date and the material were very damaging to Henry's case. it had not been a good day for the brothers. Just before 5pm, the court adjourned for the day. Thursday was a new day and though the witnesses would not be as key as the earlier ones, a further seventeen people[6] were standing by to give their evidence against the Wainwrights in the morning. It was clear that the case would be over by Christmas, but would not be over in November.

Chapter Thirteen

Day 4 of the Trial

Afurther seventeen witnesses waited in the wings on Thursday, 25 November, the most of any of the trial days, with crowds still thronging the Old Bailey. The first witness was Charles Titiens.[1] He had previously worked for Henry Wainwright for 3 years up until July 1875. He gave evidence of detecting an offensive smell in the back part of 215 Whitechapel Road. He then obtained some chloride of lime which he sprinkled on a large pile of ashes, after which the smell appeared to have gone. In September 1874 he had taken a packing case to Mr Baylis at 149 Whitechapel Road on the instructions of Henry in order to obtain chloride of lime.

The next witness was George William Rogers, who had worked as a manager for Henry Wainwright from August 1873 till April 1875. For part of this time, Rogers had lived with his wife above Henry's shop at 84 Whitechapel Road. Luckily for them, just before the fire seriously damaged it, they had moved across the road to Henry's warehouse, at number 215. Rogers knew 'Mrs King', as he used to act as a messenger taking money and letters to her from Henry. He described her annoyance about the small amount of money Henry was sending her. Rogers stated that he had seen her come to the shop about a dozen times and that they had argued with one another.

He said that Wainwright was very particular about possession of the keys to 215, as they were kept in the counting house of 84 and Wainwright always kept the keys to the counting house with him. Sometimes Rogers could not get into the building to open up on account of only Henry having the keys. Wainwright's care of the keys for 215 appears surprisingly possessive, and appears suspiciously like someone wanting to avoid anyone poking around the warehouse where Harriet lay dead.

Rogers was also involved with the chloride of lime incident on 10 September 1874. (He stated that he was sure of the date as his wife gave birth two days later). He stated that Wainwright had asked him to find out the price of the material from Baylis' for an order for, 'someone in Southend'. This was despite the fact that the firm didn't have *any* customers from that Essex town. He saw the chloride arrive that evening but it had disappeared by the next day. He also confirmed that they had never previously used chloride of lime. This leaves us wondering, what was the material for? If the Southend purchaser actually existed, then Henry could have produced him at the trial.

After moving into 215 in November 1874, Mr and Mrs Rogers became aware of a bad smell at the end of the shop soon after Christmas. He complained to Henry several times. Wainwright said that it was a pile of ashes, which he was going to have removed.

The next subject of his cross examination related to very important evidence about a revolver that he had seen in the possession of Henry Wainwright. He told the court that on July 1874 while in the 'Counting House' at number 84, Henry had shown him a 9 or 10-inch revolver in a green baize bag that he kept in his desk. The gun had either 5 or 6 chambers and Henry asked him to pawn it for him. Henry told him, 'I'm short this week; I bought it off Sawyer, and gave him £6 for it. Get £2, 10 shillings on it'.

Rogers took the firearm to one of the pawnbrokers in Mile End Road, but was only offered a paltry 15 shillings, so declined the deal and gave it back to Wainwright who put it back in his desk. Rogers had not seen the gun since.[2] The next witness was his wife, Jane Rogers.

Mrs Rogers confirmed hearing arguments between Henry and 'Mrs King'. She had heard the words, 'don't, don't', being used on a date in August when she found Mrs King lying insensible on the floor of the shop at 84. On seeing her on the floor, she spoke to Wainwright who stated that she was, 'only a little feint', and he asked her for some vinegar. Wainwright always seemed to have a ready supply of lame excuses about his suspicious behaviour.

The next three witnesses were all employed at William Dicker's Pawnbrokers in 1874 and included John Matthew Steele, George Overall and Herribin Mason Leets. They all gave evidence of rings that had been pawned. Steele produced two pawn tickets[3] from Dicker's at 1 Upton Place in Commercial Road. One was for a wedding ring in May 1874 for 10 shillings in the name of 'Ann King', of 3 Sidney Square.

The second, dated 22 May 1874, was for a 'keeper ring' for 8 shillings in the same name and address. Both items were taken out of pawn on 11 September 1874, though none of the men recalled anything else about who had recovered them. Thirteen and a half pence had to be paid in interest. The name Ann King is curious, but this was explained by Mr Steele. He stated that if the Christian name wasn't given by the person pawning, staff would call men, 'John' and women, 'Ann'.

The next set of three visitors to the witness box gave very useful evidence about hearing shots being fired on 11 September 1874 in the vicinity of Whitechapel Road. First up was James Kay, a blacksmith at Wiseman's the coach builders, at number 216, right next door to Henry Wainwright's warehouse. He had made an entry in his workbook on 11 September to say that he had been completing a very heavy job on a van at the rear of the premises when he had heard three loud 'pistol shots'. It was between 5 and 7pm when he heard the noises coming from the direction of Wainwright's premises.

He described the three shots as being very rapid and took about six seconds. At the time, James was being assisted by his brother William, as well as the 'governor', Mr Wiseman. On hearing the shots, the other two made off towards the gates at Vine Court at the rear of the premises, but James had called them back as he was just at a crucial point in repairing a wheel. He remained in the yard and they then went on with their work. He thought nothing else of the matter till September 1875 when he heard about the murder case.

Brother, William Kay, gave very similar evidence to that of his brother though he added that he knew that the neighbour on the *other* side, Mr Pinnell at number 214 Whitechapel Road, had a pistol and he had looked through the keyhole of Pinnell's gate, but he saw no one about, so went back to his work. The business owner's son, James Wiseman was the third of the trio who also recalled hearing the shots. He tapped out the speed of the three shots on the witness box.

Mary Jane Trew was the daughter of the owner, Mr Wiseman. She was in the habit of copying her father's books and had copied the dated entry made by James Kay. She read his date of the incident as 9 September and copied that into her book. It appears that the handwriting gave her the wrong impression of the date which was actually the 11th. She had not taken notice of a stroke of ink before what she thought was a nine. The attorney general only introduced this piece of evidence in a spirit of fairness to the defence. The prosecution said that the murder had taken place on the 11 September. If the date in the book had been correct, it would have proved that the shots were nothing to do with Harriet's death as she had been seen alive and well on that day.

The final witness in relation to the pistol shots was John Hood Pinnell who was the owner of the oil business next door to Wainwright's at 214 Whitechapel Road. Although he didn't hear the shots himself, he stated that he had a toy pistol, which he produced to the court. He was in the habit of firing it into the back yard for fun. The main reason for his appearing at the Bailey however was an encounter he had with his neighbour, Henry Wainwright who he had known for many years. On the 10 September 1874, he recalled Henry coming into his shop between 11am and 11.30am and buying eight yards of cord. He had seen the cord that was used to tie up Harriet Lane. He stated it was similar to the cord he had sold Henry, though he couldn't swear to it.

The next witness also brought his own gun to court. This was Charles Sawyer, a brush maker from 63 Southwark Bridge Road, and former partner of Henry Wainwright. Their partnership was short lived, having only lasted between November 1873 to January 1874. After their partnership was dissolved, Sawyer had taken possession of the keys to both 84 and 215. He stated that in the private office on the first floor of number 84, he searched a desk and, in a drawer, he discovered a packet of bullets. On discovering the items, he gave them to Wainwright who stated that they were his.

Solicitor Samuel Hessan Behrend followed Sawyer into the witness box and gave evidence of having financial dealings with Henry Wainwright. One of his clients had lent Henry money. Behrend had taken a mortgage on both properties as well as some life assurance policies as security in September 1874. Around May or June 1875, he issued a writ of ejectment to Henry, but at his request, he had not served it. After trustees had been appointed in July 1875, he immediately took possession of 215 and put in a tenant named Albert Francois into the premises. In August he rented the property to Emma Izzard. Albert told the court that he only stayed a short time before returning the key to Mr Behrend.

The thirteenth witness of the long day was Emma Izzard. She had taken on the tenancy at 215 on 27 August 1875. During this period, Henry Wainwright visited the premises every day. She wasn't sure whether he had a key to the premises as on one occasion he was 'trying the back door with a key'. This evidence is relevant as it shows that Wainwright still had access to the building by means of a key.

The last two witnesses of the day both gave evidence in relation to Thomas Wainwright and the Hen and Chickens. Walter Archer, had been employed by Thomas at the Hen and Chickens between January and June 1875 after he had started an ironmonger's business at the premises. Significantly Archer had seen Henry Wainwright at the premises about five times. In June, Thomas' business ended and the building was sold under the control of Mr George Lewis, and a new padlock was placed on the outside of the door and he kept the only key to the lock. Thomas Wainwright visited Archer at Mr Lewis' office around 2 July and he asked him for the key to the now empty building. He stated that the padlock was a common one costing 9 pence.

Accountant George Lewis said he knew Thomas and Henry Wainwright, and had lent Thomas money on the basis that he would soon be receiving money from the insurance claim on the fire at 84 Whitechapel Road. That expected windfall did not materialise, and so Lewis was left out of pocket. He confirmed that the key for the premises was missing from his office, having been removed by Thomas. He also told the court that the letter marked Exhibit 'E' was almost certainly in the hand writing of Thomas.

The court adjourned at 4.50pm[4] after a long procession of witnesses. After 4 full days of evidence, the already strong case for the prosecution was now fully in its stride and was adding to the clarity of the case against Henry Wainwright. Friday was scheduled to be another full day of witnesses with no letup in the Crown's pursuit of the by now dispirited brothers.

Chapter Fourteen

Day 5 of the Trial

Friday 26 November commenced at precisely 10am. It was to be the last day where multiple witnesses were called, but it was definitely a day of two halves. The Crown produced various seemingly less important individuals to give evidence in the morning.

As the day began, the Crier of the Old Bailey[1] called for everyone to be uncovered as the judge as well as the prisoners entered the court room. The men sat 2 yards apart and were described as looking 'paler and thinner' than on previous days. The court was again packed, with many medical men having obtained entry in order to hear evidence of the post mortems. Following on from hearing all the 'routine witnesses', the court took a decision to eject all the female onlookers from the trial. The newspaper gave details of what happened.

> If any of the ladies present in the earlier part of the day had reckoned on profiting by a clinical lecture, they were disappointed, for as the time drew near for calling the surgical witnesses, Under Sheriff Crawford requested the occupants of what may be called the 'Ladies Gallery', to withdraw. Their seats were vacated, and for the remained of the day, these places afforded additional accommodation to the sterner sex.

William Graydon was the first witness of the day. He was the manager at the premises of Rowlandson's Upholsterers business, 83 Whitechapel Road. He told the court that on the 10 September, between 1 and 2pm, he sold Henry Wainwright two yards of common black American cloth. He had known Henry for 17 years. He stated that the cloth was similar to that produced by Inspector Fox, which was the material that had covered the body of Harriet Lane.

The next witness, Henry Young, was interesting as he gave evidence of seeing Thomas and Henry Wainwright together in New Road, outside Martin's shop between 10–11am on the morning of 11 September 1875. He noticed that Thomas was looking unwell and that he had shaved his moustache off. The question was, why was he looking so ill? Had he been up half the night cutting up Harriet Lane's body?

The judge then decided that he wanted to recall the witness George W. Rogers, regarding a letter written by Henry Wainwright that he had seen. On the previous day he had not allowed this evidence to be admitted, but after a change of heart he was now going to allow it. Rogers stated that he had been called down whilst at 84 Whitechapel Road by Henry Wainwright who was with 'Mrs King'. Henry had handed him a letter in an envelope addressed to his wife in Tredegar Square.

At this point 'Mrs King' snatched the letter out of his hand. He recovered the torn letter and then read it. He described the letter as a 'piece of nonsense,' but he decided not to take it to Henry's wife. He had then thrown the letter in the fire. On day 5, he was asked to recall any details of the contents of the letter that he could. He stated that part of the letter, which was in Henry's hand, stated, 'I cannot survive the disgrace, and you will never see me no more'.[2]

Into the witness box next plodded, Detective Sgt George William Forster of 'H' Division. He told the court that he had arrested Thomas Wainwright at Parsons Green on a charge of desertion of his wife on 1 October 1875, and had taken him to Leman Street Police Station. At Clerkenwell Court the charge of desertion was dropped, but Forster then rearrested Thomas on the rather more serious matter of being involved in Harriet's murder. Thomas said to the detective, 'I suppose there will be some other charge against me in reference to the spade and axe? I was not coming forward voluntarily to give evidence against my brother, but to save myself I had better speak the truth.' He then stated that he had bought a spade and a wood cutter for his brother Henry at Mr Pettigrew's premises at 181 Whitechapel Road on 10 September 1875.

Following his colleague into the witness box was 'H' Division's Chief Inspector James Constantine McDonald. He had spoken to Thomas at Southwark Police Station, informing him that he was going to be charged with assisting Henry in the murder. At this point, Thomas asked to make a statement and was given a pen and paper to write it down.

Statement of Facts. I beg to state that on Friday 10th September, at 12.30, I was with some friends at the Black Lion, Bishopsgate Street. Shortly after, I called on my brother Henry at Mr Martin's, He then asked me if I would go and buy him a garden spade and chopper to chop wood. I then went to Pettigrew's and purchased the articles, for which I paid 3 shillings, and I charged my brother 5 shillings. I was with Mr Pettigrew, I dare say, half an hour or three-quarters. We went and had a drink together.

I then took the parcel, to my brother at 78, New Road, Whitechapel. I then left him and went to Creight's, Whitechapel Road, and had some sherry that would be about 2.30pm. From there I went and had my dinner, and then went to the Black Lion, Bishopsgate Street, and from there to Racquet Court, Fleet Street – about 4.30 – and from there to the Surrey Gardens where I remained until about 10.45 p.m.

Thomas' statement was full of detail about the day that Harriet's body was supposedly cut up. Every minute of the afternoon and evening appeared to have been accounted for. It proved to be a day of many appointments and much travelling across London!

McDonald also gave evidence of keys found on Thomas at the police station. One of the keys was found to unlock the padlock at the Hen and Chickens, although when asked about it, he stated that he didn't think it was the 'proper key'.

Ironmonger Frederick Pettigrew gave simple evidence of Thomas Wainwright buying an axe and spade from his ironmonger's business at 81 Whitechapel Road. He knew both Thomas and Henry Wainwright personally. He told the court that he could identify the axe and spade produced in court as being purchased from his shop. He marked his stock with letters 'HH'. The ones in court were also marked in this way. Pettigrew sold them to Thomas on 10 September 1875 between 12 and 1pm, though he could not prove the date through any documentary evidence of sale.

Whitechapel Road builder and decorator Francis Johnston was next. Henry was known to Johnston who, in November 1874,[3] asked him to 'stipple' a window on the front of the building which had normally allowed anyone to see all the way through to the back. In effect what he was doing was covering windows to prevent prying eyes looking through. This could have been done for some legitimate reason, but with Wainwright in all sorts of financial trouble, why would he have gone to the expense of doing 'cosmetic' work to the premises. Wainwright had told Johnston that 'he did not wish people to look into the warehouse'. One possible reason could have been to cover up any dubious goings on in the shop late at night, such as the cutting up of a body.

The following witness was Charles Grojean Rennie L'Enfant,[4] a clerk of the Bankruptcy Court. His evidence confirmed that Henry Wainwright had been made bankrupt. There had been a first hearing on 15 March 1874 where the creditors were initially to be paid 12 shillings in the pound. There was a second bankruptcy hearing on 30 June 1875. Henry was declared bankrupt at a further hearing on 10 November 1875. Henry Wainwright had been arrested between those 2 meetings.

Charles Chabot[5] was a notable handwriting expert brought in by the prosecution to give evidence about certain documents involved in the case. He told the court that he had seen;

1) 'Statement of Fact' written and signed by Thomas Wainwright at the police station. He had compared this to several documents;
2) Letter from 'Thomas to Mrs E. Lewis';

3) Letter signed by Thomas dated Wednesday evening;
4) Letter signed 'Thomas George Wainwright, 26 Jan 1875';
5) Letter dated 21 Nov

Upon examination, he found the letters and documents had all been written by the same hand. (The police had witnessed seeing Thomas write the Statement of Fact, so it was concluded that it could be relied upon for it being his genuine handwriting which could be compared to other documents).

After initially being contacted by the Treasury Solicitors, Chabot had written back to them with his findings on 5 October 1875. His three-page letter[6] is beautifully handwritten and still exists in the National Archives. He stated in his letter the following;

> I am of the opinion without any doubt whatever that the said letter to Miss Wilmore marked 'E' is the undisguised handwriting of the person who wrote the said Statement of Fact. [The letter sent from Frieake to Miss Wilmore from the Charing Cross Hotel was exhibited as Exhibit 'E'.] There is no doubt whatever that all the writing was the work of Thomas Wainwright.

He stated that the similarities of the handwriting were plainly apparent. He also demonstrated similarities of the letter 'Y' which were unusually written. There were several other similarities which were demonstrated, which proved that Thomas Wainwright wrote the letters from 'E. Frieake'.

The last witness before lunch was locksmith, Henry William French, from Kent Street in the Borough. He had been shown two keys, as well as the padlock taken from the Hen and Chickens. The keys had been separately produced by Inspector Fox and Chief Inspector McDonald.[7] French told the court that the key produced by Inspector Fox (found on Henry Wainwright), was the 'proper' key for the lock. He said that the other key from Chief Inspector McDonald, which was found on Thomas Wainwright, was not the right key, but would open the lock. He added that the lock was a very common one. The judge was unimpressed with the evidence, stating that although Thomas' key accidentally opened the lock, it could not be proved that he knew that it would open the padlock.

At this moment the Lord Chief Justice decided that he had heard enough for the morning session, and that lunch was required. The witnesses that day had so far been of the routine variety, but the main event was coming after 1pm when the evidence of the medical men would begin. As the ladies of the court exited for the day, the remaining men would have been looking forward to a lively afternoon.

Chapter Fifteen

Day 5 Continues:
Medical Evidence from the Prosecution

Frederick Larkin

Frederick Larkin conducted an examination of the body of what was, at the time, an unknown corpse.

Larkin entered the witness box at the Old Bailey to give his evidence to the packed all male courtroom. His evidence was going to be crucial to the prosecution case. He had to be able to convince the jury that the body found was that of Harriet Lane, otherwise counsel for Henry Wainwright might soon have him walking freely again down Whitechapel Road. Fortunately for the Crown, this afternoon was going to be Larkin's finest hour. His detailed and methodical evidence would play a large part in concluding the case against Wainwright.

The Attorney General, Sir John Holker, led Larkin though his evidence with added questions from the judge, while Henry Wainwright's counsel, Mr Besley, asked questions on behalf of his client. The following precis of the evidence from Larkin is taken from the book, *The Trial of the Wainwrights*.[1] He gave evidence of the various examinations he made over several days.

'I was called to see the body before 5.30pm on 11 September. I was shown 2 parcels of a female body. Some portions of the body were mummified. The parts had been separated very unscientifically. The body was divided into ten parts. The head and neck one part, the two hands, two arms, one trunk, two thighs, and two legs and feet connected.

The body had been recently divided. I could not at that time form an opinion as to how long it had been dead, no more than a long time. I made another examination early on Monday morning, 13 September.

I found that the parts put together made up a body. I made another partial examination on the 14th with Mr Smith; simply to remove the viscera, and I then observed a cut in the throat. I removed all the viscera except the brain, which was in such a soft watery condition that I could not remove it. I put each viscous into a separate glass jar for any possible subsequent examination; they were scaled up and I locked them up in the vestry and kept the key. On the 16th I made an examination together with Mr Bond.

I formed an opinion that the woman was about 25 years of age, from the condition of the wisdom teeth; All the wisdom teeth were cut except one, which was evidently being cut at the time. She was of a slender make, about 5 feet in height; the hands and feet were proportionately small with the other frame of the body; I mean they were small for the body. In order to ascertain the height, we put the parts as nearly in position as possible, and repeatedly measured them. The cutting up had been done very roughly and very recently. It must have been done by some chopping instrument. I have seen the chopper produced; the body might have been cut up with such an instrument.[22]

There was a very great deal of dirt on the body mixed with chloride of lime. Chloride of lime thrown upon a body would tend to preserve the external parts more especially. It is a disinfectant, and I believe it has a tendency to preserve anything put upon it; It retards the decomposition of those parts with which it comes in contact. Its principal agency is to deodorise. I found no quick-lime.

We found a fracture of the skull, just behind and nearly level with the top of the right ear; that was an old fracture. On inspecting the interior of the skull, we found a bullet in the back part of the brain in the portion known as the cerebellum. That corresponded with the fracture. We could trace the course of the fracture to the place where we found the bullet. We also found a second bullet lying on the base of the skull on a part known as the sphenoid bone, and by tracing the direction of that bullet outwards we found another hole or fracture in the skull, just in front and nearly level with the top of the same ear.

One of those bullets had certainly entered the head during life; The one behind the ear. I was led to that conclusion by the extravasation of blood underneath the scalp for a considerable distance around the wound, having a diameter of at least two inches, and also slightly within the skull in the direction in which the bullet had gone. That led me to the conclusion that the bullet had entered the head during life, whilst the circulation was active. There was not so much appearance with regard to the second bullet – there was slight extravasation underneath the scalp. My inference from that would be that the first bullet had penetrated the brain during life, and the second when the first had so far produced its effect that life was fast ebbing. Either of those shots was quite sufficient to account for death, not necessarily instantaneously.[3]

We next turned our attention to the cut throat.[4] It was a cut from right to left, just beyond the medial line on the right side of the neck, across the neck to a point about opposite the angle of the lower jaw on the left side. It had severed all the structures from the wind-pipe down to the vertebrae. It extended about two inches upwards and backwards, below, and opposite the angle of the lower jaw; It must have severed the carotid artery; it was too dry to dissect those parts carefully. That cut must have been made either immediately before or immediately after death. I was led to that conclusion by the extravasation of blood in and about the part. The extravasation implies that the circulation is still going on, because had it been done at a time very remote from death it could not have taken place, because it would have been congealed; The blood would not have been circulating. It is only while the blood is in a fluid state that extravasation of it can take place. That would be a wound quite sufficient to cause death in a minute or two.

I took off a pad from the back of the head and took it home[5] and examined it, and in that I found a third bullet, sticking very closely to it; there was an immense quantity of hairpins in the pad. I also took home a piece of velvet ribbon. The hair pins were bent, broken, and rusty. There was an innumerable quantity of them all over the pad, enough to have arrested the passage of the bullet. This (produced) is the pad and the ribbon. The velvet was in a very rotten state. These (produced) are the three bullets. We gave them to Inspector Fox. I gave the one found in the pad, and Mr Bond gave the others. This is the one I found in the pad; They are of a different shape. These are the two found in the head; The flattened one is the posterior one, that might be done from the way in which it entered the skull. They are both somewhat out of shape; but the other not so much. The one found in the pad is almost flattened, more so than either.

Mr Bond and I made a little examination of the remains to endeavour to ascertain whether the woman had borne a child, and I subsequently made a further examination myself.

I did not minutely examine the hair, I took some of it away with me, washed it and gave it to Inspector Fox. The washing made it a little lighter.

I noticed that one tooth[6] was decayed down level with the gum or jaw. Next was behind the eye tooth on the right side. From its position I think it might have been visible when she laughed or smiled. There were some teeth missing. With the exception of the one tooth. I should call it a good set of teeth. The remaining incisor tooth at the top indicated that it might have been slightly prominent.

I could only see the remains of one ear. I could see that that had been pierced for an earring. I think I have now described the various matters to which my attention was directed on the 16th, when I was with Mr Bond. I made several subsequent examinations for the purpose of ascertaining whether the woman had borne a child, the result of which gave me a very strong idea that the uterus was that of a person who had been a mother.

My attention was not at first directed to any alleged scar on the leg. Not until I heard it in the police court from Mr Lane. It was when he was examined before the Magistrate. I was there. The body was in such a state from decomposition that it would have been perfectly impossible for anyone to have found the scar unless diligent search was made for it. After Mr Lane had given his evidence Mr Bond and I made an examination for the purpose of ascertaining whether there was a scar or not. We made that examination in the presence of Mr Aubyn, a surgeon, who was there on behalf of Henry Wainwright. We found a scar on the right leg, about four inches below the middle of the knee.[7] It was very much puckered. It was an elongated scar, about as big as a shilling the scar itself, the scar could have resulted from some hot material. A red-hot poker falling on the place would very possibly produce it.

I afterwards heard Mr Lane and Mrs Taylor examined before the coroner. I had not said anything about the scar I had discovered before they had given their evidence. I purposely said nothing about it. I think Mr Lane, before the Magistrate, had described it as on the outside of the leg. He thought it was the right. I have seen a pair of boots produced by Inspector Fox. I have compared one with the corresponding foot, and in my opinion it would fit.

I went to 215, Whitechapel Road. I saw some remains of stains on the flags; but I could not say what they were; they might have been produced by chopping up the body.[8] I found a tooth in the parcel containing the remains, and others Mr Bond had given him. Both the upper incisors were missing from the mouth, I think the left eye tooth on the upper jaw, and I think both the lower incisors; but they were found and replaced.[9] That left the only missing teeth the left lower incisor and the right upper incisor, they have never been found. I think four were found, two are missing. Those teeth had come out since death. Upon a rough idea I should say the woman had been dead from nine to twelve months. Chloride of lime would be apt to retard the progress of decomposition.

I am speaking roughly when I say death might have occurred from nine to twelve months. It is impossible to give the exact date. The body was in an advanced stage of decomposition. I think I had made about four examinations before the scar examination.

A small portion of flesh was left on the right side of the face, but all the soft parts were decayed. The eyes were in a very shrunken condition and sunk to the back of the sockets. It was quite impossible for anyone to recognise the features unless it was the cheek bones. The brain was in such a pulpy state that I did not like to remove it, and in following the course of the bullets I only followed the direction of the dura mater, the covering of the brain. I should be guided by a little mark on the skull internally, where the bullet seems to have struck and rebounded.

I came to a conclusion. In gun-shot wounds, death may arise from a shock to the system or from haemorrhage. I cannot say so as a matter of fact, but what I contend is that if the first wound behind the ear had been inflicted shortly after death, or closely after death, I think it would have been perfectly impossible for the bullet to have got so far under the scalp as it evidently had done in this case. I could not say whether the bullet in the head was the first, second, or third shot; it is impossible. The cut in the throat may have been done with an ordinary knife. I am not quite clear as to the extent of that cut into the vertebra.

Why I am inclined to the opinion that the body was that of a person who had borne a child, is because the measurements of the uterus were greater than those acknowledged to be the measurements of a virgin uterus. Virgin uteruses of adult women are very much the same in measurement, also in weight and in general size, provided they are healthy. The external measurement of a virgin uterus, including the substance: the extreme length would be about 2¼ inches to 2¾ inches, and the breadth about an inch and a third, while this uterus that I examined was, as near as possible, 3 inches, and its breadth about 2½ inches. Another reason for my opinion is the thinness of the walls. I should say, taken conjointly, the front wall and the back wall of a virgin uterus would measure about an inch, ½ an inch one side and ½ an inch the other.

After child-bearing the walls become thinner, and as near as I could say the measurement of the walls of this uterus were ⅝ of an inch. I think it is not a fact that the walls get thicker after child-bearing, I certainly shall not admit it. I cannot explain why they should get thinner. Another ground for my opinion is, that I have compared this uterus with the several uteri in the museum of Guy's Hospital, both those of the virgin and those of persons who have borne children, and it is certainly inconsistent to think it is that of a virgin, because it is so unlike all what I see there of virgin uteri.

Another reason is, the condition of the walls of the abdomen. I gather from all this that after a woman had borne a child, the abdomen being very much stretched during pregnancy (especially the latter months of pregnancy), when the child is born, it leaves the abdomen in a flabby condition, and these scars are the result of that, the contraction of the abdomen to a certain extent.

The boots were never put on the feet; I judge from the size of the feet, they measured as near as possible 8½ inches; I cannot say that the feet were very much smaller than I should expect to find in a person of 5 feet 1 inch in height, but they were not larger, there are plenty of women of 5 feet 1 inch with feet like that. I have measured the boots. They are as near as possible 9 inches long.

The uterus weighed as near as possible 12 drachms, and one source says that a virgin uterus weighs 8 drachms. Doctor Alfred Meadows is an authority who differs. He says in his book from 8 to 12 drachms.

I took the measurement of the body from head to feet, independently of Mr Bond, and as accurately as I could. I made it 5 feet. I do not say that on the supposition of death many months previously and decomposition at that stage having set in, the length would be rather in excess of that during life, but it might be. I can understand that the decayed tooth could be seen if she laughed very much, and in smiling it must have been seen. I do not know whether that is one of the teeth the least covered with enamel, or whether that tooth is the first to decay in fifty people out of a hundred. The two incisors did not project very much, but very slightly. I should not describe the whole of the upper set of teeth as projecting very much, I do not say that by any means; there was nothing extraordinary about the teeth, except that the central incisors were slightly prominent. I have been qualified five years this month.

In my opinion, it is quite impossible for the deceased to have inflicted the wounds upon herself.[10] If a bullet entered the brain its effect upon the sensibility of the person would depend upon its position – I cannot say whether a person would be in possession of their senses and faculties with such a bullet in the brain as to enable them to cut their own throat afterwards.

Points made by Dr Larkin[11] that helped to prove the body was Harriet Lane	Facts about Harriet that matched the evidence
Body was aged around 25 years old	Harriet was 22 ½ years old
Body was a woman who had had children	Harriet *had* had 2 children
Body was 5 feet tall	This was around the height of her sister who was almost the same height as Harriet
One of the teeth that was decayed would have been visible if she smiled	The tooth next to her eye tooth was decayed and was visible when she smiled
A scar was found on the leg which matched one that Harriet had	Scar was found on her leg as her father had described in a hot poker accident
Body had been dead between 9 and 12 months	Body had been dead 12 months
Slender body, small hands and feet	This described Harriet's appearance
Slightly protruding front teeth	This described Harriet's front teeth
Velvet pad held by pins found	A pad like this was habitually worn by Harriet

Dr Thomas Bond

The second medical expert that the prosecution called, who added to the weight of the case against the Wainwright brothers, was the eminent Thomas Bond FRCS; MB; BS; (1841–1901).[12] Dr Bond followed Frederick Larkin into the witness box on the same afternoon at the Old Bailey, Friday 26 November.[13]

> I live at 50, Parliament Street, Westminster, and am assistant-surgeon to the Westminster Hospital, and lecturer on forensic medicine at the hospital. On the 16th September last, I saw the remains of this body at the dead house. Mr Larkin was present. The body was that of a female of short stature, about 5 feet in height, of slender make, limbs, and body. I thought she was from twenty to twenty-five years of age, and that the body had been dead many months. She might certainly have been dead as long as twelve months. I made four examinations altogether.

To save on repetition only the very relevant sections of his evidence are included to save duplication from Dr Larkin. Dr Bond made the following points;

- 4 teeth were missing. One tooth was decayed, and would have been visible when Harriet laughed.
- The neck wound required considerable force and was not self-inflicted.
- He found the first bullet in the cerebellum, having entered during life.

- Second bullet was found on the spheroid bone. Either bullet would have caused death.
- It was impossible for Harriet to have fired the shots.
- 'I'm inclined to the opinion that the uterus had been impregnated, and that the woman had borne children.'
- 'I didn't find the scar during the first examination on 16 September. After hearing Mr Lane mention the scar, I made a special examination. I found the scar on outside of the right leg, 3 inches below the knee.'
- Scar was size of a shilling; the skin was puckered consistent with the appearance of a burn from a hot poker.
- 'I cut the scar out; it is mounted – I have it in my pocket (producing it)'[14]
- Bullets[15] are conical, first weighed 66 grains, second 78 grains, Mr Larkin's bullet was 82 grains.
- Bond stated 'I examined hair from the body and hair found by Insp Fox at 215 under a microscope, they were similar'.[16]

Almost as an after-thought, Mr Besley decide to introduce one final and very short piece of evidence just to round off the day. James Squires was a Whitechapel gunsmith. He was another 'expert' witness of sorts. He had been shown the three deadly bullets by Inspector Fox. He was able to tell the court that they were conical bullets which were either 'central fire 320, or rim fire 297'. They would only work in a central fire or a rim fire revolver. As Wainwright's gun had never been found, this evidence didn't really progress the case. The attorney general stated that the prosecution case would conclude in the morning with one or two last witnesses. The judge rose at 5.05pm. Hopefully the ladies would be back in the morning?

Chapter Sixteen

Day 6 of the Trial

O nce again there was precious little space in the court as *The Hour* newspaper,[1] reported that 'the court was more crowded than ever'. Henry's lead barrister, Mr Edward Besley, would have needed a large glass of water standing by him that day as he had a full day ahead; opening for the defence in the morning and then interviewing the two defence doctors before closing the afternoon.

Besley, like all good barristers, needed to start well and get the jury on his side. His opening gambit, seeing that he did not have many options to choose from, was to try and illicit sympathy for the 'poor prisoners' with a strong opening speech:

> Gentlemen of the Jury: No one can envy the present actors in a trial which has now reached its sixth day. No one can envy the prisoners at the bar, whether innocent or guilty, because they have had six days of mental torture; and to them the result is of the highest importance. It means the difference between existence and non-existence, and, therefore, no one can envy them.[2]

He continued by claiming that the huge amount of press coverage of the case was prejudicial to his client and that not knowing the evidence that the Crown were going to bring made his defence, 'stupendously difficult' (In 2022, the defence are entitled to disclosure of the prosecution evidence). He then advised the jury that although the case against Henry looked grim, it was still possible to clear him of all charges if any doubt lingered in their minds:

> It is an advocate's duty not in any way to distort the facts, but rather to analyse the evidence for the Jury, and to lead their minds, if not to a state of perfect satisfaction as to the innocence of the accused, at least to that necessary doubt which will enable you to pronounce the words, "Not guilty'.

Besley then stated that the evidence was purely circumstantial, and suggested that a chain of circumstantial evidence needed to be unbroken. His main points made by are summed up below;[3]

Main points made by Mr Moody in summing up

- There was no evidence of Harriet being 'taken away' from her family in 1871.
- Henry Wainwright acknowledged the 2 children, paying for them far more than the law would compel him to pay if he had been disposed to act in an unworthy manner.
- There is no evidence whatsoever that Henry was in close contact with, or living under the same roof as, Harriet Lane.
- 'The prosecution has urged us to accept that previous to September 1874, Henry Wainwright had become weary of, and had lost all affection for, Harriet Lane. This is speculation.'
- 'The Frieake incident. The Crown are endeavouring to suggest that from October 1873, there was a deliberate, premeditated plan and scheme by Henry Wainwright to murder Harriet Lane.'
- 'Thomas Wainwright was to be impersonating Edward Frieake, a well-known auctioneer, in the East-End of London.'
- 'Henry Wainwright brought a friend to Mrs Wells, whom he called Edward. There is no evidence that Henry Wainwright ever called "Edward", Edward Frieake.'
- 'Mrs Wells was unable to identify Thomas Wainwright.'
- 'It may occur to you that if Thomas Wainwright was not the "Edward" of the visit to Mrs Wells, why should not the prisoner Henry produce that friend? But you must not assume that he is guilty because he is not able to produce witnesses to combat every little point.'
- 'Can you conceive any motive for selecting the uncommon name of Frieake, when Brown or Robinson would have answered the purpose equally well?'
- 'Mrs Wells' evidence as to identity is such that the word "frivolous" is too dignified to apply to it.'
- 'Mrs Foster failed to recognise Thomas Wainwright.'
- 'Miss Wilmore, the most trustworthy witness, almost negates the suggestion that Thomas Wainwright was the false Edward Frieake.'
- The evidence of Mr Humphries regarding the borrowing of the champagne glasses as to one or two occasions is doubtful. He has four pubs; how would he remember the lending of 4 glasses a year previously?
- Doubt was thrown on whether the disturbance in the street at Sidney Square involved Henry and Thomas at all. Or was it the real Mr Frieake?
- There was doubt over the date of the chloride of lime sale from Mr Baylis on 10 September. Was it likely that he would buy it from a man that knew him?
- The date given for the shots being fired was unreliable and was the 9th, when Harriet was still alive. The shots were probably Mr Pinnell firing off practice shots.

- The Prosecution have not proved who sent the telegrams from Dover. Perhaps the telegrams were genuine, and were sent by the man in the cab with Mrs King when Miss Wilmore saw her drive past her near the Bank of England!
- As a motive for the charge of murder, the Crown has utterly failed to prove that the prisoner had immoral relations with other women (for example, Alice Day).
- Miss Wilmore saw Harriet around Christmas 1874, in a cab near the Bank of England. Perhaps Harriet is now in Australia or New Zealand and has no idea what is currently taking place in London.
- Mr Rogers story of Harriet fainting and the snatching at the letter is a fabrication. The witness is unreliable. The letter did not exist.
- Between Christmas 1874 and September 1875, there appeared to be no expectation of Harriet's return. This is consistent with the facts that she had left the country with a rich man after having received as much money as she could from Henry.
- The discovery of the grave at 215 Whitechapel Road: A body was found but was it Harriet Lane? Everything stated by the prosecution is speculation. No one knows when the body was put there. The bullets fired were very small and would not have made much noise. No one heard the floor joists being sawn?
- Up till June 1875, Henry never shrunk from paying for his children. It did not follow that when he lacked means and was being persecuted by Harriet that he would resort to any expedient to 'dispose of her'.
- The spade and axe were sold to Thomas Wainwright on 10 September 1875. There is no evidence they ever reached the hand of Henry.
- Henry knew that the remains were there (wrapped in cloth), this is undisputable. He did not know the body was that of Harriet Lane. Knowing that Harriet Lane was missing, he knew he would be made responsible for her and be called to explain how she died.
- The prosecution has to prove Henry caused Harriet's death by violence. Why would an intelligent man ask Alice Day to ride with him in the cab? Why didn't he sent Stokes for the cab not go himself? The discovery of the body 'arose from the carelessness of innocence'.
- Henry's pretending to bribe the police into silence, I pass by. The fact of his being compromised, accounts for his conduct, you must not assume that he is guilty of murder.
- The identification of the body issue is based on 12 points:

1. Slight build
2. Five feet in height
3. Small hands
4. Small feet
5. Hair of light colour
6. Hairpad with a number of hairpins
7. Decayed tooth
8. Age
9. Woman who had had children
10. Scar
11. Wedding ring and guard
12. Two buttons

- The buttons are not proved, as are the wedding and keeper ring. The height and size of hands and feet were not conclusive. The colour of the hair could have been changed by chloride of lime. Miss Wilmore could not possibly identify the hair pad found as being Harriet's. The decayed tooth is the commonest thing, and cannot be taken as proof of identity.
- The age of the body could not be pinpointed to 10 years. The Crown evidence which says the body was that of a mother is not proved. Two further doctors will tell you that this is distinctly not the body of a woman who has borne children and, if not, cannot be the body of Harriet Lane. Burn scars from pokers are common, so is not conclusive.
- If you do not think the identity of the body is satisfactory you cannot find Henry Wainwright guilty of the murder of Harriet Lane.
- Another count on the indictment, the 'murder of a woman whose name is unknown to the jury'. This count has been added as the prosecution could not trust the identification of the body of Harriet Lane.
- If you charge him with murder of a woman unknown, no one knows the circumstances under which the murder took place and if you exclude Harriet Lane, what evidence is there that it was not a suicide?
- You cannot say there has been a murder – it may be suicide. If you cannot prove murder, would you for that take away a man's life? The judge asked what theory Mr Besley had for the suicidal [sic] person to dig their own grave and bury themselves? Mr Besley side stepped this point from the learned judge.

Mr Besley concluded the first part of his considerable day's work with these final thoughts to the jury;

I have dealt with the defence Henry Wainwright has against the charge of murdering Harriet Lane upon the two points – first, that the case has not been satisfactorily made out; and secondly, that there is a want of identification. It is for the Prosecution to make out that it is Harriet Lane; but they charge the murder of a female unknown; and, as regards that second count, I can well conceive circumstances in which a person, young and unmarried, with a brain overstrained by trouble, might commit suicide with the idea of appalling and punishing the person who had wronged her. Imagine such a man? Confronted with the body! It is easy to imagine that would be wiser to call in the police, but does it inevitably follow that such a man would always do the wisest thing?

Such a man might say that she is out of the world; it matters very little where she lies, and he might be induced for his own protection to place in an improper place the person who had committed suicide. I argue that it is not Harriet Lane, and therefore he has not committed wilful murder. If it is the suicide of a person unknown, the possession of the remains is not enough to deprive the prisoner of life by your verdict.

Mr Besley sat down after a long morning's work. His address to the jury was his big moment. Had he done enough to sway the jury? On the face of it, he came up with a number of arguable points, but on some of the vital issues he had been unable to make much headway. He conceded that Henry knew about the body and had tried to bribe the police officers. These two facts alone leave too many questions unanswered. What was the likelihood that there was a different woman under the floorboards who had committed suicide?

With his main speech now completed, he needed a good show from his medical witnesses to try and muddy the waters over the identity of the body. If only they could prove that the corpse had never given birth, he might be in with a chance. There was a lot riding on Drs Meadows and Aubyn's evidence after lunch.

Chapter Seventeen

Day 6 Continues:
Medical Evidence from the Defence

Dr Alfred Meadows

Henry Wainwright's defence team sought to do anything they could to throw doubt on the very strong prosecution case against him. Apart from bringing character witnesses who described Henry as a jolly fine fellow, the only glimmer of hope was the medical evidence. The trial might succeed or fail on the outcome of the battle of the heavyweight medical men. Drs Larkin and Bond had already landed huge blows in that department. They had to convince the jury that the body was, without doubt, Harriet Lane. If they could not, then the prosecution would fail, and the brothers would walk free.

On the afternoon of Saturday, 27 November 1875, Dr Alfred Meadows[1] was the first of two medical witnesses for the defence to step into the witness box. He was an expert in obstetrics and so had been brought in to try and prove that the female body found in Borough High Street in the possession of Henry Wainwright had not borne children. Harriet Lane had given birth to two offspring. Dr Meadows introduced himself to the court.

> I am a Fellow of the Royal College of Physicians, a lecturer on midwifery at St. Mary's Hospital, and physician to St. Mary's Hospital. I have made obstetrics a considerable subject of study. I examined the uterus at my house on the 3rd September in order to form some opinion whether that uterus was that of a person who had borne a child. The points are the size and the cavity of the walls, but more particularly the shape of the uterine walls.[2]

Meadows was not here to discuss the cause of death, or the height, legs or scars on the body. He was only interested in the uterus and whether he could say with certainty that the body had been a mother. His findings were thus; 'It is not possible to express any distinct opinion as to whether the uterus had been pregnant or not; my opinion, considering the points mentioned, is that the uterus had not been pregnant.'

This was a clincher for the prosecution. Meadows may, on the balance of probabilities, have thought that the body was not that of a mother but, in the end, his words told the court what Henry Wainwright would have preferred not to hear. He could not be sure. His presence at court had been almost worthless to the defence. The last hope of the defence was about to follow Meadows into the witness box.

Frederick George Aubyn

Frederick Aubyn[33] represented the last chance saloon for the Wainwrights' hopes of an acquittal. The Attorney General, Sir John Holker, must by now have been smelling blood as Aubyn began his evidence. Sir John would have been listening intently to his precise words to discover whether the defence had kept their best till last, or whether it was another medical damp squib. Dr Aubin then introduced himself to the court.

I am a member of the Royal College of Surgeons, and practice at 519, Commercial Road. I have been in the profession about eighteen years. I inspected the remains of the deceased woman by the solicitor for the prisoner on the 24th September, and attended with Mr Bond on the next morning at 9.30 to do so at the mortuary at St. Saviour's Church. We examined the body three or four times; it was in a very advanced stage of decomposition. From examination, I should think the age was from twenty-five to thirty, not more.

I examined both the legs. The scar produced, is the one discovered on the right leg below the knee – I discovered also a scar on the left leg which I cut out (producing it). I cannot say what it is the scar of, but from some injury, where it has been struck on this part, or it may have been from a burn. I think the skin has been destroyed. The scar is about the size of a shilling; I will swear positively that it is not the result of decomposition, but in my opinion, it is a scar.

I examined the mouth; there was one bicuspid tooth decayed down to the bone, and some others were missing.

I examined the uterus with care, for the purpose of forming an opinion whether the woman bad been pregnant or not, and the signs to which I looked were the length and the size of the cavity, the general appearance of the womb, and the thickness of the walls. I also observed the shape with Dr Meadows. I do not give a decided opinion as to the having been pregnant, but my opinion is that she was not pregnant, that the womb had not been gravid, that she had not borne a child.

I examined the hair; I did not detect any curl in it; I produce it. I have made my measurements with great care and they are the same as Dr Meadows arrived at. I measured the body with Mr Bond; it measured exactly 4 feet 11¼ inches. I also examined the feet and hands; there was nothing remarkable in them, nothing unusually small, considering the size of the body'.[4]

Sir John then rose to his feet for his cross examination. Having heard the last witness, Dr Meadows, say he could not be sure about the body being a mother, the second surgeon said almost the same thing, 'I do not give a decided opinion'. This immediately left the prosecution with an almost unassailable lead in a match that looked like it should have been stopped by the referee. Neither witness could contradict the evidence of Larkin and Bond. Having heard the, 'I'm not sure' remarks, Sir John didn't press him further on the subject. The judge had obviously noted the uncertain aspect of the defence surgeon's evidence. When he summed up later to the jury, he said the following; 'Harriet Lane had had two children, and it, of course becomes and important inquiry whether the remains were those of a woman who had borne children or not. We now have the evidence of Mr Larkin and Mr Bond in the affirmative.'[5]

The judge didn't even refer to Drs, Meadows and Aubyn, leaving the jury in no doubt that no weight was to be placed on their evidence. Aubyn did give more evidence to the court, but none of his finding made any difference to the identity of Harriet Lane being established. One wonders how Aubyn felt when he departed the witness box. He had been instructed by the defence, but his findings and that of Dr Meadows had not helped their case one jot, and Henry's life now hung by a thread.

Character witnesses for Henry Wainwright – The last chance
After the eminent doctors departed the witness box, it only remained for the last few defence witnesses to be examined. After a busy morning these character witnesses were cross examined not by Mr Besley but by Mr Douglas Straight. They were unlikely to add much, if any, weight to the defence case.

When the defence were preparing their case for trial, they needed to think carefully about any witnesses that could possibly assist getting him an acquittal. Drs Aubyn and Meadows were the only witnesses for the defence that gave any actual proper evidence.

Their usefulness at the Old Bailey had been limited to say the least, but more padding was needed to bolster the jury's opinion of Henry. One way to try and convince them that Henry was a fine upstanding member of the local community was to ask several local worthies to come to court to give good character about him. It was a kind of legal clutching at straws.

Mr Edward Martin of Carlton Villa, Upton, who carried out a corn, rice and brush business at 78 New Road, Whitechapel, was called, but he spent most of his cross examination discussing his cash books, not really helping the case much. He did state that he had taken Henry Wainwright on as a manager and that he had been 'steady' and 'well conducted', working every day from 8am – 8pm. He also described Henry as a 'kind hearted and humane man'.[6]

Independent minister, Rev John Thomas gave evidence to say that he had known Henry for 18 years and he had also found him to be 'humane and kind hearted'. Neighbour, William Thomas Good, a tailor of 213 Whitechapel Road gave similar evidence.

The defence also rolled out a further four witnesses who were prepared to commend Henry's good character.[77] These included; Donald Monroe, a member of the Metropolitan Board of Works; Mr Edward Lacy, Chemist; Mr Samuel Ludbrook, Brush maker, and William Victor Bardon, manager of a chemical works in Whitechapel.

Coverage in the official trial reports of the case, as well as the newspapers, gave hardly a mention to the character witnesses. It seems to have been widely accepted that back in his stress-free days before he met Harriet, Henry had been a popular and respectable man about town. Good character back then was not going to cut any ice with the jury now.

With a dearth of points scored by the defence witnesses, Mr Besley and his defence team were going to have to fine tune their closing speech on Monday. It was going to be a much shorter affair than the opening speech, but it would need to hit home with the jury to stand any chance of an acquittal.

After Day 6 of an exciting week concluded, the Lord Chief Justice gave the Jury an update about the progress of the case and their requirement to remain at the Bailey.[88] He apologised to the jury, telling them that the trial would not be over by Monday and that they would still not yet be going home. He was unable to allow the jury members to separate, but assured them that a trip out would be arranged to give them some fresh air and exercise. At 4.54pm precisely, the court adjourned for the day. The judge and jury were now looking forward to a much-needed day off from the courtroom.

Chapter Eighteen

Day 7 of the Trial: The Defence's Final Day

As the last day for hearing witnesses dawned, the *Evening Standard* brought news of the crowding[1] in the area of the Old Bailey. The judge had difficulty in entering the court in the chaos. *The Hour*[2] reported that the case got underway at 10.30am instead of the usual 10am. The day began with a short summing up from Mr Besley. The later part of the day was given over to the summing up on behalf of Thomas Wainwright and his two witnesses.

Mr Besley told the jury that he wouldn't be going over matters already covered. He began by stressing how important the date of death was to the proceedings. He was at his most eloquent at the start of his nautical oration;

> It is for the prosecution to make their case clear, and unless they do so, your verdict must be one of not guilty, which simply means that the charge has not been fully proved to your satisfaction. You cannot disguise from yourselves that if the 11 September 1874, be not the true date of the death of the person whose remains these are, you are inevitably cast upon such a sea of doubt that it is impossible for you to steer safely into any harbour of security.

This was the point where Besley had to attack the jury's initial thoughts that Henry was guilty as charged. After hearing the first few days of the evidence, his guilt seemed almost a racing certainty. Suddenly, however, after hearing nothing but evidence against the brothers, here was Mr Besley attacking the certainty of the Crown witnesses' evidence; questioning their memories of events, putting different angles on different incidents and lampooning any identifications. Suddenly, the jury members would have been sitting up straighter in their seats and paying more attention, perhaps more than they did late on Saturday afternoon. A good defender's job is to place seeds of doubt in the jury's mind. Were they still certain of what they thought they were sure of? Besley then mentioned the time frame of death;

> You will have noticed that the way in which the prosecution get at that date is by the withdrawal of Harriet Lane from the lodgings of Mrs Foster

on the 11th September 1874, and they not only offer no evidence as to her having been seen later, but say that the crime was committed between 5 and 7 o'clock on the evening of that day. They also fix on the place where they alleged it was perpetrated, namely, the back of the premises, 215 Whitechapel Road.

Besley had hoped that his medical witnesses could have been more certain on the issue of the body being a mother. They could only offer possible opinions rather than positive evidence as the prosecution doctors had done. Added to this, the extreme nervousness of Dr Aubyn, which seemed to throw him completely, was not helping the giving of his evidence or likely to be going down well with the jury.

Mr Besley questioned the identification of Harriet Lane by the height of the corpse, colour of the hair, as well as the situation of the teeth, and he urged the jury to find that there were doubts which should have been favourable to the prisoner's case. He also questioned whether a man like Henry Wainwright, described as 'kind and humane', displayed conduct that was consistent with a person who could be guilty of such a crime. His final words were these;

I am now about to close my task. You will retire to your room at some period now approaching, and there quietly amongst yourselves will have to say, first of all, if this crime has been conclusively proved to be the deprivation of life of a woman by another, or by herself; and; secondly, you will have to consider, are these those remains of Harriet Lane beyond any reasonable doubt?

As Mr Besley retook his seat, he must have wondered what the odds were on Henry being acquitted. He had certainly done his best in muddying the prosecuting cases' waters. He had to hope that his learned friend, Mr Moody for Thomas Wainwright, might be able to offer some assistance with his address to the jury. The final key piece of the process would then be the Lord Chief Justice's summing up. The problem was, that the whole of Tuesday was going to be taken up by the attorney general trying to persuade them of the brother's guilt.

Mr Moody's Defence for Thomas Wainwright

George Moody was the last man to speak up for the brothers. He was charged with saving the life of Thomas Wainwright. He took three and a half hours in urging the jury to acquit his client. He spoke admirably, in the best traditions of the Old Bailey and throughout made some very interesting points. Thomas after all, arguably had the best chance of being cleared. This was his powerful opening to the jury members;

> 'You will remember, gentlemen, the earnest and touching words of my learned friend, Mr Besley, in adverting to the solemn nature of the duty devolving upon all engaged in this trial. I allude to the circumstance for this reason. He treated the subject so well that I could not add anything to it with profit. There are two charges against the prisoner for whom I appear; one is that of being an accessory before, and the other that of being an accessory after the fact; and the consequence of being found guilty of either will be most grave and serious. I did not think of attempting to deter you from discharging your duty, but I do desire that you should comprehend how very grave is the charge'.[3]

Make no mistake, Thomas Wainwright's life was also hanging by a thread. A verdict of guilty to being an accessory before the fact would likely see him hang. Moody told the jury that even if a murder had been proved, it had not been proved that Thomas was an accessory. He added that if the body was not Harriet Lane, the case against Thomas would collapse, even though Thomas had purchased the shovel and axe.

The aspect of the identity of the corpse was raised again in the hope that the jury might have had a small doubt in their minds, and so ensuring Thomas' freedom. The jury would also have to pay particular attention to Mr Moody's speech as the charges against him were not as simple as those against Henry, and the fine points of what 'before' and 'after' the fact meant would have to be grasped by the members.

Moody dismissed the thought that Henry wanted to get rid of Harriet much earlier than 1874. When he first met Harriet, Henry was besotted with her, and the illicit affair kept his attention during the good times of dangerous liaisons. While she stayed hidden and was unencumbered by a child, she was his evening plaything.

That all changed when she became pregnant. He was not only going to have to pay for Harriet and her child's keep, but there was now a serious danger of the loss of his good name, not to mention a scandal which might cost him his marriage. He had much to lose. Moody continued, stating that Henry was a humane and popular man who was unlikely to have entered into such a plot as to kill Harriet.

If there had have been a plot, why would he have chosen the name of Frieake? The name certainly was a strange choice. Roberts, Brown or Smith would have been a far better one. Perhaps it was the first name that came into his head?

Henry was running two homes, as well as a failing business, and may have felt like the world was closing in on him. Henry was capable of making some calamitous decisions, and lack of sleep and the stress may have been affecting his thought process. The decision to move the body with Stokes, then leave him with the bags of body parts, before picking up Alice Day, and trying to bribe the policemen, were all choices that flew in the face of common sense.

The main points made by Mr Moody are summed up below;[4]
- The identifications of Thomas Wainwright as Frieake were all unreliable.
- Mrs Wells only saw the 'Frieake' for a few moments in January 1874 and didn't see him again till October 1875, in the dock of the court (18 months later), when she was aware that he had been 'charged with being Mr Frieake'.
- Miss Wilmore gave a description of Frieake which was unlike Thomas Wainwright's appearance.
- Mrs Foster saw Frieake on 1 September 1874. She failed to pick Thomas out in an identity parade as Frieake.
- Amelia Stanley saw Mr Frieake for but a few moments when he showed to see Harriet Lane. There was insufficient time to allow her any close observation of him.
- The judge commented about the identification evidence of witnesses, and that they gave their evidence with doubt and hesitation at the police court.
- There were doubts over the accuracy of Mr Humphries. The date in his book was wrong.
- The prosecution says that two men plotting a murder went to a pub owned by someone who knew them both, and which was opposite the house of the intended victim. They could have been seen from her house in the bar or perhaps by Harriet herself. 'Could anything more improbable be imagined?'
- Perhaps Henry Wainwright, being in financial difficulty, wished to put his relationship with Harriet on a different footing. He would have wanted her to suffer as little inconvenience as possible, but still wanted to make a permanent arrangement with her. He could not easily pay a large sum to her, as if he did, she might suspect that he had been deceiving her. Having the money coming from a friend would be better, and then that friend could terminate his ambiguous arrangement with her. He would have looked for a friend to do this but he would not have used his brother for this.
- Was the letter sent from Mr Frieake to Mrs King, where she apologised for her behaviour, in response to negotiations taking place between her and Frieake (Thomas)? If Thomas was this negotiator on behalf of Henry, does this make him guilty of being an accessory after the fact?

- Regarding the charge of murder against Henry Wainwright, there is 'every probability that he could never have been engaged in so cruel, so cold blooded and treacherous a design'. He would never have selected his brother to impersonate Frieake.
- 'Even if Thomas did take part in the Frieake episode, even then, his conduct is consistent with the theory I have presented to you. It is inconsistent with a guilty design, but is consistent with a truly laudable motive, for the advancement of the comfort of this woman'.
- The Dover Letter. 'I only asked the writing expert one question. Was the handwriting disguised? He said it was an honest letter. Don't you think the writer of the letter would have disguised his handwriting?'
- When Henry was arrested and the Frieake connection was made, while Thomas was still at large and he heard about the situation, why didn't Thomas flee when he had the chance?
- When Thomas was arrested, he made a statement to the police he saying, 'I have done no more than one brother would do for another. The prosecution should not take this as an admission of guilt'.
- 'It's not improbable that one brother might have said to the other, 'She has disappeared, and her friends have a notion I am with her, and they are coming here and making a noise, and I want to stop it. I know the person with whom she has gone away. Will you write a letter?' One can conceive a possibility of doing such a thing as this to relieve a relative from some temporary trouble.'
- The letter from 'Charing Cross Hotel' spells the name 'FRIEAKE'. The telegram spells the name as 'FREEKE'. Would the names be spelt differently if written by Thomas? Why would he send one to himself?
- On 10 September 1875, Thomas buys a hatchet and a spade from Mr Pettigrew, a man who has known him for years. Thomas takes the items saying they are for Henry. He even confirmed that 10 September *was* the correct date. If he was trying to deceive, would he have said this?
- Alfred Young allegedly saw Henry and Thomas Wainwright talking on 11 September 1875 outside Mr Martin's door, and that Thomas looked unwell, and had shaved his moustache off. I think the date was 10 September not the 11th, when Thomas was in the neighbourhood. Why did Alfred Young take so long to tell the police this evidence?
- 'The prosecution is trying to build a vague suspicion of a man having been employed for hours during the night in performing this fearful and ghastly work of mutilation'. (Cutting Harriet's body up)
- If Thomas had helped dismember the body, it would be madness to bring in a third party – Stokes – to move it.

Portrait of Henry Wainwright. (The Trial of the Wainwrights, *1920*)

Mr Harry Bodkin Poland QC. (The Trial of the Wainwrights, *1920*)

Lord Chief Justice Coburn (The Trial of the Wainwrights, *1920*)

Front door of Henry Wainwright's house in Tredegar Square, Mile End. (*Author's Image*)

Front Page of *Illustrated Police News*, 16 October 1875, featuring Thomas Wainwright (centre) and his arrest (bottom images), Mrs Foster, Mr Rogers, Mr Eels and some locations involved in the crime (top). (*Copyright The British Library Board. All Rights Reserved*)

'Tom and Henry in the dock. The spade and pick', *Illustrated Police News*, 23 October 1875. (*Copyright The British Library Board. All Rights Reserved*)

Prison Life, Illustrated Police News supplement, 13 November 1875. (*Copyright The British Library Board. All Rights Reserved*)

Left to Right: Henry Wainwright, Harriet Day and Thomas Wainwright. *Illustrated Police News*, 27 November 1875. (*Copyright The British Library Board. All Rights Reserved*)

Number 40 Tredegar Square, Mile End, home of Henry Wainwright. (*Author's image*)

Number 3 Sidney Square. After leaving here, Harriet Lane was never seen again. (*Author's image*)

Alice Day. (*National Archives, Copyright Ref 1-30-356*)

Thomas Wainwright in prison. (*National Archives*)

Edward Frieke's business card. (*National Archives, Ref TS 18-1*)

Henry Wainwright. (The Trial of
the Wainwrights, *1920*)

- 'It was alleged that a key to the Hen and Chickens was handed from Thomas to Henry, but there is no evidence on this point'. The locks are very common and other keys could have opened them. Even if Thomas had given Henry the key, what evidence of a criminal intent was there? Thomas and Henry both had a very tenuous tenure of their respective premises at Borough High Street and Whitechapel Road. If he was party to such a concealment, would Thomas have given consent for the body to be placed in his old premises?
- The prosecution has failed to show the key to the Hen and Chickens is in any way connected to Thomas. Henry was in possession of 27 keys when arrested.
- Although Thomas may have written the letter, there is nothing to show he did so with guilty knowledge. The same applies to all the other circumstances connected to him, as each one is very slight. The man who wrote the letter was the man who innocently parted with the key; every other act he committed might have been equally innocently done.
- What motive is there for Thomas to assist in the murder of a woman who did him no harm?
- The prosecution alleged that the motive for Thomas' crime was brotherly affection. Would he have covered his hands with blood for brotherly affection?

Mr Moody must have been happy with his day's work thus far. He had done his best, and the jury would surely be forced to look at Thomas' guilt or innocence with fresh eyes.

The day was going to finish with two minor witnesses for the defence of Thomas. First was ironmonger, Alexander Arkell of 291 Oxford Street, who had been Thomas' employer between 30 March and 10 October 1874. He told the court that Thomas had worked for him between the hours of 8am and 8pm and that he was often late in the mornings. His daily sheets recorded Thomas' attendance and absence. He stated that during the period of his employment, Thomas wore a dark moustache, but no beard or whiskers.

Mr Arkell was then shown the lock of the Hen and Chickens and the two keys. He said he wasn't a locksmith but did deal in locks and observed that the lock was made in large numbers and cost a shilling. He wasn't sure whether either key was the original, but both keys managed to undo the lock.

On being asked why Thomas Wainwright, his best salesman, was dismissed, he stated it was because he was often late in the morning and also because he had heard that he had deserted his wife. Mr Arkell's evidence had not helped the defence of Thomas Wainwright one jot.

The final witness of the whole trial was Charles George Graulier, who appeared near the end of the day. He was a solicitor of the Supreme Court.

Thomas Wainwright had been his client who first consulted him in February 1875, at which time he was about to open the Hen and Chickens.

He told the jury that he was employed to draw up an agreement between Thomas and Mr Moore, but that it was never completed. The lease was not executed in consequence of Mr Moore not carrying out his part of the agreement and the partnership fell through. After the failure of the business at the Hen and Chickens, he was consulted by Thomas with regard to the surrender of the premises.

Graulier only had one interview with him; that was around the 9th or 10th of August but no rent had been paid for the Midsummer quarter, and the solicitor for the lesser wrote to him and said that if he accepted the key, the quarter's rent and the costs of the lease should be paid. The earliest time at which he spoke to Thomas Wainwright about the surrender of the premises was the beginning of August, or the last few days of July. This closed the evidence for Thomas.

Final Summing Up by Mr Moody

Mr Moody had had a long day but as the time approached 4pm, he topped and tailed his case with a short address to the jury. He began by telling the jury that the last witness, Mr Graulier, had established the fact that Thomas could not have been aware that the Hen and Chickens was to be made a place 'of deposit' for the body when he was about to give up the premises. 'The first inquiries would naturally be made of the last occupier, and a man would hesitate a long time before he submitted to being made the first person to whom attention should be drawn'.

He then invited the jury to acquit Thomas Wainwright; he had no guilty knowledge of the letter and the spade. He asked whether it was likely that asking him to write a simple letter would lead to such a terrible outcome. Thomas had not suspected anything and had only done what one man would do for a brother.

Moody declared that there were grave suspicions about the evidence in the case. He invited the jury to consider 'Letter "E"', and that if they were able to find that it had been written 'without guilty knowledge', then 'it will be your pleasure to say he is not guilty; and, in asking you to give this verdict on behalf of Thomas, I may say, although, without any authority to do so, I am asking for the same verdict on the part of Henry'.

As George Moody relaxed back into his seat, Attorney General Sir John Holker rose to reply on the case. Anticipating at least a 2-hour speech, the judge decided enough was enough at 4pm, and the case was adjourned. The jury would have been glad of the early finish as they made their way back to the Cannon Street Hotel for yet another night.

Chapter Nineteen

Day 8 of the Trial: The Prosecution's Speech to the Jury Regarding Henry

As day 8 of the trial dawned, the street outside the court was again packed, and the *London Evening Standard*[1] described the scene as crowds were at times having to be repelled from both entrances by the police under the supervision of Chief Inspector Tillcock.[2] *The Hour* newspaper reported that the throng was so bad that even the judge was late arriving at his chambers at the Old Bailey.[3]

The jurors were probably looking forward to it being the final day with everything over by tea time. Alas, Sir John Holker made a serious under estimate of his address to the jury, as he spent four hours instead of the planned two, trying to persuade them to find both brothers guilty.

Sir John opened for the Crown, telling the court that he would deal with the facts in the order that they had been presented to the jury by the witnesses. He commended Mr Besley, Henry's counsel, for his 'most able speech'. The niceties of the 'my learned friend' type of language soon evaporated however, as Mr Holker laid into Mr Besley's summing up to the jury.

The devastating opening of the attorney general's speech showed his skill as not only a wordsmith but also how persuasive he could be in his arguments. He was more or less scoffing at the defence from Henry's counsel, in that it flew in the face of common sense. As you read his words, think of him on his feet in the Old Bailey, fully gowned and bewigged, with his portly stomach, long bushy sideburns, Lancashire accent and his air of authority, befitting the most senior prosecutor in the land. This is his opening salvo;[4]

'Mr Besley, in the course of his summing up, has presented to you a digest of the evidence, and set before you the defence he makes for his client, and I propose at the outset to take a general view of what that defence is.

I listened with the greatest possible attention to what he relied upon. He says that the evidence for the prosecution is incomplete and unsatisfactory – not sufficient to induce to your minds that guilt lies at the door of the prisoner he represents. He says that as regards the evidence, some of it is weak, some of it is false, some of it inaccurate, and the rest open to grave suspicion. That in its details it is not satisfactory, and in the mass too incomplete, to bring home the charge.

He then went onto say, there is not sufficient evidence to establish that the body found was that of Harriet Lane. He says a body was found on the premises of Henry Wainwright, on the 11 Sept 1875, under circumstances of grave suspicion which no doubt called for some explanation on the part of Wainwright; the explanation he gives is simply that it was not the body of Harriet Lane, but that it might be that of some woman who had received injury at the hands of Wainwright, and who committed suicide on those premises; Wainwright being induced by the horror of the moment to conceal the body; lest if it were discovered on his premises he might have a charge made against him which it would be difficult to meet.

On the assumption that the body is that of Harriet Lane he has given no explanation whatever of the conduct of this man. He has a right to say, if he thinks so, that the evidence is not conclusive enough to bring home guilt to the prisoner; but in the assumption that the body is that of Harriet Lane, there is no explanation and no theory to account for the inference you are invited to draw from the facts presented to your notice. On the other hand, supposing that it is not the body of Harriet Lane, the theory which he desires you to act upon is that the unfortunate woman, whoever she may have been, met with death by her own hand, and that Henry Wainwright, under the influence of fear, buried the body in those premises.

Just consider for a moment whether this theory can be tenable. You have the evidence before you of the injury found to have been inflicted upon the body. It is perfectly true that there was a cut in the throat sufficient to destroy life almost instantaneously, for that cut severed the windpipe, and all the structures to the vertebrae, and she had two bullets in her head and a third had lodged in the pad.

Can you imagine all those injuries to have been inflicted by her own hand? Suppose the cut in the throat was inflicted during life, how would it be possible for her afterwards to discharge these three bullets with such deadly and certain aim?

Reverse the case, and suppose the bullets were first discharged. How was it possible for the woman afterwards to inflict the wound in her throat? My learned friend contends that the wound in the throat was not inflicted till after death, but no one has advanced any reason why it should be so inflicted, and there is no evidence of any motive for inflicting it after death. What have we then? Why there in this cut in the throat, and we have it clearly proved that there were two wounds made by a pistol, one behind the ear and another before the ear, made by bullets which had entered and lodged in the woman's brain.

In addition to that, you have it that there was a third bullet, which had lodged in the pad, stopped by the mass of hair pins. How would it be possible for a woman who attempted to commit suicide first to discharge a shot into the back of the pad? Could you, gentlemen, do you think, discharge a pistol into the back of your neck, and if it could be done, do you think anyone would do it? That is not the way a woman would commit suicide. She would, you may be sure, discharge it into her forehead, her mouth, or her heart – any part of the body that she could reach with facility; its idle to suggest that she would commence at the back of her head.

But if she did not so commence, the absurdity becomes greater, for, having two bullets lodged in the brain, she must have then performed the impossible act, of discharging the third at the back of her head.

Well, gentlemen, I put it to you, is it physically possible? Try yourself to turn the muzzle of a revolver to the back of your own heads where that bullet lodged in the pad. But even if she had done so in this case, and the bullet was arrested in the pad, it must have come with such fearful force against the back of her head as to stun her instantly; and do you think she could then discharge two shots into the brain? Or, taking the reverse case, do you think she not only lodged one bullet in her brain, but followed it up with a second before firing the one which lodged in her pad?

Really, gentlemen, you must deal with the facts of this case as you would deal with any other case, by looking upon it with the eye of reason, and I will not insult our reason, by asking you to assume that the woman committed suicide. If she did not, then at the very threshold this difficulty stares Henry Wainwright in the face. There is a woman buried at 215 Whitechapel Road, under the floor of the paint-room. On the 11 September 1875, he is dealing with the remains.

Can anyone doubt from the evidence that his hand severed the remains into a number of pieces? On the 11th he is taking them to the Hen and Chickens; he is arrested; and he gives an explanation which is utterly incredible. He is found in possession of the mutilated remains of a woman who has met with her death by foul play, and it is incumbent, on him, under these circumstances, to give you some explanations; but explanation there is none!

If you disregard the theory of suicide, what explanation does Henry Wainwright give of the possession? What I submit to you, gentlemen of the jury, is, that if it was not suicide, it was murder, and no explanation is given by my learned friend who defends Henry Wainwright. The only defence my learned friend relies on is that the evidence adduced by the prosecution is unsatisfactory'.

This opening oration must have had the effect of jolting any of the doubters of Henry Wainwright's guilt back into their chairs. Suddenly all the 'good work' done by Mr Besley on behalf of his client seemed for naught faced with Mr Holker's onslaught. One can imagine the jury members attempting to shoot themselves in the back of the head with imaginary pistols. The opening had brought the jury back to reality.

Sir John's speech moved seamlessly along, and is a masterclass of advocacy. He made a catalogue of important points in the following four hours.

The main points made by Mr Holker are summed up below;
- Harriet Lane was never heard of alive after 11 September 1874 on leaving Mrs Foster's.
- During 1874, Henry Wainwright was in very serious financial trouble. He had difficulty supporting Mrs King. Bankruptcy proceedings had begun.
- In July 1874, Henry asked his manager, Rogers, to dispose of a revolver. Mrs King was having to pawn items to make ends meet.
- The introduction of Frieake (see the attorney general's clever theory about Frieake below)

Sir John questioned why the uncommon name of Frieake was chosen. Edward Frieake was an auctioneer friend of Henry's who did not know Harriet. It is probable that in conversations between Henry and Harriet, many references were made about Edward. It was natural therefore to introduce the name of someone who she had already heard of. Someone *was* introduced to Harriet as Frieake. Let's assume for a moment that *this* Frieake was not Thomas Wainwright. Then we know that a genuine gentleman by the name of Frieake went to see her and succeeded in carrying Harriet off and away from Henry.

In August, this Mr Frieake visits Harriet, and she believes him to be Mr Edward Frieake, the auctioneer of Coleman Street, as a letter from her is sent to him there in August. If Frieake has become her new lover in lieu of Henry, one would expect some feeling in her writing. Sir John explains the letter;

'My Dear Mr Frieake.' Is that the way in which a woman about to go away with a man would begin a letter to him? Her letter goes on, 'I trust you will pardon me for writing to you, but I feel I ought to apologise for my rude behaviour last evening, after the kindness I have received from you. I had been worried and annoyed during the day, and that made me so excited. I am sorry I went away so cross,' Is there anything in the language of that letter which would lead you to suppose that there was any undue familiarity existing between the writer of it and the Mr Frieake to whom it was written? There is not a word to indicate that there was anything between the two except the friendship which would naturally spring up from such a correspondence.

There was nothing in the letter to suggest affection, or that he would be taking her away from Henry Wainwright.

Further main points made by Mr Holker in his summing up are continued below;

- On 5 September 1874, Henry writes to Harriet the 'Dear Pet' letter saying that 'E.F.' is going to call on her. She leaves Sidney Square on 11 September bound for 215 Whitechapel Road and is never been heard of again, having apparently gone off with Frieake. A body is later found at 215 Whitechapel Road.
- Harriet was very fond of her two children. She was always bound to her family in Waltham. Is it credible that she would leave behind all those who were dear to her with a man who must have been almost an absolute stranger? Would she never make any communication to those who were left behind?
- Is there is any feeling stronger in human nature than the love a woman has for her little children? Can you believe that if Harriet Lane had departed, she would have refrained from writing?
- If Frieake was not Thomas Wainwright, who was he? Henry would have known all about this Mr Frieake. What has he ever told anybody about him? That he is not the Coleman Street Frieake and he visits certain pubs, etc. If there really is another Mr Frieake, is that all the detail he can offer about him?
- The defence tried to suggest that Thomas and Frieake were not the same person. It's clear that a person purporting to be Frieake was visiting Mrs King at Sidney Square.
- The identifications of Thomas by the witnesses, Wells, Wilmore, Foster and Stanley were not conclusive.
- Thomas is identified by the joint evidence of Mrs Foster, who went to the pub to get champagne glasses, and Mr Humphries, the pub owner, who saw

Thomas and Henry on 5 September 1874 at the pub, and that he saw Thomas ordering champagne. The irresistible conclusion is that it was Thomas who took the champagne to see Mrs King under the guise of Frieake.

- Add to this that Mr Arkell, Thomas' employer, noted that Thomas was absent from work for much of the 5th of September, so giving him the opportunity to visit Sidney Square.

- The 'Dear Pet' letter, postmarked 5 September, states that Frieake was visiting at 7pm that day. If Thomas was passing himself off as Frieake, it's not for me to say what the purpose was, but all the evidence suggests Thomas was Frieake.

- The date of the 5th September may be wrong, but the fact that a disturbance took place is corroborated by Foster, Wilmore and Stanley.

- The chloride of lime. The defence say there are doubts about the date of purchase and the intended use of it. Baylis' book says 10th September. Mrs Rogers fixes the date exactly due to seeing it on the day before the birth of her child on the 11th. If Henry bought it for a customer in Southend, why doesn't he tell us the details of the customer?

- The defence say Wainwright would never have bought lime from a neighbour but get it elsewhere. I would suggest to you that persons who do evil deeds do not expect them to be discovered, and that a person who bought chloride of lime for the covering of a body would not think that the murder would ever come to light, or that the use he put that chloride of lime to would ever be disclosed.

- The evidence of three shots. The men heard what may have been three pistol shots being fired in rapid succession in the vicinity of Wainwright's premises. The date of the 'shots' was an issue, but in the end It's not important. A woman did meet her death through three pistol shots. Was this evidence of gunfire another link in the chain of evidence? What is clear is that shots were fired into the head of this woman, in all probability, were they not fired on the 11th September.

- It's said Wainwright gave Harriet 10 shillings to spend on an outfit for Brighton. Where is the evidence of that outfit having been purchased? With all the publicity of the case, would no one come forward in Whitechapel to furnish details of its purchase?

- Where are the people to tell us where Harriet is? How come she has made no enquiry of her children? Why hasn't this Mr Frieake been in communication with anyone? They must have heard about this case and would have known that one word from them would see this case cleared.

- The woman must have received those shots which caused her death that night at number 215. There is no evidence, at any rate, to show where she is.

- You cannot doubt that the body *is* that of Harriet Lane, and that she met her death by means of the three chambers of a revolver being fired into her head on the 11th September.
- The Charing Cross Hotel letter sent to Miss Wilmore from Mr Frieake advised her that Harriet would never speak to friends or family again, and that they soon intended to marry. It finishes, 'we are just off to Dover'. Assume for a moment that Frieake had taken her to France. Why should the prisoner have made all these excuses and explanations?
- If she had simply left Henry for a wealthier man, he would not have been to blame. His friends knew about Harriet. Why resort to these suspicious excuses? All he had to do was to tell the simple truth, but instead of that, he gets his brother to write this letter; and a more astute or cunning letter could not have been devised to put inquirers off the scent and pacify her friends, and to induce them to be quiet.
- The three telegrams. Henry produces one to Miss Wilmore. They come from Dover Pier telegraph office and state, 'we are just off to Paris', who sent those telegrams? Was it Frieake, or was it not rather the man who dictated or wrote that letter? What tale do they tell? Was that not a contrivance to follow up the Charing Cross letter to satisfy the friends of Harriet Lane and put them off the scent?
- Henry Wainwright makes further excuses; he says Harriet had been seen by his foreman, and by one of his porters. But was that true? We have heard the foreman, Rogers, say that he never saw the woman. Mr Besley complains that we have not called the workman; but there is nothing to prevent Henry Wainwright, if the statement is true, calling that workman or porter himself.
- The defence say that Mr Johnson's evidence about stippling the windows at the rear of 215 was worthless. Perhaps Henry Wainwright had good reason for stippling the window in November 1874 – who can tell? The theory of the prosecution is, that in the paint-room at the end of the premises there was this dreadful secret – a woman lying buried whose body it was necessary for Henry Wainwright to get rid of. Would it do, then, for him to have that paint-room, and the door of the paint room, commanded by the eyes of anyone looking from the kitchen window?
- The 10 September 1875 preparations were being been made to remove the body. The cloth, the cord, the chopper, and the spade had been bought and Henry had discussed moving a parcel with Stokes. Henry then found his way to the Hen and Chickens with the body. It has been asked, why did Henry employ Stokes, and if Thomas was implicated, why did he not do what Stokes did?

- Henry Wainwright might well have supposed if he or his brother were seen carrying the parcels away, a suspicion would attach to them which would not attach to the man Stokes. Is it not reasonable that persons engaged in wicked transactions should make a mistake?
- It was also asked, why did Henry pick up Alice Day in his cab? Again, this was to avert suspicion.
- After Henry was arrested, he offered a bribe to the officers. When he arrived at the police station, having had plenty of time for consideration, he says that some gentleman whom he had met in a pub had offered him £3 to carry the parcels to the Borough.
- The defence say the body is not that of Harriet Lane. The Crown state that the body is hers for a variety of reasons.
- The height of the body. The eminent surgeons for the prosecution stated that its height, would have matched Harriet's.
- Had the body been that of a woman who had borne children? Dr Larkin thought the body had been a mother. All the doctors agreed that it is difficult, if not impossible, to arrive at a conclusion about this matter, even if you were to make an investigation immediately after the death of a woman.
- The scar on the leg corresponded exactly to what the witnesses described about a burn she had sustained.
- The hair pad. The velvet ribbon and great number of hair pins were described by Miss Wilmore and corresponded in every way with the pad found on the body.
- If Harriet went away with Frieake, then knowing that a man whom she once loved was now on trial for her murder, knowing that he faced the death penalty, would she refuse to come here and save him? Why is she silent? Because she is dead! The defence say the body is somebody else, who committed suicide. This theory is an insult to your intelligence. What account has Henry given of this woman? He must have known all about her but he says nothing from his own mouth or through his counsel about her.
- Henry was being embarrassed by his mistress importuning him for money which he couldn't pay. She comes to his premises and causes a scene. He was highly thought of in the neighbourhood and these occurrences were prejudicial to his good name. This is a motive for murder.
- Mrs Rogers gives evidence of hearing Harriet say, 'don't, don't', and seeing her lying on the floor in a fainting fit while in Henry's company. Was he threatening her? It shows that the woman was occasioning, anxiety, embarrassment, and, perhaps, dread in the mind of Henry Wainwright. This was in August 1874. On 10 September he was buying chloride of lime! On 11th September she leaves Sidney Square and is never seen again!

- I suggest that Henry introduced a man to Harriet and passed him off as Mr Frieake, a plan that had been going on well before September 1874. I suggest that this was for the purpose of carrying out a scheme, and that the scheme was the destruction of that woman, and then that the blame for her disappearance should be placed on the shoulders of Frieake.
- Sending the letters and telegrams was for the purpose of making excuses to friends, and of preventing further enquiry. Why make all these subterfuges if she had merely gone off with Frieake? The friends of Harriet Lane have concluded that she had gone off with another paramour, left her children, and perhaps they thought she had married. They ceased to inquire.
- In November 1874, Rogers goes to live at 215 and discovers an offensive smell. The premises remain empty till April 1875 and are then soon to be given up. By 27 August 1875, Henry knows the cause of the smell, and he knows that the body has to be moved otherwise the new owners might discover the cause of that smell. On 10 September 1875 he obtains cloth, the axe, and the shovel.
- Henry, that evening or perhaps in the dead of the night, takes the body out of its grave and chopped it up for convenient carriage, and put it in parcels. On the 11th he is confronted by the police at the Hen and Chickens. These circumstances which are against the prisoner and, if they are sufficient to bring home to your minds without any reasonable doubt the guilt of the prisoner, it will be your duty to return a verdict of guilty of wilful murder.

At this point the attorney general sat down, having given a fine performance covering the evidence against Henry Wainwright. He seemed to have thought of everything, and had explained to the jury some of the points where they may have had some doubts about the guilt of the prisoner. Sir John had given a masterclass in his summing up, and it would have been a brilliant lesson for any of the budding lawyers who had been crowding the courtroom. His explanation of the key facts to the jury in such persuasive tones was outstanding.

The court broke for lunch and Sir John must have gone for a well-earned smoked salmon lunch. Thomas, meanwhile, would have been back in his cell, perhaps with a battered plate, enjoying some bread and soup. Sir John may hopefully have then had a little time to consider the next chapter of his day in the case against Thomas. He had effectively ripped Henry's defence to shreds, and Thomas must have waited with trepidation as he prepared to hear what he would make of his own case.

Chapter Twenty

Day 8 of the Trial: The Prosecution's Speech to the Jury Regarding Thomas

After the break for lunch, Sir John Holker got back to his feet to address the jury in the matter of Thomas Wainwright. His morning summing up the case against Henry could not have gone much better. His brief had been to successfully convict both brothers, but especially in the case of wilful murder against Henry. Any sort of conviction against Thomas, before or after the fact, would be a good result. He began by telling the jury that the amount of evidence against Thomas was much smaller.

He hinted to the jury that their guilty verdicts should not be defeated by giving doubt to any information that was not worthy of their attention. This was code for saying that the defence had tried to rubbish the prosecution case, but without any substance to their pleas. Then with a straight face he commended the work of Thomas' counsel, Mr Moody, calling his charge to the jury on Thomas' behalf, as being of 'great ability'.

Sir John suggested that Thomas had, for some reason, whether it was due to brotherly affection or some less worthy motive, lent himself to a plot to pass himself off as his brother's friend, Edward Frieake. What was to be gained by such a plot was not for Sir John to say, but the scheme was afoot, and so he asked the jury to infer something against Thomas.

The main points made by Sir John are summed up below;[1]
- Harriet was to be 'soothed or conciliated to believe that some place was being obtained for her' and that the main objective was to get her to go to the place where her murder could be committed.
- The plan was to persuade Harriet that money was going to be obtained through Mr Frieake to obtain a suitable residence for her. She thought that Mr Frieake was the auctioneer of Coleman Street.
- The letter written by 'Mrs King' to 'Mr Frieake' contained words which alluded to some 'arrangements' being made. 'I think if you and Harry would see me tomorrow evening, we may be able to arrange matters satisfactorily. Please let me know if you will call'. It is clear from this that something had been going on in the shape of an arrangement which Harriet Lane, Henry

Wainwright and this man Frieake were to be parties. It is evident from the letter that Harriet Lane had been introduced to Frieake and also that he had called upon her at her lodgings.

- 'Frieake' knew her address, and it is clear that he had been kind to her, and also that she had behaved in an unladylike way.
- I say this letter should be sufficient to satisfy any reasonable mind that there had to be a Frieake who was introduced to Harriet Lane as the auctioneer of Coleman Street. The letter beginning, 'Dear Pet' mentioning the initials 'E.F.', shows that there must have been some business to be transacted, something to be done or arranged by Henry Wainwright, and the man, whoever it was, that was representing Frieake.
- Mrs Foster says that Frieake came to the house to see Mrs King about furniture and to get her opinion on what colours she would like. This shows that something was being instilled in this woman's mind which led her to believe that she would be established in another home, or to have, possibly, a home of her own, and that these transactions were effected through the instrumentality of Frieake.
- Was it not clear that some scheme was afoot, and that it was some person impersonating Mr Frieake, the auctioneer?
- Mr Arkell, Thomas' employer, says that he was absent from the shop on several dates in August and September 1874. There was nothing to stop Thomas getting to Mrs Foster's residence in Sidney Square on Saturday 5 September.
- The defence draw attention to the identification of Thomas by the witnesses as being Frieake. These identifications are from more than 12 months ago, so are difficult to accurately recollect, but they all said they 'believed' it was Thomas but could not swear to it.
- The evidence of Mr Humphries fixed the date as 5 September. The date he gave may have been wrong, but it does not follow that because a man is wrong about one thing that he is necessarily wrong about another.
- The occurrence happened more than a year ago, and why should he remember the date? It is a thing which would be likely to impress itself upon his memory, but not the date; unless there is something which will make the case of peculiar importance it escapes the memory. He remembers the disturbance and thinks he remembers the time. He has an entry in his diary to fix the date.
- It is certain that Thomas was in Humphries pub and took away some champagne glasses, the date may have been the 5 September or an earlier date. On that very day, Henry sends Harriet a letter, 'Dear Pet'. If Thomas was Frieake, what was he playing that part for? What was his motive?

- Thomas next appears in the matter of the undated Charing Cross letter. You can compare the writing of that letter with the ordinary writing of Thomas. You can form your own opinion as well as the expert can.
- Shortly after the disappearance of Harriet Lane, and after enquiries had been made by her family and friends, we have Thomas writing this letter.
- The theory is that Thomas was Frieake, and that the two brothers contrived a scheme to convince Mrs King that Thomas was Mr Frieake, and that he was about to find her new lodgings.
- There was no idea that Mrs King should disappear with Wainwright or should disappear with Mr Frieke; she was to be established somewhere in London or the country; she was not apparently to be separated from her friends, to lose sight of her children, or to be estranged from those who were dear to her. That is what would be in the mind of the man who wrote this letter. Thomas would know he had been playing a part – a part to pacify and soothe Mrs King.
- Mr Moody suggests that Thomas was applied to do a good turn for his brother; as 'they are asking about Mrs King, and I cannot satisfy them as to her whereabouts', Henry asks him to write this letter, and he writes it. I am assuming all along that he is acting as a friend.
- The letter which starts 'My dear Miss Wilmore, l am very much surprised at not receiving a reply to my last letter', begins with a falsehood. She had not received a previous letter. The letter continues, saying that Mrs King agreed to cut off all ties with family and friends and that they were 'off to Dover'. When Miss Wilmore saw that letter, she was to assume that Harriet Lane was permanently cutting off all her ties with everyone, including her children.
- When Thomas Wainwright was asked to write that letter, was he an innocent man? Why should he not write the letter for Henry? Because he knew he was the man who had been passed off as Mr Frieake, and that this was a lie about her going off with him. He must have known it was not her intention to withdraw herself from her friends and her children. It was not her intention to discard all her connections, her friends, and acquaintances for the future. He must have known this.
- If there was another Mr Frieake, and Henry had come to Thomas and said, Mrs King has absconded, and has gone away with Frieake, a friend of mine, and she will not come back, and I am anxious to satisfy her friends, that they may not bore me any longer with their inquiries, he might then have written such a letter as this. Why, if she had simply gone away; he could have cleared himself by simply speaking the truth?
- Was there another, a third Mr Frieake, a trusted friend of Henry Wainwright, of who we can learn nothing, but who he could have given us a satisfactory account?

- Surely, Thomas would have asked Henry, why do you ask me to put my name to a tissue of lies? What is your motive? Where is Mrs King? Satisfy me that Mrs King is alive. Satisfy me that Mrs King is being cared for. Satisfy me that there is some shadow of foundation in this story, and I will do it."
- On 17 October this letter to Miss Wilmore was accompanied by a similar one written to Henry. Later on, a telegram is sent to Miss Wilmore from Dover. Then you are entitled to connect those two circumstances together, and to assume that there was a plot between the two brothers prior to September? Who sent that telegram? I do not say it was Thomas, but it was either Thomas or Henry, both of whom knew that this woman was missing.
- If the theory of the prosecution is right, she was dead, and Henry knew it, and wanted to account for her absence by telling a tissue of falsehoods. It was not likely that Henry would have employed any fresh actor to send this telegram from Dover because the suspicions of that person would have been aroused and, therefore, the probability is that either Henry or Thomas sent it. Which was it? My learned friend has ingeniously tried to lead you to believe that it was not Thomas.
- He draws your attention to the spelling of the name Frieake on the telegram from Dover. It is a slight matter. It may have been a mistake by the clerk. Henry may have dictated it wrongly to Thomas. Thomas may simply have forgotten the spelling.
- We do not hear anything more against Thomas till we come to the time he is engaged in getting a lease of the Hen and Chickens, in the Borough. Thomas obtained the key from Mr Lewis, and that it was afterwards found in the possession of Henry Wainwright when he went to the Hen and Chickens to deposit the body of the woman on 11 September.
- If Henry was going to remove the body, what would have to be done? He would have had to either on the evening of the 10th or early morning of the 11th, take away the boards, take out the earth, remove the body and cut it up into pieces. How long would this have taken? Could he do it alone? I don't say that there is any evidence Thomas Wainwright being there. That is for the jury to consider. Henry would only have had a short time to do the job as he could not have turned on the gas lights as they had been removed and, if he had used lamps, these could have been seen from Whitechapel Road. Would he had had enough natural light from a September evening?
- There is evidence to suggest Henry did not act alone as a pocket knife was found. But was it Henry's knife? When he was searched by the police, he was found to have a pocket knife in his belongings.
- Then comes the question; was he doing the work alone? Or if not, who could be with him? Can you conceive anyone else being with him except the man who had written at his suggestion the letter from Charing Cross Station?

- Thomas Wainwright was seen the next day with Henry Wainwright and appeared to be ill, and had shaved off his moustache. You must say what, in your judgment, this points to. Then again, there is no doubt that the body was being removed by Henry Wainwright to the Hen and Chickens, where it appears that there was a place in the basement which one would choose for depositing it in. The body and these premises were in Thomas Wainwright's occupation.
- It is said that Thomas could not have formed the idea of placing the remains on his premises, because he was about to surrender them to the landlord. Does it follow that when Henry Wainwright took the mutilated remains to the Hen and Chickens, he intended them to remain? Might it not be that he intended to remove them, or that it was intended to make a grave under the floor of the cellar which would not be discovered.

Sir John had done a good job in explaining the charges against Thomas. After an excellent morning's work on Henry, the standard of advocacy hadn't slipped with Thomas, and the jury had been provided with a strong case against him.

He invited the jury to find Thomas guilty of the first charge of being an accessory before the fact. He then added the second charge of being involved in the disposal of the body and assisting his brother in evading justice. He stressed the first charge was as serious as murder itself, but then very fairly added that they could only come to this finding upon the most clear and convincing proof. He then asked the jury to choose which charge they could be sure about. In reality, he seemed to be telling them to only convict on the second, less serious matter.

As proceedings for the day ended at 3pm, Sir John would have been the happiest of all the barristers involved in the case. He had had a thrilling day presiding over the prosecution of this amazing murder trial. He was at the height of his barristerial powers, and this case would turn out to be one of the highlights of his illustrious career.

Chapter Twenty-One

Day 9 of the Trial: The Judge Sums Up

After all the witnesses and the advocates for both sides had said their piece, the mass of information that had been bombarding the jury from day one of the trial had to be sifted through. The last act before sending the jury out to deliberate was the judge's most important part of proceedings; his summing up.

This part of the legal process is important in that it gives the jury a full precis of the case, along with all the evidential matters that they need to consider. It is the judge's role to explain the law to the jury, especially, in this case, in relation to the charge against Thomas. The accessory before and after the fact situation would need to be fully understood by the jurors.

His Lordship started his submission at 10am. He told the jury that the case relied on circumstantial evidence, as no one had seen the murder take place. A motive for the murder needed to be established. He qualified the circumstances around the identity of the body, stating that even if they could not be sure that the body belonged to Harriet Lane, they could still convict for murder. He then spoke about the identification of the corpse in Henry's cab and whether the jury were satisfied as to its identity.

The judge then advised them about a unique set of circumstances in relation to the identity of the body that Henry Wainwright had been found in possession of, which the prosecution had sought to prove was the body of Harriet Lane. He warned the jury of the following;

> I am bound to tell you that if you should be of the opinion that the prisoner took the life of the body he was dealing with, even though the proof of identity should fail, it will then be your duty to convict him. It is not necessary in a charge of murder that the identity of a person killed should be established; the law throws its protection alike around the unknown and the known as far as it can.[1]

His Honour then went about explaining the different sorts of evidence. He explained that British justice relies on the presenting of different types of evidence to the jury on which they must base their verdicts. The best and most reliable evidence is 'direct evidence'.[2] **(See footnote for information about circumstantial evidence.)**

The judge mentioned that financial problems were squeezing Henry Wainwright to an extent that Harriet Lane was having to pawn her belongings to survive. This also led to unpleasant scenes at his shop where Harriet arrived regularly, looking for money to be able to feed the children. There had been angry scenes witnessed by Mr and Mrs Rogers accompanied by loud quarrelling. On one occasion they had heard her shouting, 'Oh don't, oh don't.' Soon afterwards, Harriet was seen lying on the floor of the shop. The judge stated that the defence had claimed that this evidence of the Rogers' was a vile and wicked perjury. But he queried, what possible motive did they have to lie?

The summing up continued by pointing out the danger in which Wainwright found himself. The responsibility of keeping Harriet and the children would continue for many years to come, but then when the money was drying up, she was apt to be ill tempered, and if she had perhaps drunk too much, she may had made a disturbance which could lead to an exposure that might reach the ears of Henry's wife, who knew nothing of the affair. The judge's succinct description fitted the situation perfectly. 'He lived on the edge of a volcano that might at any moment have exploded and led to disastrous consequences'.

Would Henry's debts and the instability of Harriet's behaviour, the judge asked, form a motive for murder? Was the involvement of the fictitious Mr Frieake simply a way of getting rid of Miss Lane, and could it be concluded that Thomas was an accessory before the fact? The motive for the murder of Harriet was very clear. The Frieake situation appeared to be a contrivance to stop people looking for her in England and to assume she was now abroad with a wealthy new man. Was this other Frieake an invention? If there really was a Frieake, why had he not come forward?

The letters and telegrams were a very crafty plan to throw people who were looking for Harriet off the scent. Did Henry really believe that there was another man called Edward Frieake, or was it a complete deception? If this second man called Frieake really existed, why had he not been found?

The judge next mentioned the disappearance of Harriet Lane. People were baffled, but no one initially suspected foul play. A body had been deposited at 215 Whitechapel Road, but the pending disposal of the property due to financial problems meant that the body had to be moved or face its possible discovery. The body needed to be small enough while being moved so as not to attract attention.

The learned judge suggested that with the Hen and Chickens empty, Henry Wainwright decided to move the body there, and went about acquiring items to assist him in that regard.

Henry was discovered in possession of the body by the police officers who he offered to bribe. Was this action not proof of his guilt of the crime of murder? At the police station, Henry was asked about the parcel that he had taken in his cab. He suggested that a man in a pub had asked him to move them for £5. The judge dismissed this unlikely scenario with the comment, 'I need not point out that this statement was altogether untrue'.

His Lordship mentioned that when she left 3 Sidney Square, Harriet had told Miss Wilmore she would only be gone for a day or two. Was it probable that Henry could at that time, have afforded to give her £25? Where was the evidence that he had obtained a dress for her?

The matter of the Charing Cross Hotel letter was then raised by his Honour, who stated that the letter was in the handwriting of Thomas Wainwright and that the correspondence had been craftily devised, as it effectively cut her off from all communications. Would a woman like Harriet, who was a loving mother and who was also attached to her friends and family, have agreed to cut everyone off dead? The telegrams from Dover were clearly a scheme which were to prevent further enquiry about what had become of Harriet.

Number 215 Whitechapel Road was unquestionably the grave of the body. No one could be in any doubt that it had been disinterred between 10 and 11 September 1875, and had then been dismembered.

His lordship stated later that the bullet wounds to the head were clearly the cause of death. But by whom was it done? The body had been found in Henry's possession. The judge was clearly not impressed with the suggestion that Harriet may have committed suicide and that common sense suggested who may have been the murderer; the *Morning Post*[33] gave the judge's comments on the subject;

If they found a man removing a body from one place to another, the presumption might fairly be that the man who removed it must have been the man who put it in the hiding-place, and if they found him dealing with it, and having recourse to concealment, there was still further reason why he should give a satisfactory account of how he became possessed of it. It was only common sense to say when a man concealed the body of a woman who had been murdered, 'What is your motive for concealment? Are you the murderer?'

The prisoner's mouth was not closed, he could offer his own explanation, tell his counsel what his case was, and call his own witnesses. He had listened with the greatest pains to the address of the counsel for the prisoner to see if he could offer any satisfactory explanation of the conduct of the prisoner in taking up the body in order to transfer it elsewhere, the transfer being made for the purpose of concealment. The only explanation offered, however, was the vague and wild one that the woman had committed suicide, such an explanation, however, stopping where it did, was obviously absurd.

Henry had not provided any plausible explanation to his counsel as to how Harriet might have met her end. The judge then came to the matter of the identity of the corpse. He alluded to the similarities between the body and a description of Harriet. If the body was not Harriet, where was she now? She had been attached to her family and her children. The judge then came up with the killer question;

> If the body buried in Whitechapel Road was not the body of Harriet Lane, whose was it? If it was not the body of Harriet Lane, why should the prisoner have been disturbing it and taking it up and transferring it to another place?

All the points of identity indicated that the corpse was undoubtedly Harriet. Points such as the age, slender size, teeth, and hair pointed to it being her. Her clothing, hair pad with hairpins, and buttons also tallied. The body had been examined for a scar on the leg which had found by the doctors. The doctors for the prosecution had also given evidence that the body was that of a mother. What of the chloride of lime, why did he purchase it. No customer in Southend has been produced? And the revolver? Henry had possessed a revolver and had the means to kill her in this way. Three shots were heard being fired. If the body was Harriet's, she had been assassinated.

The Lord Chief Justice then turned to the case against Thomas. His opinion was that it was not conclusive that Thomas had been an accessory before the fact, and that it would not be safe to convict him of that offence. For the jury to convict him, Thomas would have had to have known that a murder had been committed, and that his object was to assist his brother in trying to conceal it.

The judge ended his summing up, having confidence that the jury would do their duty. If they had any doubt in the case against the prisoners, they should give them the benefit of that doubt. On the other hand, if they used rational, thinking minds, and if the facts brought them to the conclusion that the woman fell by Henry Wainwright's hand, then they should do their duty, sternly and thoroughly.

The summing up seems a fair reflection of the evidence. Reading between the judge's lines, it was very clear that he thought Henry was guilty, though he could not actually tell the jury that. Thomas was a different matter. The judge had helped his cause by directing the jury that only a conviction for him being an accessory after the fact could be accepted. This was a very important concession for Thomas, especially in relation to any likely sentence. This comment could save his life. The jury retired at 3.45pm.

Chapter Twenty-Two

Day 9 of the Trial: Conclusion and Sentencing

With the case finally ending after the long Old Bailey battle, the Press hacks would have been scribbling furiously to get their copy finished in time to be out on the pavements the following morning. The conclusion of this trial was a topic of conversation very much on the lips of the Great British Public. The *Illustrated Police News* had been following the case more than most other newspapers, and their unnamed reporter wrote an excellent article on the final day of excitement at the Central Criminal Court: you could almost have been there after reading the summing up of that nail biting final act of the case.

As soon as the verdict was announced, the *IPN* reporter will undoubtedly have jumped in a passing cab to take him the mile from the court to the *IPN* offices down along Fleet Street to the Strand. As he burst through the door, all eyes would have been on him. 'What was the verdict?' may have been shouted at him as the excited staff became the first to hear the outcome 'hot off the press'. The copy would then have been finished off and edited, before being given to the compositors for turning into the typed end product for use in the actual printing process.

The final day's report from the *Illustrated Police News*[1] was worth the 1 penny cost of the newspaper alone;

'THE LAST DAY OF THE TRIAL
Few cases of modern times excited greater public interest than the trial of the two Wainwrights. The Lord Chief Justice commenced his summing up. The prisoners, on being placed in the dock, took their seats more closely together than during the last few days of the trial.

The judge had evidently before him, copious notes of his summing up, for from time to time he turned over a sheet, there was no reading; Every word of the trial seemed to be fixed in the speaker's mind, as slowly and deliberately, in a quiet, almost solemn voice, he went on delivering his charge to the attentive jury.

So perfect was the silence that the scratch of a pen or pencil, and; the crackling of a sheet of paper sounded painfully loud; the person who coughed did so in a suppressed, half stifled way; Now and again, only faintly, making its way through the double windows, came the cry uttered by the driver of some vehicle, trying to get his horse through the crowd in the Old Bailey.

Nothing could have been more calmly just and impressive than the summing up; at times the judge's voice sank very low, when he spoke in mingled tones of sadness and feeling of the disappearance of Harriet Lane.

For the most part the judge's words were delivered in a quiet colloquial form, but at times his voice became almost inaudible. At no time though, had the horrors of the affair been more apparent than now. Even when the judge went through the most revolting portions of the story, the prisoners sat unmoved.

And now once more the description given by the judge was most graphic, as he painted in vivid colours the probable way in which the alleged deed was done; the description of the probable position, the way in which the shots were fired, and the gash in the throat was given; and now for the first time was there any change in the elder prisoner's face.

Hour after hour, with the scales of justice evenly poised, the judge went on clearly, and concisely laying before the jury the various facts of the evidence for and against the prisoners, and bidding the men who would have to give their verdicts carefully weigh each fact.

The judge concluded his most impressive charge at a quarter to four, and then, in the midst of a burst of talk and confusion, the jury filed out of their box, the judge left the bench, and the two prisoners exchanged a word together'.

According to *The Evening Mail*[22] newspaper; the jury retired at 3.45pm and returned at 4.37pm. 'There was a cry of "They come!" the prisoners were ushered into the dock, to remain standing, and – ominous sign – four warders closed up behind them.'

This was *the* moment. You could have heard a pin drop. Every soul in the courtroom would have been trembling in anticipation. Henry and Thomas would both have been looking at the jury and the foreman eagerly for signs of a pending not guilty verdict. Did the jury make eye contact with the defendants? Or did they look away, not wanting so see the imploring faces of the two men begging for mercy as they were about to convict them?

For the barristers, it was all in a day's work, but even they would be hoping for a good result in order to enhance their reputations and so looked on keenly. The judge sat passively at this point awaiting unanimous verdicts, and probably

Henry and Thomas in the dock, published by George Purkess – Police News edition. (*Courtesy of Bishopsgate Institute*)

thinking about whether he would be needing to get the black cap out of the drawer in next few moments.

The police officers present would also have been feeling the tension at this point. Three months of hard work and meticulous preparation, many police hours of laborious leg work and stress in putting the case together had now reached its conclusion. Had the considerable cost of the police investigation been worth it? Reputations were on the line here too for the senior officers. They would also have glanced at the defendants, but would be more keenly surveying the jury. Not guilty verdicts would not go down well at Scotland Yard or with the Commissioner.

Another group at the trial were the casual onlookers, who came to the court for its entertainment value rather than paying to visit a vaudeville show. Though possibly not nervous either way, even these attendees would surely have felt the tension in the room. It was, after all, a capital case, and two men's lives were on the line.

The final notable section of onlookers were the friends and relatives of the defendants. For them, the next few minutes were to be the most important of their lives. Mrs Elizabeth Wainwright (wife), William Wainwright (brother), and Alice Day (friend) were all present and endured an agonising wait for the outcome. As the jury returned and the crowd settled to silence, these poor unfortunates must all have struggled to keep their composure. Hands would have been shaking and their hearts would have been beating fast.

William would have been hoping to retain the family reputation intact with a not guilty verdict. Would the money he used to fund the defence barristers have been well spent? Mrs Wainwright pondered the prospect of soon being made a widow. Alice Day also looked on with fear. Despite the fact that Henry's actions had directly led to her spending a week in prison, her fondness of the generous version of Henry made her feel pity for him.

The clerk of the arraigns, Mr Avory asked the defendants to answer to their names, and then asked the foreman of the jury two formal questions;[3]

Mr AVORY: *Do you find the prisoner, Henry Wainwright, is guilty or not guilty of the indictment, which charges him with wilful murder?*

FOREMAN: *We do all say he is guilty.*

At that moment, time stood still as the foreman took a second or two to unemotionally utter the word 'GUILTY'. The court would have been in uproar for a few seconds as the main verdict was announced. Although Henry remained impassive on the outside, inside he must have felt crushed, knowing that he now only had a short time to live. It's a surprise that his legs hadn't given way at this moment.

The focus then turned to Thomas who, having heard the guilty verdict against Henry, would now be fearing the worst as he prayed for the best. The clerk continued his questioning.

Mr AVORY: *Do you say that Thomas Wainwright is guilty of being an accessory before or after the fact?*

FOREMAN: *Not guilty before, but guilty after.*

The Evening Mail continued its report of the verdict.

> On hearing the verdict on Thomas, Henry gave a sharp angry glance round at his brother, frowning fiercely. The next he was facing the Judge, who had put on the black cap – a square piece of cloth after the fashion of a hood; and already the news of the verdict had darted like lightning from lip to lip, and was known in the street, for now, and at frequent intervals, came up the cheering of the mob to mingle with the Judges words as he asked Henry Wainwright, the usual question if he had anything to say.
>
> The prisoner took advantage of the opportunity and drawing himself up, spoke for a few minutes boldly, firmly without a quiver in his voice; The shouts of the mob mingling with his words as he called God to witness that he was innocent of the deed.
>
> One minute a short, pallid, firm man was standing calmly before Judge, the next minute the warders had closed round him, there was an ominous jingle of keys, and in all human probability, Henry Wainwright had gone for ever from the public gaze. As he disappeared, the Judge removed his black cap and passed sentence upon Thomas, who had stood with face slightly averted from his brother, and who wore still the same heavy, unchanged, stolid look that he has preserved throughout.

Henry Wainwright spoke these final words in public[4]

> Standing as I do at the bar of this court convicted of the crime of wilful murder, I declare before that God before whom I shall shortly have to appear that I am not the murderer of the remains that were found in my possession. I never fired a pistol in my life, and I could prove by witnesses that I never buried or exhumed those remains. I admit that I have been guilty of immorality, that I have been guilty of many indiscretions; but with regard to the crime of which I have been convicted, and for which I am to suffer death, my conscience is clear, and I swear that I am innocent.

It was a considered and powerful statement as this trial of trials produced yet more drama. Perhaps some had expected Henry to finally admit his guilt, but he had his story and he was sticking to it. His defence really had been doomed from the start in the absence of any explanation on his part as to who the body was, or how he came to be moving it across London Bridge. The judge, having presided over a thrilling case, did not hold back as he rounded on him with distain:

> You have been found guilty upon the clearest evidence of the crime of wilful murder of Harriet Lane, and no one who has heard the evidence that has been given upon the trial can doubt for a moment that the jury have come to a just and righteous conclusion. I can therefore only deplore that, standing as you say you are upon the brink of the grave and in the presence of that God, you should have made the statement you have made that you are innocent of the crime.
>
> There can be no doubt whatever that you took the life of this poor young woman, who had lived with you for a long time on terms of the greatest love and friendship, and who was the mother of your children. You enticed her to your house, and you there used the revolver with which she was slain. No one can entertain the slightest doubt that this was how she met her death, and that you were guilty of a most barbarous, cruel, murder.
>
> I only say what I have done for the purpose of inducing you to know that there is no hope of mercy for you in this world. I have only to warn you against any delusive hope you may entertain that the sentence of the law will not be carried into effect. So long as it remains the law of this country that he who of malice afore-thought destroys the life of another, shall die also, in such a case as this, sentence will certainly be carried out, and I now have only now to pass upon you the formal sentence of the law, which is that you be taken from the dock back to the prison from whence you came, and from thence to the place of execution, and may the Lord God Almighty have mercy on your soul.

It was clear what the judge had been thinking all through the case, and he had given it to Henry with both barrels. At this point Henry was removed from the courtroom, leaving his brother to face the last of the music. The judge was rather more measured with his comments towards Thomas;

> The jury have, in my opinion, correctly acquitted you of the heavier crime of having entered into the scheme conceived by your brother with a view to murder Harriet Lane. Their opinion, and they have pronounced it by their verdict, is that having become aware of the crime committed by your brother, you lent yourself to assist him by its concealment. No

fraternal affection, no regard or sympathy which one brother should have for another, can excuse you in the eyes of the law for assisting him.

I am ready to believe that you were actuated under the influence which your brother had over you, without which you might not have done what you did. I believe you have been his dupe and his tool, and he has in some degree your crime to answer for practically as his own. You yielded weakly and wrongly to his influence and his greater age.

He felt that the least sentence he could pronounce was that of penal servitude for seven years. The prisoner Thomas, who did not utter a word throughout the whole of the proceedings, was then removed from the bar'.

The trial then ended, after consigning Thomas to seven years of hard labour miles away from his family. The *Friend of India*[5] newspaper gave details of the effect of the verdict.

The young man Stokes, who discovered the murder, was awarded £30 by the judge – an amount which, under the circumstances, might have been much larger. Alice Day found her way into court, and feinted on hearing the sentence passed. So ends this prolonged inquiry into one of the foulest crimes, committed by a man of good education, engaging manners, and blessed with a good mother, who, poor woman, has lost her reason since the terrible disclosure.

Although Alice Day had been badly treated by Henry Wainwright, her friendship with him must have still meant something to her as the verdict was clearly a shock.

One thing that none of the newspapers reported on the day of the trial was what happened as Thomas and Henry were both taken down by the guards, so we can only guess at the situation as they descended the stairs to the detention area. As both men disappeared from view of the courtroom it was if their lights were being snuffed out, as neither of them would ever be seen in public again.

Did they come face to face with one another when they arrived in the gaolers office? And, if they did, what conversation passed between them? Would there have been shouting and recriminations between the brothers? Would there have been floods of tears? They both knew the truth about who had killed Harriet Lane, but their joint subterfuge and plan on escaping justice had come to nothing. As both were shackled for the walk next door, back to Newgate, the final slamming shut of their prison cell door that night must have felt like the end of the world.

Chapter Twenty-Three

Ellen Wilmore

This key witness in the case is one of some mystery and we know only a small amount of detail about her. What was obvious about Ellen Wilmore is that she was a true and loyal friend to Harriet Lane, as well as being a devoted surrogate mother to both of Harriet's two girls. The newspapers were full of information about her, but mostly in relation to the case. No one had bothered to ask her details of her own background, birth or family history, and the case may have prompted her to change her identity sometime in 1876 when interest and public scrutiny were starting to quieten down. We may

'Mrs Wilmore', *Illustrated Police News*, 25 December 1875. (*Copyright The British Library Board. All Rights Reserved*)

never know, but she is missing from the records before and after 1875, and it's not known what became of her or whether she ever married and had children of her own.

There are only a few crumbs of detail; one newspaper[1] claimed that her late father was a solicitor and that she ran a dressmaking business in Waltham together with Harriet. She was an important witness in giving evidence about explanations given from Henry Wainwright regarding the disappearance of Harriet in September 1874. She was clearly not in favour of Harriet's dangerous association with Henry. Perhaps she could see through his facade of respectability that Harriet couldn't?

Harriet Lane's Children

The matter of the children following the guilty verdicts at the Old Bailey was one of importance to a number of parties. Around this time there was a great deal of sympathy for the various children who were left behind after the dust settled. Henry Wainwright's children had lost their comfortable lifestyle as well as their father. Thomas Wainwright's had lost a father for seven years (in reality, they'd never see him again), and were soon to lose their mother. Harriet's children were about to lose the second of their parents. It was an uncertain time for all of those children, whose lives would be changed forever as a result of this infamous case.

The *Illustrated Police News*[2] stated that Miss Wilmore and Harriet's children, being in a destitute state, had been taken in by a Mr Couzens of Maryland Street, Stratford. The children looked healthy and had evidently not suffered any hunger, this being due to Miss Wilmore pawning all she possessed.

After the trial, the judge and under sheriffs set up an account to benefit Miss Wilmore, calling it 'The Wilmore Fund',[3] with subscriptions being paid into London Joint Stock Bank, but one thing that can always be guaranteed to draw attention is the giving away of cash.

The York Herald[4] reported a sudden change of heart in Harriet's parents as to the long-term future of her young orphans. With the smell of money in the air, John Lane wrote to Ellen Wilmore asking for them to be handed over to him. One wonders if he had simply decided to do the right thing or was it instead the prospect of the money that prompted him to send her a letter asking for the girls to be handed over. The newspaper was in no doubt as to his motives as they were only interested in taking the children now, when 'they firmly refused to take them off her hands before'.

By the early Spring of 1876, the *Morpeth Herald*[5] reported a collection of £280, which, as of 2021, would be worth around £33,141.[6] One wonders what John Lane[7] did with the money?

The Globe newspaper of 3 December 1875 gave details of a visit by their intrepid reporter, who found Ellen and the children in a snow-covered Maryland Road, Stratford.[8] When summing up the case, the judge expressed regret that the rules of evidence had forbidden the hearing of Miss Wilmore's testimony as to what Harriet Lane said to her immediately before their last meeting.

The Globe thought that it was in the public interest that the readership should know what the evidence was that Miss Wilmore was prevented from giving. She stated that before leaving Sidney Square, Harriet had told her that 'she was going to Henry Wainwright's residence in the Whitechapel-Road'. Harriet had added that 'Mr Frieake was very kind-hearted, but nothing on earth should ever part her from Henry.'

Chapter Twenty-Four

After the Trial

Henry awaits his execution at Newgate

After arriving back in his cell following his sentencing, Henry would be wondering how much time he had left, as well as what he was going to do with that period where he was in limbo. There were people to see and final letters to write.

Soon after his trial, the date of his execution had been fixed and preparations begun. The hangman would have to be informed and there would then follow a period of intense activity. The *Belfast Weekly Telegraph*[1] gave details of an unwelcome visit from the prison officials. One morning, a deputation of officials including the governor crammed into Henry Wainwright's cell to inform him of the date of his last day on earth. (A drawing of this scene appeared in the Supplement to the *Illustrated Police News* on 18 Dec 1875).

Wainwright must have known what was coming. He was duly informed that the date of his execution was to be Tuesday 21 December 1875 at 8am. Wainwright conducted himself with extraordinary fortitude without displaying any emotion when the date was read out to him. There was to be no Christmas presence for Henry. There was no mention of Wainwright's reaction when the deputation had left. Condemned prisoners were always considered by the authorities as a suicide risk, so Henry was would have been watched day and night to prevent such an occurrence.

Henry spent almost three weeks as a condemned man being guarded by warders. It would have been fascinating to have been a fly on the wall in those final days as he received visitors, wrote letters and sat with the warder. He would surely not have sat in stony silence all that time? One wonders if the warders ever told tales in the pub about the time they sat with the infamous Henry Wainwright, listening to the story of his life.

One of the visitors that he received was from his solicitor, Mr Pelham.[2] The *Belfast Weekly Telegraph*[3] gave details of the visit:

On Monday, Wainwright's solicitor had an Interview with him in Newgate in the presence of the Governor. The time was entirely occupied with private business matters, chiefly relating to the prisoner's

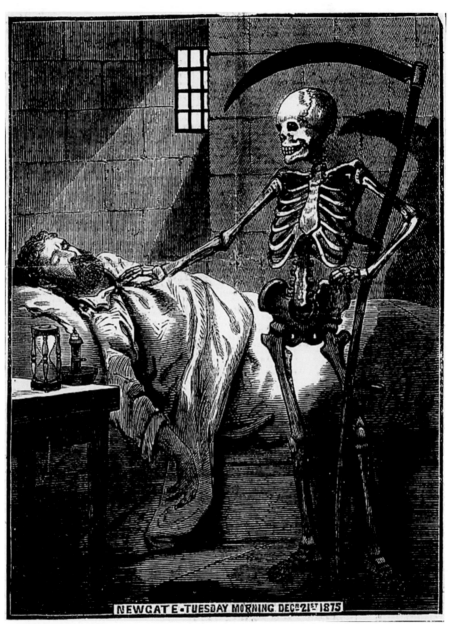

NEWGATE-TUESDAY MORNING DEC 21ST 1875

'Death' watching over a sleeping Wainwright at Newgate, 1 January 1876. (*Copyright The British Library Board. All Rights Reserved*)

life policies. One of these has been allowed to lapse, and of the other the renewal is said, about due. It may prove to be the case that the violent death to which he stands condemned is not a specified exception to his life policy.

The convict was desirous that his solicitor should see his brother Thomas, and accordingly Mr Pelham made application at once to the authorities with a view of obtaining an interview with Thomas, who has not yet been removed from Newgate. Thomas Wainwright had an interview with his wife on Tuesday. Nothing in the nature of a confession has been made by either prisoner.

The question of Henry's life insurance is a very interesting one. Presumably the policy was taken out by him on his own life at some point to ensure that if the worst was to happen, his wife and family would have money to tide them over without being thrown into poverty. Perhaps the policy had been taken out in better times before he met Harriet. Anyone who has taken out insurance will be aware that there are always clauses in the policy to prevent people 'taking advantage'. For all we know, a clause in the policy may have stated the following;

EXCLUSION: Should the policy holder be convicted of murder at a criminal court, and be sentenced to death, the termination of their life having been ended by his lawful execution, the paying up of the policy will become null and void.

This clause is possible, but unlikely. It's probable that a general exclusion covering criminal behaviour might have avoided a payout. Even without one of those, the insurance company may just have looked at Henry's suspicious fire insurance claim and thought better of it. Policies were not generally designed for murderers to benefit from.

A condemned man was allowed visitors in his final days in order to say his goodbyes. The visit of his elderly mother would of course have been painful for both parties. The *Diss Express*[4] noted the following about her final meeting with Henry.

Mrs Wainwright, who was attired in mourning, remained a considerable time. The Governor of the gaol and the Ordinary were present during the interview, which, it need hardly be said, was in the utmost degree painful. Mrs Wainwright bore up well.

Henry Wainwright had also been visited by some of his former friends who were trying to offer financial assistance for his wife and family who now had no means of financial support. The same newspaper cast its opinion on the matter, concluding that offering money to the loved ones of the murderer was akin to an immoral life insurance. The *Diss Express*[5] takes up its air of superiority on the case:

> The WAINWRIGHT CASE. Most people must approve of an adequate public subscription being raised on behalf of Mrs Henry Wainwright, but there is a possibility of the thing being overdone by too many offering to take up subscriptions and a danger of mischief, present and prospective, resulting from an outbreak of what has been appropriately called "sensational charity." A dangerous precedent, having a tendency to cause murder to be regarded as a species of life assurance.

The exertions of the Rev Alfred Conder threw more light on his efforts and his thoughts about the fall from grace of his former friend, Henry Wainwright. An article[6] published in Spring 1876 gives more details of the collection as well as the story of Henry's regrets.

> **WAINWRIGHT AND HIS CHILDREN**. The number of subscriptions to the Wainwright fund is 1,032, ranging from £50 downwards, and the total amount obtained £1,232. The Rev Conder, in publishing his report as to the fund, quoted from the letter of a subscriber who says the cause of Wainwright's downfall 'He got amongst a clique of card-players and a set of public house politicians, by whom not only this unfortunate man, but many others, have been destroyed.
>
> Night after night he was gambling with these men, much older than himself, and of course was unable to attend to his business. He was then making a clear profit of £1,200 a year; it soon fell off, and his habits and character deteriorated.
>
> From one of the last letters he wrote to Mr Conder gives the following: I thank you above all for your kindness on behalf of my wife and children; your act removed the load of grief which weighed down my sorrowing heart. Yes, it is a sorrowing broken heart, when I reflect what was, what I might have been, and what I now am. I truly thank the merciful God, that the sins of the father are not visited upon the children.
>
> May mine never know who their father was! Oh my God! I who loved them so, who was so beloved by them. My dear wife, poor soul, was with me today. She said, "I should not have minded this if you had been a cruel husband to me, but you have not." Poor thing, she never knew of my wickedness till the world knew it too, and now even she forgives me. May God be merciful and kind to her, be her protector and her friend.' In concluding, Mr Conder adds that Mrs Wainwright hopes, with the assistance of the fund, to support her children by giving lessons in music.

Henry Wainwright was going to his death with his reputation in tatters as far as most of the public and the press were concerned, but there was a sizable feeling in some sections of society that he was to be pitied. The *Glasgow Herald*[7] had no sympathy for Henry's crimes and excuses, or his supporters who regarded him as their '*darling idol*'. He was thought of by them as 'good looking, amiable and clever' and they wondered, 'Is it possible that Henry Wainwright could have been guilty of such a horrible crime? The idea is perfectly monstrous!'

The Rev Conder's[8] collection for Mrs Wainwright was to secure her and the children's future for the rest of her life. The family changed their names to Worthington, and lived out their lives comfortably, living at 104 Goldhurst Terrace, South Hampstead. The children all did well but only one of them ever married and no children from the family members were ever produced. Elizabeth Worthington died on 2 April 1924 and is buried in Hampstead Cemetery.

The Herald stated that the 'confession' made by Henry in which he denied the actual murder was 'entirely in the line of his undoubted dramatic talent', adding 'he knew how to put his case in order to tickle the ears of those who have shed a Thames-full of tears over him, and emptied their purses on behalf of his children.'

The paper was unimpressed by Henry's ambiguous final statement and they added, 'He sins in particular, and confess in generalities.' Henry had left out all the gory details and had given a 'theatrical confession'. Henry was admitting to being a weak philanderer rather than a cruel murderer. His charm offensive, which may have been aimed towards his family and friends may perhaps have won him some sympathy, though the editor of the *Glasgow Herald* was in no way taken in.

The Herald did not mourn Henry's execution, stating that he had 'died a more disgraceful, if less cruel death than did Harriet Lane'. The paper stated that the whole affair was a lesson to everyone, and that his 'wandering-eyes' and the desperate desire to save his reputation had resulted in his ruin. His pride had cost him his life.

Petition to reprieve Henry's life

When Henry heard the words 'guilty' being uttered by the jury foreman on 1 December 1875, he knew that his days on earth were numbered. The judge had specifically told him that due to his malice aforethought crime, there could be no chance of a reprieve. But what if he could be saved from this terrible end and the judge was wrong?

The newspapers announced the inevitable sentence, but there were those who considered that Henry was either innocent of the actual murder, or who in any event did not deserve to go to the gallows. Many of his supporters thought that he should be saved from the clutches of the hangman.

With no time to lose, the great and the good of Whitechapel and Bow immediately got to work raising a petition to present to the Home Secretary to try and preserve Henry's life. The petition, which still survives in the National Archives,[9] was addressed to Home Secretary, Richard Asheton Cross.[10]

Many of the petitioners who begged for the mercy of Henry's life had known him from childhood. This was no ordinary prisoner, or a rough, uneducated criminal who awaited death. The document painted a very *worthy* picture of Henry, describing his 'abilities as an educationalist and lecturer'. It also mentioned his being a 'kind husband and affectionate parent'.

The plea for mercy acknowledged that whilst Henry was involved in the murder, he was not guilty of committing the actual murder. The document ended with a plea that the matter should be reconsidered and that a commutation from Queen Victoria should be passed on Henry Wainwright. It was an appeal that would go unheeded.

The petition was only signed by forty-two people, though the document had been endorsed by many people of importance in the Whitechapel and Bow district. Interestingly, none of the signatories were women. The list contained all manner of people of standing in the community; there were no shoe blacks or costermongers among them. It did, however, consist of thirteen church officials, including four ministers as well as eight merchants.

One of Henry's rival brush manufacturer friends, John Horsey, had also signed the petition, as did a professor of music, Alfred Carder, and Mr W. Marsh of the Guardian of the Poplar Union. Perhaps the most interesting of the petitioners was surgeon Mr John Liddle[11] of 80 Bow Road. He was the Medical Officer for Health in Whitechapel who campaigned for improvements in the appalling overcrowded slum dwellings in parts of the area.

Many of Henry's supporters wrote to the police as well as the Home Office asking for clemency for Henry. Some thought that Henry was not the actual shooter of the revolver, suggesting Thomas was the culprit, while others simply disliked the idea of any man being executed by the state.

An interesting plea was received by the Home Secretary from the 'Workmen's Club', Ham Lane, Stratford, asking for respite from the death penalty. Mr John Richard Tamahill of Stratford made representations about the case, particularly in respect of Miss Wilmore. The petition mentioned that they believed that Miss Wilmore went by the alias of 'Mrs Clair' and 'Miss Borrowdale', hinting at some unspecified impropriety on her behalf.[12]

As Henry, his family, his solicitor and supporters nervously awaited the decision of the Home Secretary, some impatient souls visited the Home Office on Sunday 19 and Monday 20 December: 'many excited persons presented themselves at the Home Office saying they attended for the reprieve of the condemned man'.

The efforts of Henry's supporters were doomed to failure. A short and succinct formal decision statement was released. *The Derby Mercury* of 22 December gave the details. 'LATEST PARTICULARS. Several petitions having been preferred to the Home Secretary that the execution might be stayed in order that evidence might be procured which would exonerate Henry Wainwright from the actual commission of crime, the following letter was sent from the Home Office to Mr Pelham, the solicitor for Henry Wainwright'.

Sir – Mr Secretary Cross having had before him the memorial presented by you on behalf of Henry Wainwright, under sentence of death for murder, I am directed to express Mr Cross' regret that after full inquiry and careful consideration of all the circumstances he can discover no grounds to justify him in advising Her Majesty to interfere with the execution of the due course of the law. I am, A. F. 0. LIDDELL. By *ELECTRIC TELEGRAPH.*

The die was cast. Henry's time was now almost up. All avenues of appeal had fallen on deaf ears. His appointment with his maker was now fixed in stone. Call for public executioner, William Marwood.

Chapter Twenty-Five

The Wainwright Brothers' Joint Interview

Even after the trial had finished, both men still protested their innocence as to who the actual murderer was, so the Governor of Newgate took the unusual step of hosting a meeting between the brothers to once and for all establish who had pulled the trigger on the gun that killed Harriet Lane. Thomas had previously stated that he did not wish to have any further communication with his brother: 'I wish I was going to be hanged! He committed that murder – I knew nothing of it until last May.' This suggests he would not have been happy to be in the same room as his brother once more. It was not to be a cards-on-the-table meeting. The notes below record the questions and answers.[1]

Henry: I want to ask you some questions. Will you answer me truthfully honestly and candidly? I am writing a narrative – your name has not as yet been mentioned. Will you answer me? Truthfully candidly and without hesitation? Answer me yes or no.

Thomas: As far as I can I will.

Henry: Did you fire a revolver?

Thomas: I don't know.

Henry: Yes, or no?

Thomas: I don't know.

Henry: Did you pawn that revolver?

Thomas: No.

Henry: Not in the name of Rogers?

Thomas: No certainly not.

Henry: When you bought the spade and chopper, where did you take them?

Thomas: 78 New Road.

Henry: Whose pocket knife was it that the police found?

Thomas: I don't know.

Henry: You have given your answers. Of course, now, I shall mention your name in my statement and the affair of 84? (*This meant the fire at number 84 Whitechapel Road*)

Thomas: You may mention what you like. I have said enough for you, only mention the truth. I have seven years penal servitude through you.

Henry: Through me?

Thomas: Yes.

Henry: Don't say so.

Thomas: I do say so.

Henry: And you say you told the truth?

Thomas: yes.

A pause

The Governor: I wish you to take this opportunity of saying all you have to say because you may not have another.

Thomas: I say this, that you gave instructions to your attorney, 'Whatever you do, get me off'. You tried to get me executed and save yourself. My solicitor told me that Mr Pelham told Mr Besley to do whatever he could to get me executed and get you off. It was most cruel of you to do this. You tried to put me in the place of yourself. First of all, you told my solicitor that Alice Day committed the crime, then Rogers, then you wanted me to put Moore into it. I have nothing more to say. The witnesses have proved where the chopper went to.

Henry: Young.

Thomas: Is it not a lie to say that Young saw me talking that Saturday? It is a lie, you know I was not there.

Henry: Why five witnesses saw you although you have altered so very much. Did you not tell me that you never saw Young in the house with me?

Thomas: I never saw him in my life before.

Henry: You are not Frieake then?

Thomas: Good God, what do you make me out. You are the greatest villain I ever saw in my life. The Lord Chief Justice told you so.

Henry: (Laughingly) You are not Frieake?

Thomas: I was not identified. You tried to make me out Frieake. You may make me out what you like. I have suffered enough through you. Mr Jones the chaplain says you are the most hardened man he ever came across. If there was any heart in you at all, you would have tried to exculpate me.

Henry: How could I when I was arrested. You might have got away for you had 3 weeks.

Thomas: How could I go away. If I had anywhere to go I would do so.

Henry: I have had your reply. That is all I wanted to know

Thomas: You are the greatest villain unhung!

Signed: Sidney Roberts Smith, Governor, 8 December 1875

A letter[2] had also been written by Henry to Thomas, urging him to consider his position. This sensational letter again points the finger of being the actual murderer away from Henry. Teasingly, Henry suggests that 'a partner of HG & Co' could have been responsible. But who was this partner? All we know is that Thomas never received the letter.

Letter from Henry Wainwright to Thomas Wainwright – Document A

Dear Tom,

I have been informed that nothing now can alter your sentence, by giving you a longer term, nor can we be tried again. It remains now with yourself, whether you will speak out truthfully, to remove any (*illegible word*) that has been cast on me. You know that I would willingly have died for you. I was earnestly hoping you would have gone entirely free. I should then never have opened my lips to a simple soul. Now it is otherwise. For myself personally I have no object in life, I think of the everlasting disgrace to our family it would be.

You, if you chose, can say what you know of the entire affair, you know a certain individual of course, I mean the partner of HG & Co, who could say as follows:

- I arranged with Mrs King to leave Sidney Square.
- I met her as arranged, and we went to 215.
- I and no one else shot her with a revolver.
- I afterwards pawned the revolver at (where ever it was).
- I put the body in a box and nailed it down.
- Some weeks after, I dug the grave and buried the body.
- I dug open the grave, cut up the body, tied it up with American cloth bought by HW by my instructions.
- I did this because Mrs King was doing all she could – as she herself told me – to effect HW's ruin and disgrace, because he had so neglected her.

I have made a confidante, great extent of one [sic] who I am sure, would have been glad to have seen us both acquitted. He will assist us now. The very fact of his present kindness proves it. It now remains with you. I leave myself in your hands.

Make enquiries yourself, if anything you may say, can possibly be detrimental to you, in prolonging, or altering your sentence.

I suppose you will only be here a few days. Awaiting your reply, I am yours. Received from Henry Wainwright …11 Dec 1875 Signed Sidney Smith, Governor Newgate

NOTE (in red ink): 'Thomas has never seen this'

* * *

After the face-to-face meeting on 8 December had failed once and for all to reveal the murderer, both brothers took up their pens to record their own full, and hopefully frank, accounts of the case. Thomas wrote a modest 1,100-word résumé of his version. Henry must have been up several nights penning his huge 37,000-word statement.

Before Thomas could be moved to a different prison, the visiting magistrates interviewed him individually in order to illicit more information from him. In the interview, Thomas' written statement was to be read out to give his side of the story.

Chapter Twenty-Six

Thomas Wainwright's Interview by Visiting Magistrates (48007/13 – Document D)

In this first record, Thomas produced his written statement. During his interview he reads out his evidence, but with the prison officials asking several easy questions to try and clarify matters. It's a shame, however, that they didn't probe him further about his account as they leave many questions unanswered. Had Inspector Fox been present, his training would surely have led to more probing questions.

The interview gives astonishing explanations of Thomas' role in the case as well as some detail about the murder, the telegrams, the identity of Mr Frieake, the fire claim, the Hen and Chickens, as well as the pistol. Having never heard Thomas' voice explaining matters in court, this document is an astounding version of events.

Gaol of Newgate – 10 Dec 1875[1]
Present: Mr Alderman Finnis and Mr Alderman Hadley – Visiting magistrates – The Governor – The Ordinary. Thomas Wainwright was shown in.

Finnis: We will hear any statement you wish to make.
Thomas: There is a most dreadful thing. Since the trial my brother has accused me of being the murderer.
Finnis: We cannot go into that.
Thomas: I have made a statement which I should like to refer to. That statement is true.
Finnis: Is there anything further you wish to say beyond this? You can read this over to us and if there is any statement you wish to make you can do so. Mind, we don't ask you to do so.
Thomas: [Then read this statement as follows]:
For several years I had not been on friendly terms nor had I seen any of my relations until one Saturday in March 1874, when I met my brother Henry in Fenchurch Street.

'Interview with Thomas Wainwright', *Illustrated Police News* supplement, 18 December 1875. (*Copyright The British Library Board. All Rights Reserved*)

I told him that I obtained a situation with a Mr Arkell in Oxford Street. A few weeks after this he said he was short of money and asked me if I could sell a lot of brushes (about £100 worth) for him.

He came up the next day and I then took him to a man in Marylebone Lane who bought the brushes; my brother paid me a commission of £3 or £4 for introducing him. Some-time after this he called on me, short of money and asked me to get a bill discounted – and which I did at the Mutual Loan Office in Covent Garden (and of which is unpaid). I've received £1 for my trouble.

From May until I left Mr Arkell in October, he was continually calling on me he said he had nothing particular to do as his partner had thrown the business into chancery. I went to dinner and on three occasions he brought Alice Day with him.

One day in September, we went to a tavern I frequented in Oxford Street, The Victory.[2] He asked me if I would write a letter for him. I said, 'yes'. He pulled out a piece of paper and dictated a letter to me and I wrote it and signed it 'E. Frieake'. This was the letter that was put in at the trial. After I had written it, I said, 'what is the meaning of it'? He said 'the fact is, I'm keeping a little woman. Her friends keep bothering me and want to see her, and I don't want them to know where she is or they will perhaps take her away'. I gave the letter to him and thought no more about it.

I left Mr Arkell's about the 12th October. On the 16th October I went to see my brother at Whitechapel Road, he said 'would you like to go to Dover?' – I said, 'what for'? He replied, 'only to send over a telegram'. I said, 'I don't mind' and promised to go the next day – he then gave me 2 telegraph papers filled up – one to Miss Wilmore and one to himself. He gave me, I think £2 to pay expenses – instead of going myself – I went to Charing Cross Station saw the guard of a train that was going to Dover and asked him to hand them in at the office. I wrote out a telegram so that I should know the others had been delivered. I of course thought these telegrams were for the same purpose as the letter – viz to prevent the friends of the woman he was keeping from seeing her – or worrying him.

Finnis: Was the guard known to you?
Thomas: No. I gave him 3 messages.

After I left the employ of Mr Arkell, I was frequently at Whitechapel Road sometimes all day, assisting him to raise money – which I did by selling goods or getting bills discounted (which are very numerous), he taking all the money. People have an idea my brother was paying me money to assist me in some way, whereas, I was assisting him all I could to keep him out of his difficulties – raising money to keep him afloat.

In January 1875 a man named Moore whom I had known for 8 years proposed that I should go into partnership with him, saying he would invest £1,000 – in February we took premises at the Borough, the Hen and Chickens, which we stocked with ironmongery. Moore at this time was travelling for W.B. Osborn, iron merchant of Birmingham. He had been with him for some time. Moore and myself bought goods off Osborn. About a fortnight or three weeks after the place was opened, I received a telegram from his firm at Birmingham that Moore had absconded and had embezzled £600 or £700, so it placed me that

I could not carry on the business for want of capital – hence the collapse. This Moore is the man my brother wanted me to say committed the murder.[3]

My brother and Rogers frequently came to see me – about February he obtained the contract to supply the Metropolitan Police with brushes, but a surety for £500 was wanted to ensure him carrying it out. He put my name down, but I was not accepted. He comes to see me to know what he shall do. I got a man named Guy of Queen Victoria Street, to be security and my brother paid him £20 for so doing.

All this time he is getting into worse difficulties. One day in May or June he came to see me – and seemed very unwell – he then told me that he had caused this woman's death and had buried her at 215 Whitechapel Road and that and that he was afraid that he would have to give up the premises and that it would be found out. I then knew that I had been innocently assisting him to hide his crime. I declare to God when I wrote that letter and sent that telegram, I had no more idea a murder was committed than you had.

He asked me to assist him to remove the body – I told him I should not do so. After I left the Hen and Chicken's I saw very little of him I was travelling for a house in Newgate Street and he had gone into business with Mr Martin. On 7 September 1875 he called at Newgate Street to see me. I was not in so he left a message asking me to go and see him – I did so on the 9th.

Then he told me that the lease of the premises, 215 Whitechapel Road had sold and that they would be taking possession of it in a day or two, he was in a fearful state of mind – he asked me to let him remove the body to the Hen and Chickens and in a thoughtless moment gave him the key. I can scarcely say a thoughtless moment perhaps, for of course I knew what it was. He wanted me to assist him but I refused[4] – but I certainly did wish to prevent him being found out so that the family should not be disgraced.

I did not know until this year that he had gone by the name of Percy King! Although I wrote that letter to Miss Wilmore in which it states about not seeing King any more. I really had no idea what the letter contained until it was brought into the police court. When he was in difficulties, he had a little money which he drew from several customers, and his account at the London and Westminster Bank was closed. He asked me what he should do, he was afraid his money would be attached.

I said open an account in another name and he opened an account in the City and County Bank in the name King. That was in February 1875 and then I knew that he went in the name of Percy King because I had one of his cheques.

I never went to Sidney Square in my life. I did not know until the trial of the existence of a person of the name of Harriet Lane!

I have never at any time assumed the name of Frieake! I don't say that those persons came up falsely swearing, but they made a mistake. The detectives went about with my photograph. Humphries never saw me in his life. He stated he knew me for 4 years. Why did he want to go to Newgate to recognise me? That part of the case is a conspiracy by the police.

Governor: You say you do not know him?
Thomas: No. My brother told me first of all that it was Alice Day who assisted him, and then he said it was Rogers, and then he asked me to assist him in putting it on my late partner, Moore who he knew had absconded – and which I refused to do. Rogers was the man he asked to pawn the pistol.

In the dock at Southwark, my brother said, 'I will give you £300 if you will say you cut up the body. I have banked £100 to draw upon. If you say that, you will be sure to get off' – This of course, I also refused to do.

My solicitor came to me one day and said to me, 'your brother Henry's wife is putting it about the family, that you murdered the woman. Pelham says so. He is to get you executed and get him off.' I said, 'What is the use of your wife saying I did the murder?' He replied, 'when she came to see me one day she said, 'I don't believe you committed the murder but Tom could.''

With respect to the date of the murder, I shall be able to prove I was behind the shop counter serving customers at the time. I wished my brother William to write to Henry to fix the exact date of the murder and the time it was committed and that he was not to tell his brother Henry who wanted information, but write as from himself.

Governor: His brother did write that letter which I received last night with a memorandum from William; This is the letter (Reads).
Great Garden Street, – 9 December 1875. Dear Henry, can you send me the exact date of the murder and the time of the day it occurred? Yours truly. W Wainwright
Governor: I took that letter to Henry and he wrote on the back, this.
'Friday 11 September 1874. Between 5 and 7. I knew it about 7. I am sure of the day of the week, but not of the date, either 10th or 11th September'. H. Wainwright.
Governor: That he is certain it was Friday, but not as to the date.
Thomas: I should like the visiting magistrates to allow me to have an interview with Mr Arkell. I want him to write a letter that I

could shew it to the magistrates. Anybody might call on him, that would be enough.

Ordinary: 'What do you want him to do'?

Thomas: To write a letter stating that I was behind the counter at the time.

Ordinary: I suppose the counter books will shew that.

Thomas: The books will shew that.

Ordinary: Might I suggest if Mr Governor would call upon Mr Arkell, he would shew him the books and verify anything for production to you.

Finnis: Upon your own confession you knew of the murder.

Thomas: I knew after the murder and assisted him, that is quite right. I don't want to walk out of this prison and be pointed out as a murderer. If it was the last word I had to utter, I declare to God I am not the murderer.

Governor: Would you like to say anything to the magistrates as to what took place at the interview when Henry asked you those questions?

Thomas: I almost forget what the questions where?

Governor: He asked you if you fired the pistol.

Thomas: And I said no. Then he asked me whether I pawned the pistol in the name of Rogers, and I said no.

Ordinary: You never heard anything about pawning the pistol?

Thomas: I knew nothing about it until I was in court.

Governor: You told him that he was a great villain?

Thomas: And so, he was. And I said that that instead of bringing me into it, he ought to try and exonerate me.

Governor: You said he was the greatest villain unhung?

Thomas: So, I did, and I say so again.

Finnis: Was this man Moore very intimate with your brother?

Thomas: He has taken behind the scenes at the Pavilion Theatre and many times by himself.

Finnis: Did you say Rogers saw you at Southwark Police Court?

Thomas: The day I was charged at Southwark. Rogers was my brother's late foreman and he was a witness against him at the trial. He came to identify my handwriting and when he came to Southwark Police Court, he shook hands with me, and he said I know who Frieake is, he is a man named Tarrant or Farrant.[5]

Finnis: The real Frieake appeared on the trial. Did you know the real Frieake?

Thomas: No. I never saw him before. I knew that there was a man of that name of Frieake or passing as Frieake, because I had my dinner once with Henry at the Kings Head and he introduced me to a man as 'Teddy Frieake' and he introduced me to this man as 'Arthur Williams'. He often used to call me Arthur. He was fond of aliases.

Governor: Was this Frieake the same person as he introduced you to as Arthur Williams?

Thomas: No.

Governor: Rogers did not know where Tarrant came from?

Thomas: I only tell you what occurred. He told me no more about Tarrant. There a great many things I could say if I could think of them. Of course, my brother is writing some statement, and if the statement goes forth to the world about me, I might as well be executed too.

Governor: He told you he was writing a statement, first of all he said your name would not be mentioned, but after asking you those questions he returned to you and said 'now I have something to tell you. I shall mention your name, and in the statement will have to be mentioned the affair of 84. The affair of 84 will have to be explained.

Thomas: The affair was this. At 84 Whitechapel Road he had a fire. I assisted him to make up his claim and I knew it was what the Fire Assurance officers call an excessive claim. I knew that it was fictitious. I knew he was claiming more than the stock on the premises.

Thomas: My only object is to elan myself of this charge that he made against me. My life has not been a very moral one, and a great many people would rather believe it was I who committed the crime than he. My relations would very much rather me be in the position than him.

Governor: Why?

Thomas: They give me the credit for doing such a thing and not him.

Governor: The fact is, you have been a black sheep?

Thomas: That is so. My relations did not know my brother had been in an immoral state of life. He has been in the East End all his life. He has been a great deal worse that I have, and it was not known, he has been keeping up a respectable appearance at Tredegar Square while I have been leading a Bohemian life.

All these people came up to speak of his character for 18 or 19 years and I could hardly get anyone to speak of my character for one year, and the statement that he made in court calling upon God to witness that he never fired a pistol in his life may induce a great many people to say directly, 'you committed the murder', and that he never could do such a dreadful oath to a lie.

Governor: The magistrates have sanctioned your writing and I will take the letter to Mr Arkell. If that is clearly proved that will relieve your mind.

Thomas: I am quite satisfied in my own mind it will. I am much obliged to you.

Finnis: The Governor will take the letter to Mr Arkell and ask him to let him see his counter books and he will report to us.[6]

Newgate Gaol – 3 December 1875 – True statement made by – Signature Thomas Wainwright
Received 3 December 1875 – Sidney Roberts Smith – Governor

Footnote

Thomas made a number of admissions in this statement. He admitted to writing the letters as well as arranging for the telegrams to be sent, but stated that he had no idea it was for a criminal purpose. He also states that Henry had admitted to killing Harriet. Could this be relied upon? He then tells us that Henry asked him to help move Harriet to the Hen and Chickens but that he refused. The fact that he wasn't involved in the removal seems to support this part of his story.

The suggestion that Henry asked Thomas in the dock at Southwark that he would give him £300 if he would say he cut up the body seems a little far-fetched. Henry had no money and no prospect of getting out to pay Thomas, though he did have a habit of trying to bribe people.

An interesting suggestion apparently comes from Mr Rogers who tells Thomas that the actual man playing the part of Frieake is a man called 'Tarrant or Farrant'. This sounds another convenient story from Thomas' point of view. He gives no other detail leaving us no further forward. His last admission relates to the fire at number 84 in that he assisted Henry in making a false and exaggerated claim.

Thomas' statement gives some very interesting information and admissions, more than was admitted in court but, being a self-written statement, it only goes so far, and only gives a one-sided explanation. It's a shame that the prison officials didn't make a better job of questioning him. It was a missed chance. Henry's statement was likely to offer a lot more in the way of sensational revelations. And not all of them would have been to his little brother's liking…

Chapter Twenty-Seven

Henry Wainwright's Prison Statement: The Truth and Nothing But the Truth?

While Thomas perhaps took an hour or two to write up his prison statement,[1] Henry was more interested in a 'chapter and verse' approach, wanting to leave a full explanation behind for his family. This heavy weight and well written account from Henry is a fascinating chronicle of his rise and fall. He was certainly able to tell a story.

We are fortunate that this document, which was denied to his family due to Home Office Policy, still exists so that we can, almost a century and a half later, actually hear Henry talking through his many pages. It's a story which you could almost see him performing on stage to a hushed and eager audience.

What we have to decide is how much of it is true. His forty-eight pages have the ring of truth, but it's the fine detail which matters, and he had no one to correct this version or to challenge it. At the time of the trial, defendants were not permitted to give evidence at their own trials, and it's certainly a shame that he could not have been cross examined in court.

What you are about to read is the most sensational document of the many hundreds relating to the case.

Henry Wainwright's Statement

At the earnest solicitation of one for whom I entertain the profoundest esteem, I here relate a candid, truthful, account of that episode of my life, which has changed a flourishing man, one occupying a good position in society, respected and esteemed by a very large circle, into what I am at the present moment!

Till the year 1871, not a happier man existed. I was in possession of every comfort, and could have every wish gratified, successful in business, with an income of £500 to £600 a year, a happy, comfortable house, a loving and attentive wife who anticipated every wish, who welcomed me with joy each evening on my return home, who, if my little finger ached, would bestow greater kindness and attention, oh Gracious God! Take her under your special protection! Be kind and tender to her, who has suffered so much, and done nothing to deserve it.

Sometime in the middle of 1871 some customer bought some small article, who, after being supplied, I spoke to her probably about the weather and she left. It was my usual custom every evening to have a cigar a little before 8pm and wait at the door. While waiting, the same female frequently passed. I generally bowed to her. One evening she came and purchased some article and brought a female friend. That friend was Mrs King. Alias Harriet Louisa Lane, and the only name I ever knew her as, Louisa Varco.

Many evenings while walking home I overtook them, and I frequently walked a short way with them. Soon after they told me that they were living together in Campbell Road, Bow, they were dressmakers. They had been in business together in Waltham, but they came to London to get employment as dressmakers. For 2 or 3 months in the summer I had for several years taken my family to a farm house at Broxbourne, Herts. Which is only a short distance from Waltham. One evening the two females called and purchased hand brushes.

The ladies chose brushes to match their hair; Mrs King very fair, Wilmore very dark. I asked them if they knew Broxbourne which they did. I told them my family was there.

Told them I spent Sundays and Wednesdays there. On arriving at Broxbourne Station, the following Wednesday, I saw Mrs King on the platform. She said she had come to meet her friend at the Crown Hotel. The gardens first spoken of are perhaps some of the prettiest gardens in England. I used to spend half an hour there and prior to returning to town and purchasing one or two bouquets to bring home to present to my relations or friends.

On arriving at the gardens, I saw Mrs King, she said her friend had just gone. We had some refreshment and returned to town together. We had small talk on the train. I asked her if she intended to marry and other frivolous questions. I took up a bouquet, and her hand grasped mine[2] and held it – for a moment – our eyes met. Would to God that at that moment I had been struck with blindness. We had some refreshment at the station. We parted but arranged to meet the following evening. The place of meeting was the Temple Bar. We went to the Strand Theatre. Then had some supper at some room in The Strand. I sent her home in a cab.

The next morning brought reflection. I hated myself for my actions of the previous night and resolved never to see her again. I did not see her for a week or so. She then used to pass my business sometimes alone, sometimes with her dark friend. I always took care not to see them. And when they had been waiting for me on my journey home, I immediately crossed the road and walked quickly on.

In August 1871, a message arrived by cabman, stating that a gentleman, staying at the Green Dragon Hotel, Bishopsgate,[3] wished to see me immediately on very important business. I went back with the cabman. I went to the Green Dragon. I was shown into a sitting room, and there was Louisa Varco (or Mrs King) She rushed right into my arms and said she couldn't live without me. She knew it was very wrong. She had just come from Waltham and intended staying at the Green Dragon for the night. We had some refreshments and I was about to leave. She said that she was sorry to ask a favour but coming from the station, had had her pocket picked, [and] lost her purse which had £9–10 in it. Would I lend her a few pounds till she saw her friends at Bow? I gave her what she asked for and left.

Vice is a monster of such frightful surprise, that to be hated needs but to be seen, yet seen too often familiar with her face, we first endure, then pity, then embrace.

A week or so later she met me, her friend had found it all out, that she (HL) had been staying with a gentleman at the Green Dragon Hotel, that they had discarded her and turned her out of the house, and they would never receive her again. And what was worse still she said she had a baby coming, what was she to do? Believing it to be mine,[4] I at once accepted the responsibility, I engaged a couple of rooms for her, and supplied her with every comfort. She continually repeated to me that her family had deserted her, but it was brought out in evidence, at trial, that her own mother and sister nursed her during her confinement and were well paid for doing so; if they received the money, I gave Mrs King.

About a month after this I found out her frightful propensity for drink and she had notice given to leave. From there she went to Sidney Square where she removed at least a dozen times. I'm not (?) by vindictive feelings, far from it, I wish and intend to be guided by the truth.[5]

At the time I resolved to sever my criminal connection with this woman, though I intended to support the child and take care of the mother till some circumstances might arise when my aid would not be required. It was then arranged that the child was to be put out to nurse and that she was to live at some distance that we should not see each other again. Where she removed to, I did not know, but Miss Wilmore in her evidence said it was in Bedford Square.

When the child was 5–6 months old, I received a note to meet her at Temple Bar. She was with a friend introduced to me as Miss Wilmore. She told me the child was getting on very well and gave her address as Lupus Street, Pimlico. I was to pay Miss Wilmore herself and not Mrs King. I used to send or take the amount to her in Pimlico, I invariably sent a note saying when I would make my next visit.

When going there on one occasion Miss Wilmore was out, but Mrs King was in her room. We had not met for some time. Mrs King said she had heard I was coming, so she came herself to see me again. She had sent Miss Wilmore out for a walk. 'Go and get a bottle of champagne' she said and 'don't run away immediately'. I went and got the wine. This was a short time before Christmas 1872.

She told me that she had been invited to spend Christmas with friends in the country. I replied that it was where her family lived and I was glad that they had become friends. 'Oh!' she replied, 'we are not friends and if I went there, they would kick me out of the house, I am going to stay with a lady friend recently married who keeps a public house near there'. She then asked for some money as she wished to make a present for Miss Wilmore for her kindness. Miss Wilmore shortly came home and I left. (I must here candidly remark that Miss Wilmore was a thoroughly truthful witness.)

The next I heard of her was about February 1873, she was staying at Cecil Street, Strand, where I frequently sent a postal order. She had frequently written to me constantly asking me to come and see her if only for 5 minutes or meet her somewhere. She never visited me at my business premises, as far as I know, nor came near where I lived.

In March (1873) she asked me to meet her at Temple Bar and not to come to Cecil Street. She had some important news for me which she was certain would be very acceptable. I met her and she informed that a gentleman, who was living in the same house, had given her great attention, and given her several handsome presents. She told me his name, which I refrain from giving; it might possibly do him harm. I accompanied her back to Cecil Street, and was induced to go in, as she said, 'only for 5 minutes'. She showed me a liqueur stand containing several kinds of spirits and several dresses being made which she said had been given to her by her friend the gentleman she spoke about. Her dressmaker was there, I recognised her as her sister, Mrs Taylor.

About two months after this, she wrote me a letter asking me to come and see her. The gentleman who had been paying such attention who had offered to keep her as a lady, had gone to the country for a week or two. I went and she said she was not well she did not know what was the matter with her and asked me to send a doctor. I sent her a doctor from Whitechapel. I saw the doctor a day or two later afterwards, he informed me that she was 'enceinte', (French word for pregnant) and also suffering from a contagious disease,[6] this was about June 1873.

From that time on I never visited her at Cecil Street or replied to any of her letters, which now began to increase in numbers. For the last 6 months especially, and indeed also from the birth of the child, the fear of disgrace and exposure kept me in a continual worry, and a nervous excitability. I was in partnership with my brother William, and had been since 1860, when my father retired from business, over profits from £1200 to £1500 PA.

I quarrelled with my brother, and dissolved our partnership by which was arranged I was to pay him about £4,000. One child was born, another was coming. Soon after, one old traveller, one of the best on the firm, and who had been with me for many years, gave me notice to leave. He joined my brother William in partnership, and took with him most of the connections. A traveller I engaged proved a defaulter, I lost my fondness in business, even living. I became irksome, I was robbed by my secrets, lost all self-control, and drifted to the devil.[7]

Letters at this time were continually coming from this woman, requesting an interview. I sent no reply. At last, one evening, just before leaving business, a note was delivered by hand, stating that unless I came out then to see her, she should come to my business and ask for me. I went out to her, she was partially intoxicated, and said she wanted some money. This was about August 1873.

I told her to return to the friend at Cecil Street, she said, he had left about a month or two before, she had written to him but had received no answer, adding 'It's just like all you men, and now he's gone, I mean to stick to you, come and have some brandy'. I sternly refused, she became very excited and I was afraid of making a scene, to keep her quiet we went down some bye street to a quiet public house. She then said, 'I've got another baby coming, and you'll have to keep it old boy, or else I'll know the reason why'. I told her I should do nothing else for her; she had forfeited all the regard I had for her. How could she expect me to see her, or assist her after the life she had been leading the last few months. She said, 'I don't care about that, I'll make you keep me, and attend to me too.' She became dreadfully excited and abusive, a crowd began to collect, I left her, jumped into a cab and drove away, in almost as mad a state as she was.

The following day, a letter came from her, couched in the most subtle terms, imploring my forgiveness, and asking me to see her once more, as she intended to end her miserable life. After any scene like this, the following day always brought a letter – which she so well knew how to write – expressing deep contrition. Asking to be forgiven and promising never again to be guilty of such behaviour. I sent no reply.

I became ill – dejected, miserable. My business which required even more attention than usual, was avoided. Many friends remarked my haggard, worn-out expression, and I heard once, one friend remark to another, 'He's not the Harry Wainwright that he used to be'. I felt myself an outcast. I had frequently wandered for hours, at night, along deserted streets, bewailing the wrong, I had done my family, pondering my very wretchedness.[8]

Another letter came, asking me to see her for the last time, so say good-bye and she would never see me again. She was then living in Islington. I went to see her. She threw herself on her knees, and prayed for forgiveness – she would always be so good – she would never annoy me again – I had always been so good to her, don't leave her till her confinement was over – she hadn't a friend in the world to look to. Then she said, 'Oh Percy, although I have been very naughty, it is yours'. (The baby).

After a long pause I agreed to support her till after her confinement – but all intercourse should cease between us, I would take apartments for her, but she was to be my sister-in-law. These apartments were taken at the house of Mrs Wells, St Peter Street, Hackney Road.

From the time she went to Mrs Wells till after the confinement, she kept her word. I visited about once a week or a fortnight to pay what expenses had been incurred. She never annoyed me, in any possible way, she seemed grateful for my attention and I willingly paid the expenses. About a month after her confinement, the lurking devil showed itself. She became absorbed in one passion, the passion for drink, and when under its influence – infuriated, wild – mad! The reason for receiving her notices to quit from all her residences, was intoxication. The only two landladies examined as witnesses stated this fact.

'The Frieake episode', began soon after Mrs King's confinement at Mrs Wells'. I had resolved firmly to omit all mention of the name of my brother Thomas during this account. I fully intended to mention only the name of Edward Frieake, and let those who read this paper form their own judgement with reference to the identity of the individual who assumed that name. This morning, 8th December, by permission of the authorities I had an interview with my brother Thomas, in the presence of the Governor. Previous to seeing him I had taken great pains to ascertain that any admission he made, or that any remarks he uttered, could not possibly affect him, or alter any way the sentence that had been pronounced on him. Unless I had been assured beyond all doubt, I should never have asked him a single question.

I made enquiries of the Governor, and my own solicitor, who all informed me that my brother could not be tried again in this transaction. His name would never have been breathed by me, but after this interview with him – things have changed. Far be it from me to excuse a single error, or sin, of which I have been guilty. Nothing can alter my impending fate. What I now intend to state is not done to create sympathy on my own behalf, but that the world may know the exact truthful particulars, let that world judge!

(The interview was repeated as per the Chapter Twenty-Five, The Wainwright Brothers' Joint Interview)

Thomas George Wainwright then began to abuse me – accusing me of being the cause of his imprisonment of 7 years – and that if I had been half a brother, I should have tried to have taken the blame from off his shoulders. That I was the biggest scoundrel living, that Mr Jones, the Ordinary, told him I was one of the hardest hearted men that ever came into the prison. My reply was, 'I shall now speak the entire truth, keep back nothing, and your name will be brought in'. We then parted.

These incidents in which he and I alone knew, the world, but more especially our own family, can only judge by our own special assertions. Who is the liar! I have no personal object in telling a lie. My fate is irrevocably sealed. He has the world before him, (such as it is), he no doubt wishes to go again with the world as an injured man, the victim of circumstances, into which he was irrevocably drawn.

As he writes to his mother, 'I have got into this mess, through writing a letter or letters'. The above remark was told me by my brother William, or my wife, when making a visit, by that letter, he acknowledges in effect himself to be the author of the letters signed E. Frieake. This was however sufficiently proved at the trial to be his handwriting, yet he states in the presence of the Governor, that he 'never went by the name of Frieake'. The evidence of Mrs Foster, Wilmore and Wells, though apparently contradictory, points to the truth, which I here again emphatically say – there was only one individual who personated 'E. Frieake' and that was Thomas Wainwright.

He denies ever going to 3 Sidney Square. Some person of his description, and though not positively sworn, was firmly believed to be the 'Teddy Frieake' who visited there. It was hardly possible to recognise him in consequence of the great change in his appearance. If he is not – who then is the person known to so many witnesses as 'Edward Frieake'?

He denies all knowledge of Mr Humphries, also that he has never been in any of his public houses in his life; Mr Humphries has been well known to us for many years. We have not only been to the 'Princess Alice', but much more often to his other house in Whitechapel, the 'Queen's Head', as well as the Red Lion in the Strand. He denies that it was his pocket knife found by the police. He was the only person who went to 215 from the time the spade was purchased till I went with Stokes. Whose knife was it?

He now denies having the revolver. He had frequently told me the revolver was quite safe, one day during the trial, while waiting to go into court, he told me he had pawned the revolver and he had got the ticket quite safe.

Could it not be ascertained where the revolver was pawned and that he might be identified?

He said the Rev Jones the Ordinary, had told him, that I had one of the hardest hearts, that he had ever met with in prison. In the presence of the Governor, I asked Mr Jones whether it was true or not. His answer was 'I never said so, it is an abominable falsehood'.

I have decided, that every answer he gave was a foul, wicked lie. I have denounced him a bad, wicked son – a cowardly lying brother – a cruel heartless husband – the chosen associate of thieves – card sharps – and a murderer. May the light sentence he has now to undergo, damage his stature, and when that sentence has expired, may he live a better life, and try and redeem the past.

But though he may live a long life, the memory of his brother, whom he has so wronged, the memory of that brother who helped him, when no member of his family would assist him anymore; for the manner in which he has treated his poor dear old mother; the memory of that brother who came forward and assisted him, when all his friends had deserted him, the memory of the brother will haunt him till his dying day; For the cruel, cowardly and wicked lies he told in the presence of the Governor of Newgate. When I am no more, may he speak the truth, for those I leave behind, God forgive him.[9]

In January 1874, Mrs King came to my business to see me, I had sent her money by my man Rogers. She said that she didn't mean to leave me, and she meant to make me keep her like a lady. I told her to remember her promise, that she would not force herself on me again after her confinement. She said she would be very good if I came to see her once a week. I arranged to keep the children and they were put under the care of Mrs Austin, Hackney Road. Mrs King however after some time, wished to have the children back, and I gave her the nurses address and she fetched them home.

About this time, Thomas had been for a very long time, not in regular employment. He had been frequenting races, as clerk to a bookmaker, and became associated with a not very reputable clique. He occasionally called at 84 Whitechapel Road on each occasion he invariably borrowed some money which he has never repaid.

One evening, Mrs King came in, I went and spoke to her, gave her a sovereign, and she left. I then told Thomas the particulars of the connections. I said 'What would you do if you were me?' He replied, 'Let the bitch run loose'. I told him I couldn't do that; I didn't want the exposure. We had a long conversation and it was arranged that he should be my lawyer, and endeavour to make the following arrangement if possible: That I should keep the children; Allow her one pound a week for 12 months, after which I should consider myself no more responsible for her, but I would still keep the children.

For this purpose, he assumed the name of Mr Edward Lewis. We went to see Mrs King, at Mrs Wells' one afternoon. I left him in the parlour, while Mrs King went upstairs, and presently she heard Mrs King say, 'Edward come up'. To prove he went by this name, a letter written to me, was found by Mr Sawyer my partner. The handwriting was of Thomas Wainwright.

Mrs King would not accede to this proposal, and we left. His constant advice was 'Don't give her any money at all, the most you would have to pay would be 10 shillings a week, kids and all'. I replied, 'it's all very well for you, separated from your wife, not to feel what shame is, but for my own part, exposure would be ruin, and I shall pay her whatever will keep her quiet.' He replied, 'You're a damn fool! But I can get a man to marry her for £20.'

I went to Mrs Wells to pay her account. She said, 'Oh, Mrs King is so ill, she came home last night quite intoxicated, with your friend, Edward and I had a dreadful bother to get her up the stairs'. I saw Mrs King, she laughed and said, 'Your friend Edward is a jolly fellow, I quite like him, he made me tight. You won't take me out anymore but he says he will'. Thomas called a day or too later and said he had taken the little woman to the Alhambra and introduced her to a friend of his, who would marry her for £40. He said 'It would be a damn cheap way of getting rid of her.' I told him the idea was perfectly preposterous, he replied, 'Is it? If I get her married, will you give me £50?' I said, 'Yes and glad of the chance, but I must be present at the ceremony, and so must Mrs Wilmore.' Mrs King, about April, moved to Mrs Fosters', Sidney Square.

Thomas frequently took Mrs King out to different places of amusement and said to me – 'Your little woman is getting quite "spooney" on me' (sentimentally amorous).

About this time, I met Miss Wilmore by accident. She said, 'I know who your friend is, how much his eyes are like yours – he is an auctioneer, and his name is Frieake'. This was the origin of the introduction of the name Frieake – he was called 'Edward' while going under the name Lewis – and from that time he kept the name of 'Edward or Freddy Frieake'.

In July I regained possession of my businesses, moving about £2,500 to be paid by installments, and possessing a stock of rather more value than that amount.

Thomas frequently came to me on a Saturday evening. We often went to the Pavilion Theatre, and on one or two occasions took money for me to Mrs King at Sidney Square. I used to go with him to Mr Humphries, the 'Princess Alice' on the corner of Sidney Square. He would say, 'I must take her in partaking', and that something was generally a bottle of Champagne. Both Mrs Foster and Miss Wilmore stated that I NEVER visited Mrs King in Sidney Square. This is correct, I never did.

On leaving Mrs King one evening and joining me as usual at Humphries, Thomas said, 'This is getting too hot, your woman is too spooney on me, she has been doing the kissing business again tonight. She always does when she is half tight. I'll tell you what, I'll do, I'll marry her myself. I'm damn hard up, will you stand me £50 if I do? Of course, I will do it, in the name of Frieake'. I said 'You wouldn't be such a consummate fool, as to run such a risk'. 'Ah', he said, 'You have never been so hard up as I have, you don't know what a man wouldn't do, when he's skint'.

'The Relieving Officer has been down asking me about my wife's support, I want to keep her quiet. You stand the £50, leave it to me and don't bother yourself, and in less than a month you shall see a copy of the marriage certificate'. I lost myself to this vile deception, little imagining what the sequel would be, and I truly believe that no other idea was in the brain of Thomas. I believed he fully intended to go through this ceremony himself as he himself said, 'I must have some money somehow, or I shall have to leave Arkell's'. He then asked for £20 to make a few presents to make her believe, he thoroughly meant it. I let him have the money. This was about the 20th or 25th August 1874. A day or two later, on the Saturday, I met Thomas. He went to visit Mrs King.

By the evidence given by Mr E.W. Frieake, of Coleman Street, he received a letter on the Monday, a letter he could not understand from 'L. King'. That mysterious letter, upon which so many ingenious theories have been based, is easily explained. Mrs King imagined that her friend, her lover, with whom she was about to live with, and (?) she and Miss Wilmore and others knew as Teddy Frieake, was a Mr Frieake of Colman Street.

She writes to Mr Frieake this letter headed, Sunday night. She expresses regret – for her behaviour to him, 'last night' (Saturday), she promises to be better for the future and behave more ladylike, and adds, 'I am sorry I left you so cross, after your kindness to me.' What was that kindness, undoubtedly, the champagne he had brought with him, presents or money he had given her – and the belief she had that this Edward Frieake intended either to marry her, or keep her like a lady; as she knew that I did not intend to support her in the way I had done, very much longer. She then writes, 'If you and Harry will meet me tomorrow evening, arrangements can then be made, as the time is getting short.' What was this arrangement? Simply this! That she, Mrs King would go with Edward Frieake and I was to arrange with Miss Wilmore to be responsible for the children; and pay her 25 shillings a week, this explains this 'mysterious letter'.

Mr Edward Frieake of Coleman Street, having received this letter, its contents, and purpose were at this time unknown to Thomas, the fictitious Teddy Frieake or to myself. On the following day, 1 September is one of the utmost importance. At 8 in the evening, I was at my desk in the office when Thomas entered, I was putting away my papers, the desk was open and Thomas saw the revolver, and picked it up, and asked if it was loaded. It was not.

He said after looking at it, 'It's quite a new one'. I said 'Yes, it has never been fired.' I then told him I didn't want it, and was for sale, and asked him if he could find me a customer. He replied that no doubt that he could, and he asked what it had cost. I told him it cost £6. He then replied that he would take it, and do the best he could, or if I liked, he would deduct five pounds off the amount I should owe him, when he married the woman. I gave him the small tin box containing about 50 or more cartridges. NOTE! I kept this revolver at 40 Tredegar Square; My wife found the revolver in one of her drawers, she gave it to me and said 'I wish you would sell this; I don't like it in the house'. That is how the revolver came to be in my desk in Whitechapel.

We left together and went to Sidney Square for him to make the necessary preparations for his marriage to Mrs King. We walked towards Whitechapel Road when we met Mrs King in a state of intoxication. Thomas accompanied her back to the house, while I waited on the corner. She wouldn't go in the house unless 'Teddy' came in with her. I then came forward and tried to induce her to go home, but without effect. The remainder of the scene is told by Mrs Foster and Miss Wilmore in their evidence.

Thomas said 'It's no use talking to her in that state. I shall write to her and tell her to come next Saturday to make the final arrangements. About this time, I received a note from Mrs King asking me to meet her and Miss Wilmore at the back of the London Hospital. There I agreed to become responsible to Miss Wilmore, for the maintenance of the children, by the payment of 25 shillings a week. This fact is very important. Mrs King was always in the habit of coming to 84 Whitechapel Road, whenever she wished to see me – she now wishes to see me at the back of the London Hospital, away from my business premises. Why was this?

She had arranged to go and live with 'Teddy Frieake' and no doubt did not wish to be seen with me where I was known. She also knew she intended leaving me, by bringing Miss Wilmore to meet me, to shift the responsibility of the children, entirely from her own shoulders, and, make me personally responsible to Miss Wilmore. I accepted that charge, she said 'Then for the future I have to look to you, for the money for the children.'

These incidents prove with some great force, the change she intended to make, and that change arranged by 'Teddy Frieake.' Saturday 5th September arrived, 'Teddy Frieake' and I went to Sidney Square. I waited in the Humphries private bar. He went across to Mrs King. He returned and informed me that she had received notice to quit I asked him if he had everything arranged. His reply was as usual whenever I asked any questions, 'leave it to me'.

He called on the following Wednesday, I was at 215, I was clearing out the premises, and sending the stock to No 84 – I was about to let 215 – or sell the lease.

Thomas asked if I could spare one of my packing cases. I said 'Yes half a dozen if you like.' He selected one and it was put on the side for him.

He asked me where I could buy some chloride of lime. He wanted half a hundredweight. He said, 'I wish you'd buy me half a hundredweight'. 'I'll send for it in a day or two.'

I asked him how he had got on the previous Saturday. He said 'Oh all right, we've got two days' grace. I don't want to be seen any more in Sidney Square. I want you to lend me the key of the private door.' There were two keys for this door, and I gave him one of them.

On the Friday, he came about 4 o'clock. He said 'I don't want her to see you when she comes, you go away for an hour or two.' I went to East London Billiard Rooms, and stayed there a couple of hours, and came back to 84 about half past six.

He came about 7, rather intoxicated, and excited and said, 'We have had twobottles of champagne, and she got so drunk; and she won't trouble you anymore'. I said 'What do you mean?' 'Why I've shot the bitch and a damn good job too – Did you think I was such a fool as to marry her!' I called him a scoundrel, and I almost feinted, He said 'Don't be a fool and come and have some brandy'. I said 'Have you killed her?' He said 'I expect so, I've given her three shots'. I asked where she was. He said 'Upstairs, on the floor in the kitchen.' I said 'I should go for Dr Llewellyn.' He said 'If you do, I will bolt and then you would be in a nice mess. Perhaps she's not dead, come and see'. I went upstairs, she was lying on the floor sweltering in a pool of blood. I tried to speak and fell onto a chair. He said, 'Wake up there is no time to lose.' I said 'What are you going to do?' He replied, 'Put her in that case I looked out the other day, the lime.' I became frightened – lost all self-possession. On recovering a little, I thought of the awful position I was in, but yielded to his devilish influence.

'Will prevent it smelling for some time, and I shall send it off to Australia.' I said I should go, He said 'You can't go, you must help me upstairs with that case'. I did so and left him. It was raining in torrents. When I opened the door, two of Frieake's men, with a cart, who had come for some goods for the sale, I gave them some money, told them the goods were not ready, and would not be for a day or two, he went away with the empty cart.

I went and fastened up 84, and went to the Royal Oak and there waited for Thomas as arranged. He came about 9 and said it was all right. He called me a soft-hearted fool, and said 'We must not leave the box up in the kitchen. It must be brought down to the warehouse; you must come and help me.' I went to 215 and we put the case down in the warehouse. We left the place and parted. He promising to come the following evening.

For days the case with its frightful contents remained at 215. On the Tuesday or Wednesday following, Miss Wilmore called, to see me, and asked where she could send to Mrs King, as she promised to see her in two or three days. This interview came out in Miss Wilmore's evidence which was substantially correct.

I wrote to Thomas to see me immediately. He came and I told him of Miss Wilmore's visit. He said 'All right, I'll write her such a letter, that will keep her quiet'. He wrote to her, and wrote to me also, to make the affair appear genuine.

About this time, and for months afterwards, he was continually coming to see me and often brought a lady with him. We generally went and dined to Mr France's, Weavers Arms,[10] where I was in the habit of dining nearly every day. This lady he introduced to Mr and Mrs France as his wife.[11] She was always introduced as such. His then employer thought her his wife, till his own wife called, and Mr Arkell was compelled to discharge him.

As Mr Arkell himself told me, when I went and asked him why he discharged him, He said 'Your brother cannot afford to keep two wives on the salary I give him, so I was compelled to discharge him, though he was the best salesman I've ever had, and another reason, he has lately taken to excessive drinking that I couldn't keep him'. Mr Arkell also complained to me that 'Thomas seems to have some other important business in hand. He received a great number of letters, was away a great deal and came very late in the mornings.' I endeavored to get him reinstated but Mr Arkell was very firm and refused to re-engage him.

A week or two had elapsed, when he called at 215, when he saw the case there, after some little conversation, it was arranged that the contents of the case should be buried. He fastened himself in the warehouse. I went to number 84, put the duplicate key in my pocket, that some of the men should go to 215 to distract him.

After some hours work, he came and said it was all ready. I went over with him, and we turned the contents of the case into a hole he had made. He replaced the boards, nailed them down and left the premises. I took the selling of the premises off of Mr Frieake's hands.

Thomas commenced his continued application for money, on some occasions when the amount I gave him didn't satisfy his demands, he hinted about, telling the circumstances of some of his friends. Among these members was one, who was known as the 'Brighton Doctor'. He knows dozens of men they sometimes employ at horse races, who would do anything for a fiver. I was then compelled by his threats to become his security for £25 to a loan office in Russell Street, Covent Garden. I was also obliged to give him bills for £92 which were discounted by Mr Lewis whose evidence was given at the trial.

After getting all the money he could, and coming down day after day, dining with me at France's and very often bringing the person he called his wife. I told him I could not give him any more, and at last it was arranged that when I obtained the money from the insurance office, he was to have £300. He promised he would go to America and never trouble me anymore. What was this money paid to Thomas for? Why was I his continual security? For years he had lost his sense of shame, all human feelings – He left his wife and children to starve, or live on workhouse support. The money alone he had from me, would have well-kept a large family. He knew the victim of his murder was buried in my premises, and he could escape all blame. He knew he intended to deceive me, respecting the whole transaction.

Months rolled on, I was made a bankrupt – and I saw Thomas at less frequent intervals. One morning he called to see me. He said 'I see the place (215) is for sale. That thing at the end of the warehouse will get us in a mess, if we don't remove it. There's a cellar at my old place at the Hen and Chickens where it would never be found. And if it is found nobody would know how it got there, or who it belonged to.'

He then arranged to come on the following Friday, about 12 o'clock. He said 'Get me some couple of yards of American cloth, and some stout string and meet me at the Royal Oak a little after one o'clock. I will go and buy a chopper and spade'. We met at the Royal Oak. The Royal Oak is by the back door of the premises, 215, you must pass it to get to the door. I went back to business and had dinner with Mr Martin. Mr Martin and all his men, and even Stokes should be examined to prove first that neither the spade or chopper or parcel whatever was left at Martins for me. If so, they must have seen. Second, that I never left the premises the whole of the afternoon. I arrived at Martin's the following morning at 8.30 and Saturday being our busy day – I never left the premises till I left with Stokes at about 4 o'clock.

On the Friday above mentioned, Thomas came to Martins about seven, he told me it was all done, and packed in two parcels. He then left saying he would be with me the following day to arrange the removal. I then went to meet Miss Wilmore about half past seven. I left her to catch my usual train to Chingford at 8.8 – the last train.

Then comes the question – Who cut up the body? It is proved that it was thoroughly impossible for me to be there! I answer fearlessly and truthfully; Thomas George Wainwright.

The witness Henry Young said he saw us together at Mr Martin's door on the Saturday morning about 10 o'clock and Thomas was 'looking very ill'.

Thomas then arranged to meet at four o'clock on that Saturday afternoon and he said, 'If I cannot be at "Duke of Clarence", Commercial Road, by half past, bring the parcels over in a cab, I will meet you outside the Hen and Chickens.' 'You had better take our key, so as not to be kept waiting'. He then gave me the key, I used it to open the door of the Hen and Chickens.

When the police searched 215, they found a spade, a chopper and a pocket knife. My knife was taken by the police that same evening. Whose was the knife? It belonged to the person who cut up the remains, that person is Thomas George Wainwright.

A few days after my arrest, Mrs Wainwright (my wife), met Thomas and his partner and friend of 78 Newgate Street, Mr Henry George, alias Benjamin Gosling and with a dozen other aliases. They both, and especially Thomas, implored my wife to take me in some poison, when I was in Horsemonger Lane. Why? That my mouth should be closed and he could be safe.

When my dear mother came to see me on Wednesday, in the presence of the chaplain and other officers, she said entirely unasked by me, 'Henry has always been a kind and affectionate son. I have not seen Thomas for more than three years, he has been a bad, wicked son to me, and a cruel husband and father.'

It may be asked, when he first shot the woman, and came across to 84 and told me, why did I not at once give him to custody? He laughed, and said 'Who would believe you?' I then felt my awful position, and left him alone, I deserve my punishment for not denouncing him at the time, and allowing myself to be ruled by such a devilish spirit.

I commend this paper to the Governor of the goal – that it may be placed at once, with the hands of my brother William,[12] and immediate publicity be given to it. I have been accused by those, whose word I implicitly believe, that my wife and five children, will be well provided for, that takes away the load from my heart, and removes the grief which has weighed so heavily upon me, and with the hand of my maker, I place my soul, believing that he will be merciful; and though my sins have been many, he will abundantly pardon!

Signed: Henry Wainwright. Received this from the convict at 12.20 pm this 11th day of December 1875, Sidney Roberts Smith,[13] Governor.

Footnote

The statement from Henry must be one of the most exciting but frustrating documents in the history of late Victorian crime. The statement makes us question everything we thought we knew. Having heard all the evidence from the Old Bailey trial and now having read the statements of both Thomas and Henry, has your thought of who actually murdered Harriet Lane changed? Both brother's statements are well written and, in their own way, both are convincing. One thing is certain. The body under the floor boards was Harriet Lane, but which one of the brothers pulled the trigger? Both men knew who fired the gun. One of them is telling the truth, but the other is telling the most monumental lie. Both men leave out a lot of information in their accounts; the fine detail. Plainly a lot of the background information is probably true, but which brother was being stitched up?

Following the verdicts, both men still had reasons not to admit to the murder. Henry, being an educated gentleman, wanted to retain what little reputation he had left; he was going to his death but he wanted to be thought of only as an adulterer and not a murderer.

Henry writes such a lot of shocking accusations against his brother. One must, of course, wonder why neither brother used any of the information they provided in their accounts in court to incriminate each other? Both were clearly heavily involved in the crime but who can we honestly believe? Henry could have offered a statement implicating his brother, stating that Thomas had shot Harriet without his knowledge or approval. Perhaps both men were not telling the full truth in the hope of them both getting off? It certainly appears so since they both turned against each other once their guilty sentences had been passed.

Their plan to keep everything hidden had badly backfired. They both knew who killed Harriet, and the killer could have used a cut-throat defence to try and have the other brother convicted. Family loyalty may have prevented this from happening, as both sought to stay more or less silent and take their chances with the jury.

Whatever the truth of the matter, the die was now cast and nothing could change the sentence of either man, especially now that neither man had himself admitted the killing.

I ask you now, you the jury, having heard the statements of both defendants as well as all the court witnesses, do you find Thomas or Henry guilty of murdering Harriet Lane? Answers on a postcard, please!

Chapter Twenty-Eight

The Execution: Tuesday, 21 December 1875

The twenty days between sentencing and Henry's execution may have passed quickly for him, as he still must have held out some hope of a reprieve from various petitions, but he was not to see another Christmas Day. The newspapers all carried reports of the death of Henry Wainwright. In Victorian Britain, execution was part of the legal criminal process, though there were many abolitionists who viewed it as a barbaric punishment.

Public executions had ended in 1868. They had traditionally drawn huge, often disorderly crowds, which were much despised by Charles Dickens and others. But the ultimate sentences continued for the best part of a century, until being abolished in 1965.

Being accompanied by prison warders could not have aided his sleeping, and his sleepless nights must have left him feeling tired and depressed. He was a man with no future, only a shocking past. With nothing to live for, he may have wanted the end to come sooner than it did, but he appeared to have resolved himself to his fate.

The lack of privacy in his cell could not have made his final meetings with loved ones, saying the things he needed to say, easy. It is possible that he may have told them the truth of the murder, but with prison officers also sharing the tiny cell, telling Elizabeth the truth without being overheard may have been rather difficult.

We can only imagine what this final meeting with poor Mrs Wainwright was like. His affair with Miss Lane had brought the whole family crashing down. Did she still love him? What were their parting words? At this point I again ask for your indulgence to speculate on *what might* have taken place during that emotional appointment. We have some basic known information regarding his incarceration, but what is written below is not fact, but is speculation, built on evidence as well as more guesswork. It's not historically evidenced but it could still be true?

Elizabeth Wainwright, dressed all in black, arrived at the gates of hell that was Newgate Prison. Her visit was expected, and the formalities of her entry into this imposing structure were soon completed. The mood of the place was that of strict discipline. The prison officers were an imposing collection of formidable men; they exuded a stern exterior while on the premises, and jokes and pleasantries with them would not have been appropriate.

The account of Newgate Prison warder, William Thomas:[1]

I started the day shift promptly at 6am. Morning was a busy time, getting prisoners up and slopped out. Every day at Newgate was different, but also the same. The same prisoners with the same routine and the same troublemakers. You needed eyes in the back of your head. You also needed strength and stamina to be able to be on your feet all day and to be able to face up to belligerent convicts. You could never trust them. Our main goal was to prevent escapes and to preserve order. Every day I worked with criminals, many of whom would have happily knocked me down given half a chance. This particular day was going to be different, as I had been ordered to deal with the wife of our most infamous inmate.

I received Mrs Wainwright at the pre-arranged appointment time at the main door to the prison. She was dressed all in black and looked tired. After the formalities of her being searched and signing her in, I brought to her attention the rules for visitors to Newgate. This was soon completed in a businesslike manner. She neither smiled nor spoke to me about anything, other than to confirm her personal details.

Wainwright being visited by his wife. *Illustrated Police News*, 23 October 1875. (*Copyright The British Library Board. All Rights Reserved*)

I then escorted her to the Governor's office for a short meeting about arrangements for Henry's final days, and timing for the execution. Mrs Wainwright was trying hard to retain her composure as she was advised of when her husband's final moments would be. She was also informed that his clothing could not be returned to the family, and that it was forbidden for her to see the 50-page statement written by her husband. She pleaded to see it but this fell on deaf ears with the Governor. He said that he could not go against the laid down Home Office rules in this instance.

The Governor, Sidney Smith, who had personally been involved in the custody of both the Wainwright brothers, rose from his red leather seat without smiling and said to her, 'this way', and bade her to follow him through a never-ending series of barred doors. The clanking of my large set of keys and especially the slamming shut of the doors seemed to make her jump slightly. Finally, we reached Henry's cell.

Mr Smith then took a large key from me and himself unlocked Cell number 11. He looked at her blandly as he opened the door and beckoned her to go in. She timidly entered the small room, just as the warder who had been guarding Henry Wainwright got up. He then told Mrs Wainwright, 'You are allowed 20 minutes'. She then looked around further to see her husband sitting glumly against the wall on a wooden stool. It seemed to me that twenty minutes was a short time to say all that needed to be said. Henry looked worn and unkempt, though his face did brighten on seeing Elizabeth.

As Henry slowly rose to his feet, Elizabeth looked round the sparse cell area, it was probably nothing like their former delightful terraced town house in Tredegar Square. His clothing looked crumpled, as did the man himself. I noticed that his beard that had previously been so luxuriant and strokable when he first arrived at Newgate, now looked more like a bird's nest.

As she looked at the father of her children, his eyes moistened and he struggled for a few moments to compose himself enough to be able to speak. Henry then embraced Elizabeth with the grip of a drowning man, he shook as he sobbed aloud. It was a point at which myself and the other warder wanted to be anywhere else. No one wanted to look at the unhappy prisoner or his wife, it was a sight too pitiful to contemplate.

Eventually, Henry was able to compose himself and he was able to speak quietly to his wife and to discuss the children as well as the money that had been collected for them. As the time approached the twenty minute mark, Henry stood, and again embraced Elizabeth. He whispered an apology and told her that he loved her. I could not discern her reply. She remained composed and strong throughout the meeting. Mr Smith, after consulting his watch again, looked at Mrs Wainwright and said, 'the time is up, and you have to go now'.

Elizabeth appeared to be a lady of mild manners but seized the courage of the moment and looked Smith imploringly in the eye.

She addressed him as if they were in a parole board hearing. 'Mr Governor, you have been so fair and kind towards my husband, we will be eternally grateful towards you, but I need a few minutes more with my husband, I beseech you, please have pity on me'. Smith was normally a robust and decisive man who would not think twice about making tough decisions about Newgate's old lags. This though was deeply personal. This well-educated young mother of five was imploring him for a few more precious minutes. I was glad that I was not the person having to decline her request. She was right there in his personal space, looking him in the eye. He must have wanted to say no, but like me, he could probably see her heart was breaking, and the longer he took to reply, the harder it was to refuse her. He relented, giving the couple a few minutes alone, saying simply, 'very well, but it can't be too long'.

As we all shuffled outside the cell, Smith looked at me with eyes that told me that he was going against the Home Office rule book, but that his humanity forbade him from refusing the prisoners grieving wife. Ten minutes later, as Smith reentered the cell, he motioned Elizabeth to the door, Henry again took her in his arms and clung on to her. He began to wail like a person who had just been informed of the sudden death of an adored wife. Mr Smith was a busy man and he really needed to get back to his office. 'Time really is up now, Mrs Wainwright.' She thanked him for those extra precious moments.

As she tried to free herself from Henry's vice-like grip, the other warder gently pulled him away from his wife and placed him back on his chair. As Elizabeth reached the other side of the cell door, she looked back to see Henry, now collapsed on the floor shouting out 'Elizabeth, I'm sorry, I'm so, so sorry'. It was time to move and to do so quickly, to avoid prolonging the agony any longer. We could hear Henry's repeated pitiful cries as we strode behind Mr Smith down the long corridor, she didn't look back.

On the agonising return journey back along the passages to the prison gate, Elizabeth's mind must have been racing, full of emotion and with sadness for the plight of her errant husband. She had seen him for the last time in her life. She must have felt for him in this deathly situation, but did she hate him for his betrayal and dragging the family fortunes almost to the door of the workhouse?

She did not reveal to us how she was feeling. Perhaps she had once loved him utterly, and the ending of their relationship within the thick prison walls must have been a bitter pill to swallow. After unlocking the main gate for her, Mrs Wainwright departed Newgate for the final time, emerging into the weak winter sunshine and her renewed freedom. I wondered how the poor woman would survive, as the heavy door of Newgate crashed shut behind her.

Henry had fallen into a fit of depression after his wife and brother's visits on Friday 18th. His children had been forbidden from entering Newgate, and knowing that no friendly face would ever see him again, Henry's spirits plummeted. On Sunday 20th he visited the chapel for the last time and had been allowed to choose all the hymns.[2] Alas, he was overcome with emotion and had to be helped back to his cell.

That night, Henry's last sleep was to be a fretful one. The *North British Mail* of 22 December 1875 reported that he slept from 9pm till 1am and lay awake for 2–3 hours before finally awaking at 6am. He was asked by the warder how he had slept, to which he replied, 'It doesn't matter, I am about to enter upon a long sleep'. He wore the same black frock coat and vest that he had worn at the trial.

One account of the execution was vividly described in the *Cheltenham Chronicle*'s, 28 December 1875 edition. It was an eye witness account from an unnamed reporter which ended with a condemnation of the process of what he referred to as 'legal homicide'.

The reporter had spent a long night being unable to sleep, but by 7am he started out for the prison under cold grey skies, and was thinking that Wainwright only had one hour to live. He had to arrive at Newgate between 7.30 and 7.45am and produce his 'ticket' from the Governor which had been signed by the Sheriffs in order to gain admittance. A crowd of men had already gathered outside the gaol. Once inside the massive walls, the reporter entered the courtyard where in the north west corner stood a shed where the execution was to take place. About 100 people were present, including members of the press 'hurriedly scribbling in blue pencil', as well as artists from the illustrated newspapers. Also among the crowd were some city gents as well as prison workmen. This was a show not be to missed. The cold but fine morning with an easterly wind[3] may have had Henry shivering as he stepped into the yard.

The morning of the execution had arrived and the executioner and prison warders were coming, ready or not, to collect Henry Wainwright for his last walk. The Governor, chaplain, hangman, sheriff and a gaoler accompanied the 'Whitechapel Murderer'. He faltered as he saw the gallows. He glanced at the crowd of witnesses in the yard. His hair and beard blew in the wind.

The Norwich Mercury[4] took up the story;

Wainwright was wearing a spotless white shirt and low-cut waistcoat. He had been pinioned with leathern bands. He walked forward nervously. He stood at the fatal spot unassisted and without exhibiting any symptoms of failing spirit.

Marwood, after drawing a large white hood over the convict's head, proceeded to adjust the fatal cord. As the Chaplain concluded the last word of the service, 'In the midst of life we are in death', Marwood stooped and drew the bolt, the platform fell, and Wainwright was swung into eternity. The drop was about six feet, and in falling the wretched man's neck must have been broken with a fearful jerk of the rope.

Execution of Henry Wainwright, *Illustrated Police News supplement*, 25 December 1875. (*Copyright The British Library Board. All Rights Reserved*)

It had only taken 90 seconds from his emergence into the yard to the moment of death. An estimated 5,000 people had assembled outside Newgate, and when the black flag raised to denote the execution had taken place, a cheer went up from the crowd.

After being left to hang for an hour, Wainwright was cut down and a coroner's inquest was held. The Governor, Mr Smith, told the journalists that Henry's statement had been handed to him at 11pm the previous evening, but he wouldn't reveal what was in the document.

The Governor stated that Henry wanted to thank the Governor and the prison staff and added that;

> 'He placed his trust in a merciful God, and hopes that his transgressions might be blotted out for the sake of the Blessed Saviour, whom he had so long neglected. He then acknowledged the justice of his punishment, and that he deserved it, though he does not absolutely confess to the murder.

These last words from Henry were unsatisfactory. He threw no more light on the murder itself or on the question of who had pulled the trigger. Do we believe it wasn't him? Was he simply trying to remain a 'gentleman' who had sinned like so many others and yet still enjoyed a full life? Did he want his children to cling to the idea that he was not a fully paid-up murderer? The wording is interesting, 'does not absolutely confess'. It makes it sound as if he was there when Harriet was murdered, but watched somebody else do it. What we should not forget is that thousands of criminals stand in courtrooms claiming their absolute innocence when their evidence is later proved to be nothing but a pack of lies. Some humans have a great ability to lie through their teeth with a straight face in a bid to save their own skin.

Wainwright's imprisonment and execution were of huge interest to the press. The *Illustrated Police News* artists were again busy in December 1875 creating images of Wainwright's final few hours. The 11 December front page was dominated in the central area by an inventive drawing of a sleeping Henry being watched over by a seated warder. Above his head is the image of what he is dreaming about. The first picture is of happier times, showing him dancing with Harriet; the next is of him shooting her in the back of the head. The last of the drawings shows a sullen looking Henry, head in his hands, lamenting his fate.

The eager readers of the *Illustrated Police News* were treated to a Christmas special on the front page of its 25 December edition. This one carried several interesting sketches on its front page, including;

- 'The last sleep of Wainwright', showing him asleep and being watched by a warder
- 'An urgent appeal', where he is being ministered to by a clergyman
- 'Procession to the scaffold', displaying officials escorting Wainwright to the gallows
- 'The process of pinioning', the tying of the hands and legs of Wainwright (See footnote 1)
- 'The Inquest', the jury view the deceased in his coffin for the formality of the inquest
- 'The burial place for murderers – Newgate'. The most interesting image of all, showing prison staff digging a hole in the caged area where all the executed prisoners were buried. The coffin is open and has had holes drilled in it, and quick lime (see footnote 2) is being shoveled into it. A watering can stands nearby.

Supplement to the *Illustrated Police News*, 25 December 1875. The whole of this edition, which came free to the readers, was fully taken up with a single drawing.

- 'The execution of Henry Wainwright'. The final look at the face of Henry as the 'cap of doom' is pulled down over his face by the executioner Marwood. The noose hangs limply around his neck.

The final jobs to be completed at Newgate that day was for the formal inquest to be completed and Henry's body to be buried. The *Lloyds Weekly*[5] *London* newspaper gave details of Henry's condition after being cut down: 'At nine o'clock, the body was cut down and unpinioned. He was still in the black clothes which Wainwright wore when he was arrested. The hands were cold, but the forehead was still warm. The mouth was not quite closed.'

Before burial, the formality of an inquest took place and was led by the same coroner who had presided over Harriet Lane's inquest three months earlier, Mr William Payne. It took place next door to Newgate Prison in Court 3 of the Old Bailey. The jury viewed the deceased body of Henry Wainwright. The Governor of Newgate, Mr Smith, gave evidence of the conviction and execution of 37-year-old 'H.W.'. The surgeon, John R. Gibson, certified the cause of death as 'suffocation by hanging', with the jury finding that the death had been properly and legally carried out. Henry's death was registered[6] the following day by the coroner, describing Henry simply as a 'brush manufacturer, prisoner in Newgate'.

'Burial places for murderers, Newgate'. *Illustrated Police News*, 25 December 1875. (*Copyright The British Library Board. All Rights Reserved*)

The New Year's Day 1876 edition of the *Illustrated Police News* gave further particulars of the disposal of Henry's body:

The body was divested of the whole of his clothing, in the presence of Robert Mapperson, the principal warder, and the Governor, and the shell was filled up with quicklime, in which the body was completely enveloped. The lid was then screwed down and Henry Wainwright was forever removed from our mortal eyes. It was buried in one of the gloomy passages of the goal.

The effect of the quick lime upon the naked corpse, would be to entirely destroy it in the course of a very short space of time, and if the prisoner had used the same material at the time he buried the corpse of the unhappy girl, Harriet Lane, instead of chloride of lime, the effect would probably have been that his crime might never have been discovered. Every vestige of the clothing of the prisoner was subsequently destroyed by fire.

Many more newspaper articles from Fleet Street and beyond gave eyewitness accounts of the execution. The *Belfast Weekly News*[7] published an interesting account of the reporter who had spoken to an 'eyewitness'. He described the chemical process following the death:

> A quantity of quick lime was thrown in to fill up the coffin. Buckets of water were then poured in when the lime, becoming hydrated, bubbled up and fizzed, and the work of annihilation commenced. The coffin was then nailed down and buried a depth of four feet six inches. A mason subsequently came, and carved the letters 'H.W.' on the wall immediately above, the pavement was relaid, and the place restored to its normal appearance.
>
> At one of Henry's interviews with his wife an observation fell from her that showed the true woman. She said, 'Tell me, Harry, did you really love her?'.

This question is one that we would probably all liked to have asked him. The answer to this question was tantalisingly not recorded in the article, but we can imagine the scene. Henry was about to die. His wife wanted to know before his departure, whether she as the mother of his five children, was the only one he had ever loved, or had he truly loved Harriet as well. One might add another question. 'Harry, did you love Alice Day?'.

We can speculate on the answer that Henry gave. It's likely that he would have promised her that Harriet was a moment of madness, of blind passion alone, and not true love, and that he never actually loved her. If you were in his shoes when the difficult questions were being asked, what would you have said?

Knowing that he was about to die, he would probably have tried to redeem himself by at least denying that he actually loved Harriet. This would also have made the pain easier to bear for his wife Elizabeth. Henry was a convincing liar, so one final lie would not have been difficult, especially if it was to convince her of his undying love to her alone before his death. It's likely he would have dismissed Alice Day as a mere plaything and platonic pal who would accompany him to shows and restaurants while Elizabeth was at home with the children.

Rules and regulations on the disposal of bodies of felons at HM Prisons were laid down by the Home Office in the following document;

INSTRUCTIONS TO BE OBSERVED IN BURYING THE BODIES OF EXECUTED PRISONERS.[8]

The Home Office regulations stated that the plot of ground in the prison had to be '9 feet by 4 feet, and the grave will be from 8 to 10 feet in depth'. Once coffins were added on top, the last one could only be 4 feet below the surface. Further coffins on top could not be made till 7 years had passed. Any removals of bodies had to be completed with discretion and no publicity. With a maximum 3 coffins in one grave, it noted that 'exhumation is neither a simple nor desirable task'.

Wainwright was consigned to history under an alleyway at Newgate, expecting to remain there for all eternity, but as the new century approached, the area for murderers was practically full up. Newgate was also about to be demolished, all of which meant that all the bodies would have to be moved. In March 1903, Wainwright and all the other corpses were loaded into black coffins and transported in the dead of night to the City of London Cemetery, Ilford, where they were buried, 'without ceremony'.[9]

William Marwood (1818–1883),[10] developed the 'long drop' technique of hanging, which ensured that the prisoner's neck was broken instantly at the end of the drop, resulting in the prisoner dying of asphyxia while unconscious. This was considered more humane than the slow death by strangulation caused by the "short drop" method. In his nine years as a hangman, Marwood hanged 176 people.

Wainwright ended up with many other murderers in an unmarked grave in Ilford. The remains of all the Newgate bodies are now in Square 340 at the City of London Cemetery. Unfortunately, none of the names of the prisoners appear in their burial registers. All the remains were brought from Newgate in unmarked containers.[11]

Plot 340[12] is on Woodland Avenue opposite the junction of Glade Road if you want to visit. What was left of his corpse may have been mixed up with all manners of criminals. It was an ignominious ending to his story.

Chapter Twenty-Nine

Thomas Wainwright Serves His Sentence

Petition to be released from Prison

When Thomas wasn't involved in moving Portland stone about, especially on a Sunday when no work was done, he would have thought a lot about his remaining time in prison. In truth, it wasn't much of a life. Being in the company of rough criminals and working long, hard days in the bitter wind in the draconian Victorian prison regime was too awful to contemplate.

Circumstances being what they were, Thomas decided to petition the Home Office for release on 18 October 1876, maintaining his innocence of the charge which had resulted in his 84 months sentence. He would have spent much of his 'day off' filling in his petition form; he was an educated man and so his three-page application reads well. His message was simple: He had 'innocently' written the letters, and someone other than him had impersonated Frieake.

The request, on prison form number 413C and submitted to Home Secretary Richard Cross, was written and signed by Thomas in his own hand. He stated that he had been wrongfully convicted and that his sentence was unmerited and that the rest of his sentence should be remitted. He wrote the following; 'I now petition for remission of the unexpired term of my imprisonment on the grounds that I was unjustly convicted, the jury having arrived at their verdict entirely on supposition'.[1]

He then gave further details, stating the following; Someone who assumed the name of Frieake called several times on the house of Harriet Lane. Miss Wilmore received a letter signed 'E. Frieake', stating that Harriet Lane was under his protection. It was said that he wrote that letter, and it was entirely on that he was convicted, as the judge in his summing up to the jury said, if you think that Thomas wrote that letter at his brother's request to conceal a crime, you must find him guilty. He was precluded from explaining at his trial about the letter, as his counsel was instructed to suppress everything that might incriminate his brother.

He had never seen Harriet Lane or assumed the name Frieake. The four witnesses stated that they saw Frieake visit Harriet. These women were shown

Thomas' photograph and also saw him at Leman Street Police Station and they all failed to recognise him, but say he was much like the man that called. The publican Humphries committed deliberate perjury, saying he had known him for four years and that I called at his pub for champagne. I don't even know where his pub is?

In September, Henry asked him to write a letter for him, saying he was keeping a little woman and he didn't want her relatives bothering him. He believed what he said and handed him the letter and did not imagine it was to be the means of assisting to conceal a crime. The only evidence against him was obtaining a garden spade and a wood chopper for Henry.

The judge expressed his sorrow for having to pass sentence on him, and said that he had been made a fool of. He said he was innocent of the crime and did not deserve the punishment and asked that the 'petition would receive the Home Secretary's merciful consideration'.

Whether the Home Secretary gave it much consideration isn't known. For him to even think of considering remission, he would have to be convinced that there was some new and important evidence. After all, criminals often plead their innocence after conviction, knowing full well that they actually did commit the crime.

It's a shame we don't know what happened when Thomas' petition landed in the Criminal Petitions 'in tray' at the Home Office. The civil servants would have been aware of the case; the whole country knew about it. Almost a year after the trial, Thomas was asking for his release. As the 'men from the ministry' read his form, would someone be checking the original case file and court transcript? Would a criminal lawyer have seen of the petition?

What is clear is that the identification evidence of the witnesses who saw the 'imposter Frieake', was weak. Very weak. In addition, the method of witness identification of suspects in those days was woefully unreliable and would not be accepted today. The Police & Criminal Evidence Act 1984 strictly controls the rules on suspect identifications, and is there to ensure that the rules are fair, and prevent miscarriages of justice.

There were four witnesses who had seen the mysterious Mr Frieake. Jemima Foster, Harriet's landlady at 3 Sidney Square; Amelia Stanley, a friend of Mrs Foster; Ellen Wilmore, Harriet's children's nanny; and James Humphries, who owned the pub in Sidney Square. The fleeting looks that the three women had made for unconvincing evidence of recognition.

Mr Humphries was the only witness that had positive evidence to give. He stated that he had known Thomas for about 4–5 years. Although he had not seen him regularly over that period, he had seen him on the day he bought champagne from his pub for 'Mrs King' and also on the same evening that he witnessed a disturbance outside of number 3 Sidney Square. Having known Thomas for several years, it's fair to say that Mr Humphries would recognise him. Thomas claimed this evidence was perjured. It seems a case of either he knew Thomas or he didn't. One of them was lying.

Either way, Thomas had a point. Whether he was 'Mr Frieake' or not, without proper, positive identification of him, the evidence of him being that man, and therefore being an accessory to murder, fails. The problem was, Mr Humphries' identification of him appeared conclusive proof of Thomas' involvement.

Thomas perhaps considered that his trump card was his comments about the writing of the letters. He did not deny writing them. His explanation was simple enough: Henry spun him a 'believable' story that he was having some trouble with a lady and he wanted him to write some innocent letters for him. He didn't know that it was to do with a forthcoming murder, so he just helped him as a brother would.

It sounded simple enough when taken on face value. Did Thomas not think to ask more questions about the 'woman trouble' Henry was having, or the details of the letter? He didn't mention the telegrams in his petition. If he wasn't the pretend Mr Frieake, then who was? Did Henry have another reliable person he could get to act out his deception as Mr Frieake? Indeed, if someone else had impersonated Mr Frieake, why didn't they simply reveal his identity?

It's a shame that his defence team didn't play a tougher part at the trial, and the decision to defend both brothers as a team and not to say anything to incriminate Henry in Thomas' defence may have cost him his freedom. It's also frustrating that Thomas didn't enter the witness box at the Old Bailey to give his side of the story. Writing your own version of events on paper in the comfort of his prison cell is not the same as being cross examined by an experienced barrister in the dueling chamber that is the Old Bailey. It's hard to know the truth, but could what was written in the petition have made a difference to Thomas' verdict if presented to the original jury?

In Portland Prison

While Henry awaited the gallows, Thomas began his seven-year sentence in gaol for his trouble. His prison record from the National Archives[2] makes fascinating reading from the perspective of prison conditions as well as his attitude to his situation.

Following on from his conviction at the Old Bailey, and while resident at Newgate Prison prior to his move to Pentonville, it was reported that he had had a visit from his wife, Caroline.[3]

'The wife of the prisoner Thomas Wainwright had an interview with him on Tuesday, at Newgate. The interview only lasted the ordinary period in accordance with the gaol regulations, about 20 minutes, and she will not have an opportunity of seeing the prisoner again until six months have expired. Thomas Wainwright kept to the usual work of a convict in his first servitude, namely oakum picking'.

Before his brother's execution, Thomas' penal situation had been reported on 11 December by the *Illustrated Police News*. The article reported that he was now subject to all the normal restrictions and discipline of convicted prisoners, including a close-cropped prison hairstyle and that the removal of his facial hair.

During his incarceration, Thomas was moved between Horsemonger Lane, Newgate, Pentonville, Brixton, and Millbank prisons, but the vast majority of his sentence was spent at the imposing Portland Gaol in Dorset. Built in 1848, the prison is surrounded on 3 sides by the sea on the Isle of Portland, near Weymouth.

The prison is still in use today on a huge site by the village of The Grove.[4] Prisoners here were used to hew the famous Portland Stone rocks as the prison was very close to a quarry. The prisoners also provided labour to build local structures such as the enormous Portland Harbour Breakwaters[5] as well as the nearby Verne Citadel.

The Newgate Penal Record for Prisoner B1239 reveals many secrets about 5'7", 10 stone Thomas, who was described as 'sparse but muscular'. The record showed that he spent almost 5 years at Portland, from 22 September 1876 to August 1881, and also that he was employed on outside 'public works' where he was described as a 'labourer'.

Though the prison made no mention of it, a newspaper article[6] reported that Thomas had been transferred to Portland in the company of the notorious 'City swindler', Richard Banner Oakley,[7] and that he was in robust health, despite being employed in the quarries as a 'barrowman'.

Thomas' prison records cover several topics, including points awarded and pay; medical matters; punishments and letters. His medical record stated that he suffered from rheumatism and occasionally diarrhoea, and, interestingly, that he bore the scars of syphilis.

Prison conditions were harsh and discipline was inhumanly tough. Thomas regularly had his name taken for various misdemeanours, eleven times in all. These included seven cases of 'continuously talking'. Other offences included being 'idle on public works', 'improper conduct to deceive his officer' and 'having a piece of pencil on public works'.

To encourage good behaviour, prisoners were given points to decide which class of prisoner they would be. This was a sort of penal 'snakes and ladders', where inmates could go up and down a scale depending on behaviour; the better they behaved, the more regularly they could send and receive letters and visits. Thomas' appearance in the punishment books would lead to a 42-point reduction[88] on his score card, which was the difference between being in class 1 or 2 (of 3 classes) and a loss of the right to send letters.

On his arrival at Portland, a form, 'Convict Establishment 341C', would have been brought to his attention. It would not have made for happy reading. The form began thus:

Convicts are permitted to write one letter on reception and also at intervals of 3, 4, or 6 months, according to the class they may be in. They may also receive one letter at the above-named periods. In the case of misconduct, the privilege of receiving or writing a letter may be forfeited for a time.

All letters of an improper or idle tendency, or containing slang, or other objectionable expressions, will be suppressed. The permission to write and receive letters is given to convicts for the purpose of enabling them to keep up a connection with their respectable friends, and not that they may hear the news of the day'.

So, one thing that you wouldn't want would be for one of your less than respectable friends to send a three-line 'wish you were here' postcard from Southend, thereby preventing a two-page letter from your wife arriving.

The form went on to add that convicts were not allowed any articles to be sent to them at the prison, and the final piece of bad news was that visits could only be made every three, four or six months, and even then, the duration of any visits was a mere 20 minutes and could not be made on Sundays. Portland was 146 miles from Whitechapel, so anyone coming to see Thomas would have made a huge effort to get there and back, especially considering transport at the time, all for the benefit of a paltry 20 minutes. Unfortunately, no notes of his visits exist in the Portland records.

The report does record letters that Thomas sent and received, although some were marked as 'suppressed'. He wrote to his wife, mother, mother-in-law and his older brother, William Wainwright, during incarceration. Two of the letters he penned survive in the file. They give a good insight into Thomas' state of mind during his imprisonment. The fact that these letters were still on the file suggest that they were possibly never sent.

You could almost hear Thomas crying out from the letter to William, saying, 'I am convicted of being an accessory to the murder of a woman I have never even seen'. He went on, 'My future is perfectly horrible to think of, I have committed no crime, yet I have to pass seven years of my life in slavery in company of the acme of depravity and ruffianism'.[9] Thomas' fragile mental health is apparent from the line, 'When I lay down at night, I often wish I might sleep to wake no more'. Thomas felt like a man plucked from polite society and thrown in with the dregs of a criminal underclass. He didn't think he deserved to be in prison and the prospect of working for seven years moving rocks around must have seen him contemplate suicide in his darkest moments. He signed himself off in French as, 'your unhappy brother'.

The unhappy experiences of the unlucky Wainwright brothers continued with brother William, who Thomas had been writing to from Portland. In October 1892, 53-year-old brushmaker William Wainwright was found in the first-class carriage of a train at Dalston Junction. A revolver lay on the floor. The newspaper article, headlined, 'SAD SUICIDE OF WAINWRIGHT'S BROTHER' tactfully stated that he had 'blown his brains out'. His wife had recently left him, and he had since turned to drink, becoming depressed. The inquest found that he killed himself during 'temporary insanity'.[10]

The second letter in the prison file, dated 13 March 1877, was addressed, 'My Dear Carrie' (Caroline), to Thomas' wife. Thomas started by saying he had received her letter of last September (6 months previously) and enquired after the health of the children. Significantly, he asked if Carrie was 'feeling better' and that he had never forgiven himself for his unkindness, and his 'accelerating her illness'.

It is at this point that the story reached an unexpected twist. Henry Wainwright was a serial womaniser who paid the ultimate price for his philandering. His brother Thomas also seems to have had a skeleton, not under the floorboards, but certainly in his cupboard. A newspaper report[11] gave the first hint of a scandal by announcing that Thomas had been arrested for neglecting to provide for his wife and children who had been chargeable to the Parish of St. Pancras.

Thomas was at pains to point out that although he had acted unwisely; people were now reading false statements in the newspapers about him. He added that these reports had been 'concocted by a heartless woman'. He added that this woman had been 'financially successful'. Although he did not mention her by name, we can safely assume that he was referring to Henry Wainwright's widow, Elizabeth. He also insisted that his sentence was unjust.

Further bad news arrived when Thomas was informed of the death of his wife from tuberculosis on 7 April 1877, in Kentish Town,[12] aged only 31.

What would become of his children? (For further details on Caroline and the children, please see Appendix F)

As Thomas approached the end of his sentence, he was to be released on licence more than a year ahead of schedule. News of his impending release created a flurry of correspondence, as a Mrs Nina Ellis of 9 King Street, Brighton, wrote to the gaol asking when and where he was going to be released. The prison authority released prisoners on licence on the basis that they would be going to a 'suitable' address. With this in mind, the prison governor, George Clifton, wrote to Brighton Police on 7 July 1881, asking them for information on the mysterious Mrs Ellis. The response from Chief Constable James Terry was brief and to the point. 'She is a woman of bad character and keeps a brothel'.

Thomas was a complicated personality. Before his arrest, had been consorting with a Mary Jane Raper, who lived at The Rosamunds, Parsons Green. There were several rumours about their relationship, mainly that Thomas was staying with Mary Jane when her husband, Alfred, was away in America on business, and had been known to refer to Mary Jane as Mrs Wainwright. The Rapers' marriage broke down under the strain of these 'rumours' and, curiously, a check of the 1881 census tells us that an 18-year-old Florence Raper was living with Nina Bell, described as her daughter, at 9 King Street. Mrs Raper and Florence, along with Alfred A. Thomas, a son born to Mrs Raper in 1875 (not long after her rumoured affair with Thomas), eventually emigrated to Australia.

Thomas was eventually moved east to Millbank Prison in London, in preparation for his release back into society. The Governor had marked his papers to the effect that he would not be needing the assistance of the Prisoners' Aid Society and it was confirmed that he was to be released to his mother's home at 6 Albert Square, Commercial Road, London.[13] He was released in August 1881.

Thomas would no doubt have been glad to have been freed, but what life awaited him? His wife was dead and his children were being cared for elsewhere. He had no job, money or prospects. His infamous name was still in the public memory, so trying to blend anonymously back into society was going to be a challenge. It has been impossible to find any trace whatsoever of Thomas after this time. No marriage, death, census or other records can be found. Indeed, his daughter applied for probate[14] on his estate in 1909 but gave the date of his death as 'on or since 19 August 1881, at [a] place unknown', which seems to infer that she had no idea what happened to him following his release.

The only tiny piece of evidence this author has uncovered about Thomas' movements after his release from prison comes from a book published 40 years after the case was concluded. In this book,[15] a minor witness during the trial, Mr John Matthew Steel, told the author a small crumb of possible information about Thomas. It read, 'I do not know what happened to Thomas when he came out of penal servitude, but I believe he had something to do with a public house'. It's not a lot to go on.

It's possible that Thomas could have returned to life in London, but without his wife and his respectability, did he decide to follow through with the threat he made in prison to end his life? More likely perhaps is that Thomas either changed his name or moved abroad, or both, possibly emigrating to America or Australia under a new assumed name, Thomas 'Dyson', where he set up a brush business.

Chapter Thirty

Reviewing the Evidence

Was Henry Wainwright a Psychopath?

Anyone looking outwardly at Henry Wainwright in 1870 may have seen a charming and successful man. The 1875 'laid bare' version of Henry had been revealed to be very different, with his grand exterior gone and his life in ruins. Investigating this story leads the average person to enquire, how did things come to this? How could it have gone so wrong?

The Cambridge Dictionary succinctly defines psychopathy as 'a condition in which someone has no feelings for others, and does not feel bad about anything they have done'. This definition certainly fits the personality of Henry Wainwright.

By listing all the behavioral traits associated with psychopathy (below), we can assess whether Henry Wainwright could be classed as a psychopath. The NHS website[1] states that psychopaths are considered to have a severe form of anti-social personality disorder.

Behavioral Trait – signs of a psychopath	Henry
Repeatedly being deceitful	✔
Being impulsive and failing to plan ahead	✔
Repeatedly breaking the law	✔
Being irritable and aggressive	✔
Having a reckless disregard for the safety of others	✔
Being constantly irresponsible	✔
Lack of remorse or guilt	✔
Exploit, manipulate the rights of others	✔
Blame others for problems of their lives	✔
Superficial charm	✔
Narcissism	✔
Need for excitement	✔
Tells lies to get out of trouble	✔
Parasitic lifestyle. Takes advantage of others financially	✔
Promiscuous sexual behaviour	✔

In order to assess whether Henry was a psychopath we should look at each trait in detail.

- **Deceitfulness:** From the moment he met Harriet Lane, Henry's life was a whole series of deceits, including inventing an alias and failing to admit his adultery to his wife. He was also having a questionable relationship with Alice Day which he would not have disclosed to Mrs Wainwright.
- **Impulsive:** Was the decision to kill Harriet an impulsive one? When he was with Alfred Stokes and the body of Harriet was in the bags, why did he go off to get a cab instead of sending Stokes? His failure to plan the disposal of the body sounds impulsive and unplanned.
- **Law Breaking**: Henry's murder of Harriet and his 'probable' arson attack on number 84 Whitechapel Road shows his disregard of the law.
- **Irritability:** It's hard to know how irritable Henry became, but it's likely he wasn't best pleased when his plans were running out of control. When he invited Alice Day to share the getaway cab to move Harriet's body, he was quite rude and dismissive towards her, ordering her not to talk to him as he was thinking.
- **Safety:** Henry's 'probable' plan to set fire to 84 Whitechapel Road, showed a complete disregard for the safety of neighbours, especially the hundreds of customers at the Pavilion Theatre.
- **Irresponsibility:** He had a reckless attitude to his personal life as well as the action of murdering Harriet. He would risk his future on not only Harriet but also his dalliances with Alice Day.
- **Remorse:** At no point during his trial, or in his 50-page written statement did he show an ounce of remorse for the death of Harriet Lane. Even when he was convicted at the Old Bailey, he failed to show any emotion or admit his crime.
- **Manipulative:** Henry had the problem of an expensive and inconvenient lover, as well as disastrous financial issues. In order to try and alleviate himself of Harriet, he enlisted the services of his brother Thomas, probably the only person he could turn to in order to get rid of Harriet. Did he use coercive tactics in order to involve his younger brother?
- **Blame:** Henry was blaming Harriet for his financial predicament, when in fact he had been the architect of his own downfall in this regard. He also tried to blame his brother Thomas for killing Harriet.
- **Charm:** Henry was superficially charming towards the ladies in his life as well as to the people he performed for. He seems to have been universally respected in 1870, but his bonhomie may have only been on the surface.

- **Narcissism:** The traits of narcissistic behaviour definitely apply to Henry. He had a grand sense of self-importance, superiority and power. He loved being the centre of attention, on stage or with the ladies of the Pavilion Theatre.
- **Excitement:** Henry certainly had a love of excitement. He would enjoy illicitly taking Alice Day to the theatre, spending the night with Harriet in a hotel, and may even have enjoyed the thrill of 'possibly' setting fire to 84 Whitechapel Road.
- **Liar:** He was a seasoned liar over several years. He would have lied to his wife and children about the existence of Harriet and his two illegitimate children. Presumably he would have confidently lied about where he was when he was with Harriet. Even when the overwhelming evidence found him guilty of murder, he refused to accept the blame.
- **Parasitic:** Henry would likely have felt no shame in taking money from his brother William or asking business associates for credit or discounts. He would have taken advantage of many customers when bankruptcy was looming but without any sense of shame.
- **Promiscuity:** He had an eye for the ladies, but was prepared to risk everything in order to satisfy his sexual needs. He fathered two children with Harriet but at the same time was prepared to chase other women from the nearby theatre, all whilst his wife was at home with their children.

The above observations suggest a psychopathic personality, but does labeling Henry as a psychopath explain what he did and why? Whilst psychopathy is indeed a common trait of many murderers, it's important to remember that not all murderers are psychopaths, and vice versa, but the traits that lend themselves to a psychopathic personality, such as a lack of empathy or remorse and impulsivity, certainly would make an individual more likely to commit a murder.

The main points against Henry

This book puts details of a wide-ranging Victorian criminal investigation by the police into the murder of Harriet Lane on record. There is a large amount of evidence available, but for you to come to your own decision about the guilt or innocence of the Wainwright brothers, it may be useful to look back at the basic evidence relied upon by the prosecution. You, the jury, should look at all the evidence and then decide whether it has convinced you, beyond a reasonable doubt, that Henry was guilty of murder.

To convict someone of something as small as stealing a tin of baked beans from a supermarket to committing a murder, you have to be sure of their guilt, and any doubt as to the guilt of the person always has to be afforded to the accused.

Many murders are committed in private, being witnessed by the murderer alone, so that no direct eye witness evidence of the crime being committed will ever be available. In these cases, it's the circumstantial evidence that has to be relied upon. With such evidence, there often comes a tipping point when the amount of circumstantial material is so large that the case and the evidence itself becomes compelling.

So, here are the main points of evidence to help you decide for yourself:

1. Henry was carrying on a secret affair with Harriet Lane.
2. If the affair had been discovered, a scandal would have ensued, causing Henry to lose his good name.
3. By 1874, Henry's financial affairs were in a terrible mess, leaving him with very large debts.
4. The £5 that Henry was paying to Harriet Lane to look after their children was now unaffordable, so his payments to her stopped or greatly reduced.
5. Harriet was calling at Henry's business premises looking for money which was embarrassing.
6. Harriet was drinking, and generally making a nuisance of herself regarding the lack of money.
7. Her behaviour was making her unpredictable with the worry that she would eventually 'let the cat out of the bag' about their relationship. These points make a motive for murder.
8. With Henry's financial worries and bankruptcy looming large, a 'mysterious' fire took place at his insured premises at 84 Whitechapel Road. He expected a large insurance payout but, 'smelling a rat', the insurers refused to pay a penny.
9. Lack of funds meant that Henry would have to move out of his fine house in Tredegar Square and move to a very humble address in Chingford.
10. Henry was involved in a conspiracy of inventing a false Mr Teddy Frieake who was sending telegrams and letters supposedly to say Frieake and Harriet were going to France.
11. Henry owned a revolver.
12. Henry told Stokes, 'She's a nuisance. I wish I could get rid of her'.
13. On 11 Sept 1874, Harriet went to meet Henry and was never seen again.
14. Three 'gunshots' were heard at the premises next to 215 Whitechapel Road on the day Harriet disappeared.
15. Henry lied to Harriet's relatives and friends about her going away.

16. In September 1875, Henry bought, or had bought for him, items such as American cloth, rope, chloride of lime, a chopper and spade.
17. The sale 215 Whitechapel Road coincided with Henry needing to move two packages, which were later confirmed to contain the decomposed body parts of a woman
18. Henry was then caught 'red handed' by the police with the body parts entering the Hen and Chickens, which he had no right to use.
19. He tried to bribe the two police officers regarding the dead body.
20. At the police station, Henry lied, saying that a man had asked him to move a package to the Hen and Chickens for £3, no questions asked.
21. At Henry's warehouse, a 'grave' under the floorboards was discovered.
22. The stone flooring had marks on it in the warehouse indicating something may have been chopped up there.
23. Jewellery identified as Harriet's was found at the scene
24. Hair found at the scene appeared similar to Harriet's
25. Blood stains were found at the scene.
26. A freshly dug 'grave' was discovered at the Hen and Chickens, presumably ready to receive a body.
27. Three bullets were found in Harriet Lane's head by the doctors.
28. Henry's brother Thomas had access to a key to the Hen and Chickens.
29. Henry was a man who was living a double life with the deceptions that went with that life.
30. Henry was using aliases when liaising with Harriet.
31. He and Harriet gave false details to the Registrar on the birth of their children and also placed a false wedding notice in the newspaper announcing their wedding which had not taken place.
32. Henry was used to 'acting' during his public engagements and was a seasoned liar.
33. Harriet and Henry had been seen having altercations.
34. Harriet Lane would never have left her children to go away with 'Frieake'. On leaving Sidney Square she had no luggage with her.
35. Henry told enquirers that Mr Frieake was to marry Harriet, but only on the condition that she did not see her old friends again. A very useful thing for anyone trying to 'hide' Harriet, cutting her off from all communications.
36. Edward Frieake was a highly unusual name, what were the chances that Henry knew two people with that exact rare name? The real Mr Frieake was unaware of anyone with the same name as himself. If there was another Frieake, why had he not come forward?
37. Henry had the means, motive and opportunity to murder Harriet.
38. If Harriet had committed suicide, why did Henry not explain it?

The matter of premeditation was also very important in the case and the assembling of the tools for the murder job showed clear premeditation. The *Illustrated Police News*[22] wrote an interesting editorial about the case;

> He was flush with money when he met her, and it flattered his vanity to think that he could keep both a wife and mistress. He was good-natured enough while his money lasted, and so was his paramour, for the same reason; but there is no sign of genuine affection. It is only a loose man and a loose woman who have come together for the moment. As soon as the purse is empty they snarl and fight; the man gets tired of the expense when the freshness of the debauch is over, and the woman is afraid that she will lose her maintenance and have to work for herself. Wainwright murdered his mistress because he was a weak, selfish fellow, and she worried him; and he displayed the characteristic stupidity of criminals in thinking there was no other way of getting rid of her but by killing her.

Leaving aside all the above points of evidence, the plain fact is that both Henry and Thomas admitted that Harriet was the person who had been buried in number 215. One of the brothers was the man who pulled the trigger on the gun which ended Harriet's life. We have to ask did one of them act alone in taking the life of a young mother. If so, which one?

You might also like to consider whether both men were present on the evening where Harriet met her end? Were they both there with the conspiracy to murder in their minds? If that was the case, then they would both be guilty of murder and both would hang, even if one of them only stood by while the other shot Harriet.

As we've discussed, the brothers both accuse the other of the actual murder itself in their respective statements. It's a perplexing situation. Were both men in it together at the moment Harriet died? Did Henry act alone or had Thomas taken the matter into his own hands and himself killed Harriet?

Did one shot see her slump to the floor and the extra two shots were to finish her off as she lay face down? Was the throat cut by the shooter or a second assailant? What happened to the pistol as it was never recovered? There are still several vital pieces missing from the Whitechapel Road Murder jigsaw. Its likely that the full truth will never be known.

The main points against Thomas Wainwright

The points of evidence against Henry are long and convincing. He certainly had a motive for murder, and it's hardly surprising that Henry was convicted.

Thomas had no such motive. Compelling evidence was stacked against Henry and little was offered by his counsel as a defence. His guilt must have been fairly easy for the jury to decide upon.

His younger brother Thomas was a different matter entirely, and was a lot closer to call. He was charged with being an accessory to murder, but not being the murderer himself. Several correspondents wrote to the authorities suggesting that it was Thomas Wainwright in the warehouse with the revolver. But that suggestion was never put to the jury. There was, of course, little evidence to connect Thomas with the actual murder.

That leaves us with the question as to whether Thomas was an accessory before or after the murder. There was a considerable difference in the two possible charges and likely punishments.

Suppose for a moment that Henry had told Thomas that he planned to kill Harriet Lane sometime in the future, but then wanted Thomas to help him by buying some tools for the job and some assistance in the future to move the body. This would be a clear case of being an accessory before the act of murder, even though Thomas would not have been involved in any way in shooting Harriet.

A second scenario could have been that Henry told Thomas out of the blue that he had just killed Harriet. He then wanted Thomas to help dispose of the body. This would have made him guilty of being an accessory after the fact.

One thing is clear, and that was that Thomas was 'involved'. What we must decide is how involved? Although Thomas' barrister never admitted it in court, Thomas later stated that he had written a letter impersonating Teddy Frieake. Did he act with guilty knowledge?

Henry was a man in both financial and personal hell. His way of life was under threat as his empire crumbled around him. He needed a plan to turn things around. Who could he turn to? Contemplating a murder was not a thing you could discuss with a casual friend. But a brother was another matter.

He couldn't go to his other brother, William, who had dissolved their business arrangements previously, but his less than straight forward brother, Thomas, was an option. He would be very unlikely to expose Henry to the police and he could help with a plot to 'prove' that Harriet had gone away after having actually been done away with. The plot involved Thomas pretending to be a man named Frieake. Henry could have sold him the idea by saying he wouldn't have to do anything really bad, and would only have to write a few letters and telegrams and to perform some acting in meeting Harriet Lane.

The main points of evidence that support the charge of Thomas being an accessory to murder:

- Thomas wrote letters and telegrams on behalf of the fictitious Teddy Frieake to Miss Wilmore and Henry Wainwright to suggest that Harriet had gone away to France.
- Thomas bought a spade and an axe used to dismember Harriet's corpse. (His counsel accepts this evidence).
- Handwriting expert compared the letters written by 'Frieake' and found them to be the same as Thomas' handwriting. (His counsel did not deny it was his writing).
- Several witnesses actually saw the fictitious Teddy Frieake who was visiting Harriet at her lodgings and stated that the man was in fact Thomas. (The identification evidence to support all the witnesses was challenged by the defence as being unreliable).
- Although Thomas was not involved in the moving of Harriet Lane's body, it is significant that the premises chosen to rebury her, the Hen and Chickens, had recently been occupied by Thomas.
- Why did Thomas give the key to the Hen and Chickens to Henry? What possible reason was there to allow him the key, especially as Thomas was no longer operating his business from there.
- How did Henry know that there was a basement with a convenient hiding place for a body to be placed there? Could Thomas have told him?

The evidence against Thomas is nowhere near as strong as his brother Henry, but it seems inconceivable that Thomas wasn't involved in helping a brother in distress. Following his conviction, Thomas felt aggrieved at the length of his sentence for what he saw as only innocently sending some letters without knowing the truth of Henry's plotting. Are we to believe that?

The truth is that anyone assisting a murderer must expect a severe sentence. Thomas took no steps to report the matter to the police, which ensured that he was to be locked up at Her Majesty's Pleasure when the case concluded.

The courtroom evidence and the brothers own written statements lead to the conclusion that both men were involved in the conspiracy to dispose of Harriet. The only remaining question is who was the actual shooter? Henry accuses Thomas of the shooting which throws a doubt over who actually pulled the trigger. You the jury have read all the evidence and the statements. Has it made you change your mind on who was responsible for Harriet's death?

Conclusion

Throughout this book we have gone back and forth between the evidence and the possibilities of how Harriet was killed and by who. Was it indeed Henry, as the court decided, or did his younger brother actually do it, leading to a monumental miscarriage of justice where Henry was concerned? It's been a long road to get here. This case has required no stone to go unturned, with all available material having been consulted and discussed.

That being said, we have reached the point where, before you finally close this book, you should be able to decide if Henry Wainwright was guilty of murder. It's a question this author has asked himself continually while writing this fascinating story.

Having had the advantage of reading not only all the witness evidence but also the Henry and Thomas' statements, along with all the other additional details and Henry's mental health. With most of the evidence being circumstantial, as it would be in court, in the end, it must also come down to how we feel about the personalities involved and the bare facts.

I am here to tell you that Henry killed Harriet Lane.[1] Let's briefly look at the reasons why:

- Henry had a motive, along with the opportunity and means to carry out the murder.
- Henry told a pack of lies to the police.
- Thomas had no motive. Would anyone with no motive kill someone so casually as Henry described? It's unlikely. Thomas was many things, but a cold-blooded killer he was not.
- Henry's lifestyle had collapsed dramatically, losing status and money and everything he had achieved. He was about to be undone as an adulterer and bankrupt. He was completely desperate, and was prepared to do anything. Being backed into a corner and at risk of losing everything he gambled on a premeditated killing of Harriet.
- He was the sort of person that would risk seeing hundreds killed in a theatre fire, so killing Harriet was not beyond him.

- Henry was a seasoned liar. His fifty-page statement is beautifully written, and contains many truths, but his skill in creating the statement was in leaving out all the incriminating details, as well as adding uncorroborated false evidence against Thomas.
- Henry fits the profile of a psychopath. He had a complete lack of remorse for anything, other than his own predicament.
- Thomas' version of events in his statement and his prison writings are much more plausible than Henry's.
- Henry never once accused Thomas of being the murderer until he had been convicted.
- You may disagree, but my verdict, on the balance of probability, is that it was Henry that killed poor Harriet. It makes so much more sense. What is undeniable is that this case is one of the most fascinating crimes committed during the reign of Queen Victoria, and was lapped up by the British public who seem to adore a good 'whodunnit'. I sincerely hope you have enjoyed it too.

Appendix I

Assorted Subjects

A. The Press

The year is 1875. There are no televisions, radios or internet to spread the news of the day to the masses. As the populace was hungry for information on what was happening locally and abroad, the newspaper was king. The nineteenth century was the heyday of national and local papers, and Britain abounded with vast numbers of newspaper titles.

Many papers came and went over the years but some are still going strong after 150 years or more. *The Times* and the *Illustrated London News* were some of the most important. They gave 'quality' news from the four corners of the world. The archive of old newspapers in the UK is astonishing in its size and variety. The British Library holds all the old bound copies of our local gems, everything from the *Aberdare Times* to the *Yorkshire Post and Leeds Intelligencer*.

These papers document the history of our towns and cities with local information about births, marriages, deaths, accidents, elections, markets, all manner of court cases, not to mention sport, flower shows, war casualties and a host of advertisement's. All of life is there, and this goldmine of a resource is currently being digitally scanned, and saved for the nation. The collection of newspapers is perhaps the finest in the world, so the British historian has a lot to be thankful for.

We all know the old saying, don't believe everything you read in the newspapers. It's still a true adage, as reporters are human and make mistakes. The point of this chapter is therefore to celebrate the huge benefit that hundreds of years of newspaper reporting has given us, but tempered with the notion that what we read isn't always 100% correct. Mark Twain may or may not have made an amusing reference to the truthfulness of the newspapers. He may have said, 'If you don't read the newspaper, you're uninformed. If you read the newspaper, you are misinformed.'

There are literally thousands of articles in the press on the Wainwright case. This book would not have been possible without the British Newspaper Archive. The case was reputedly the biggest crime story of the year, 1875. The newspapers were full of 'ordinary' murders every week, though the run of the mill ones would quickly fade from the public memory. The Wainwright case occupied a lot of column inches in the autumn and winter of 1875. The papers followed the case from arrest to execution. It was a regular pot boiler.

The average matricide or drunken pub brawl murder did not have much to catch the public's imagination, unlike the Wainwright case, which had a one secret ingredient; scandal! Especially when the case involved a pillar of the community, a well to do 'toff', being caught playing away from home. The case got more interesting with the famous 'cab chase' with the mutilated corpse, as well as the involvement of Alice Day and Henry's brother Thomas, and the elaborate plan to spirit Harriet away to the continent. The case had everything it needed to titillate the average reader, and so it sold many extra copies that year. Special editions were issued and even ballads were released to mark the murder.

As the Wainwright case burst onto the news-stands, *The Penny Illustrated Paper*'s edition of 25 September 1875, not only distained 'other' titles but blew their own trumpet by pointing out that their staff had been 'helping' the police with the investigation. One of the *Illustrated Police News*' rivals, the *Penny Illustrated Paper* reported the following interesting article;

215 WHITECHAPEL ROAD. The exterior and interior view of this house was sketched by our artist the day that an important link in the chain of evidence was discovered, and it was our representative who found and handed to the police the massive gold keeper which poor Harriet Lane, is said to have worn.

The same artist had the privilege of sketching the scene in the cellar of the "Hen and Chickens," whilst the police were examining the hole in the wall which has been the occasion of not little suspicion; The accompanying portraits we believe will prove a far more generally acceptable souvenir of the Whitechapel tragedy than will the many repulsive and purely imaginary sketches published in the blood and thunder prints.

The *Illustrated Police News* (IPN) (1864–1938) stands out above most other papers, purely because of the sensational and melodramatic drawings that it always produced on the front page.

In 1886, the *Pall Mall Gazette*[1] published an article where it described the *Illustrated Police News* as, 'The worst newspaper in England'. The paper sent a reporter down to 286 The Strand to the *IPN* offices to meet with the proprietor, George Purkess.[2] The *Gazette* hack informed the owner of the award of the title, the 'worst newspaper'. He apparently received the news with 'great good temper'. Purkess added that he had six artists on his staff in London and also had a list of 70–100 artists in other parts of the country on which he could call.

Purkess gave an insight into how important the accuracy of the illustrations was to him. 'We take great trouble and incur considerable expense to secure good portraits. While I have given as low as sixpence, I have paid as high as £50 for a portrait. The £50 was paid for Wainwright's portrait: Only one man possessed it, and unfortunately, I went to him, instead of allowing him to come to me'.

The importance of a case like the Wainwright one can be seen from the circulation numbers that were reported by Mr Purkess. On a slow news week, circulation at its lowest would be from 150,000–200,000 copies. He stated, 'it has two or three times reached the enormous number of 600,000, as when the Wainwright and Peace[3] trials excited popular interest'.

The Wainwright Murder must have been a cause of much rejoicing in the *IPN* offices. This 'Whitechapel Tragedy', as it was often referred to in the press, was going to run and run for several months. As a result of the case's popularity, the front page kept producing more sketches to fill up the space and entice more readers.

From the start of case in September 1875 when the first Wainwright drawings appeared on the front page of the *IPN*[4] till the last one on 29 January 1876, no fewer than twenty full page blocks appeared, 6 of these were special supplements to editions. The number of individual drawings of the case is astonishing. There are 120 separate images within the 20 blocks. Henry Wainwright's execution[5] commanded a powerful full-page sketch showing the noose and hood being placed over his head.

The second *IPN* edition[6] to feature pictures is entitled the 'Whitechapel Tragedy' and contains eleven pictures. The stand out image of this edition is the large central one of (Henry) 'Wainwright the prisoner'. He is a very imposing figure with his wavy hair and full beard. Below his portrait however, is one of the coroner's inquest, with jury members viewing Harriet Lane's body Harriet Lane in her coffin. The coffin has a convenient little 'window' in it so that the jury can see the face of the poor victim.

This edition carried the first image of the victim. It also showed a drawing of Alice Day, which they reported had been engraved 'from a photo executed expressly for this paper'. As Alice had been released from court, it is within the realms of possibility that an *IPN* artist may have persuaded her on the court steps to accompany her to the nearest photographer's studio.[7]

If one had a criticism about the drawings, it would be that PC Turner, one of the arresting officers in the case, was depicted in the bottom row with his collar number 'M48' on show. The paper gave names to all the other characters on the page while on this image they only described him, rather dismissively, as 'policeman'. It's possible to imagine PC Turner paying his one penny for a copy of the *IPN* that week, eager to see what his sketch had come out like. He would probably have been happy with his portrait as he appears a fine-looking man with a superb moustache, but the lack of a name would have left him less than pleased. The lads back at the station would no doubt have been teasing PC Turner that week.

The newspaper business was a chain from the owner and editor, to the journalists and compositors, down to the printers and delivery drivers who moved the papers around. The very last link in the press chain was the street corner paper boys. The East London newspaper, *The East Wind*,[8] wrote an amusing article about the sellers at one of London principal railway stations on the day of the verdicts in the Wainwright trial when everyone travelling home that night would be itching to discover the outcome. The small article (4 Dec 1875, P5), entitled 'Paper, Sir?' illustrated how the enterprising young scallywags were not averse to making a fast buck when the opportunity arose.

The paper boys at Fenchurch Street Station had seen a chance to make a killing on the evening of the Wainwright verdict, knowing that all the commuters would be dashing to buy a paper with details of the outcome of the trial. All the young sellers had got together and were *only* selling The Echo which they were flogging at one penny, double the usual price of a half penny. They had cornered the market and were set to make a killing. The cry of 'trial and "werdick" o' Wainwright'[9] rang out by the station entrance.

These young fellows were out in all weathers flogging their newspapers every day, coming home with grubby inky hands. They would not have been earning much, but the huge interest in the Wainwright case and the forthcoming verdict, saw one young lad see an opportunity to earn a bit extra in time to make Christmas a bit more enjoyable. It was a risky enterprise, perhaps the customers would baulk at paying the extra, but everyone wanted to know the verdict.

So, the bumper *IPN* sales period of the 1875 Wainwright period was over, but Mr Purkess must have started the new year of 1876 very satisfied indeed with how the paper had flourished with this one big story. It would be another twelve years till the next big Whitechapel murder case exploded onto the scene and got the printing presses and the crime artists fully employed once more. A certain Mr J.T. Ripper was then making the headlines.

B. Fire, Fire!

This chapter covers the suspicious fire that took place not at 215, but at number 84 Whitechapel Road. The details help form a better picture of Henry Wainwright and his probable state of mind two months after Harriet's death.

As we've previously discussed, Henry Wainwright was desperate. His financial affairs had spiralled out of control with too many expenses, gambling losses and loss of business income. He was still far too short of money to see a way out of his current financial crisis after many months of living a double life.

With creditors closing in, Henry required an 'Act of God' to help him in his hour of need. At around 10pm on Friday 27 November 1874, one of his two business properties, 84 Whitechapel Road, mysteriously caught fire.

On the following day, the *Daily Telegraph*[10] carried the story of what happened. It stated that a fire had originated at the rear of number 84 on the ground floor. This news was serious enough, but the building was right next to the Pavilion Theatre where the play, 'Formosa' was still being proceeded with 'before a crowded house'.

Most of the theatre goers remained calm, hoping to see the final act, and fortunately no one was hurt. Some of the patrons may have been happy to have made an early exit. The play had not received good reviews when it later toured the country, with the *Scotsman*[11] newspaper reporting, 'its literary quality being very poor', and that some of the 'dialogue was other than of an entertaining character'. In truth, the fire next door had been a very real threat to a large number of lives.

An eye witness to the fire at the Pavilion that night was actor, J.B.Howe. Henry's neighbour in Tredegar Square, who also acted frequently at the Pavilion, was still in mid flow on stage when voices from the audience, and not of the 'bravo' variety, alerted the auditorium to something serious. J.B. takes up the story in his book, *The Cosmopolitan Actor*;[12]

While I was on the stage in the third act, I heard a woman's voice in the gallery shout out 'Come on Jack, come out, the theatres on fire!' In an instant there was a general rise of the audience, but I quietly walked down to the footlights holding up my hands, and exclaimed, 'Don't be alarmed, ladies and gentlemen, there's nothing to fear, there's no appearance of fire in the theatre, it's a false report,' but in another instant several men began to rush out of the pit and stalls, bundling over women and children in their headlong flight, and making for the front doors, while George Yates, came on to the stage, and between us, we assisted several women and children to rise from the stall seats on to the stage, crying out at the same time 'Come this way some of you.'

At this juncture, the excitement near the front doors had somewhat subsided, many returned to their seats, and the piece proceeded to the end, when the frightened audience departed, considerably thinned of its former proportions, which fortunately was not great on that evening, or who can tell what the result might have been. When I left the stage, I asked what had happened, 'Harry Wainwright's house is on fire!'

A fire engine arrived at 10.30pm but was 'unable to check the conflagration in any perceptible degree'. With the fire threatening to destroy the theatre, the Bishopsgate engine and seven or eight others arrived and managed to bring it under control by midnight. Number 84 was completely gutted and the adjoining houses partially damaged by fire and water.

Henry must have viewed the fire as pennies from heaven. The premises had been gutted, but this potential catastrophe was, in fact, a chance to bring in some money as the building was insured against fire. Unfortunately for Henry, his claim for £3,000 compensation was resisted by the Sun Insurance Company[13] who had questioned the legitimacy of the fire's origins. In 1875, Henry started proceedings against the company and a case was to be heard at the Royal Courts of Justice on 5 November.[14]

Forensic science at fire scenes was not very advanced at the time but the suspicion against Henry was hard to refute. He had both motive and the means to have carried out such a crime.

The insurance industry has always had to deal with fraud, and companies would often refuse to pay out to clients who they suspected had tried to swindle them. With large sums of money at stake, companies employed investigators to look into the suspicious claims. A motto for the fraud investigator may have been then, as now, 'where there is insurance, there will be fraud!'

With few other avenues open, and gambling having seen him on a losing streak, the chance of a major pay out from the Sun Insurance Company may just have saved him financially.

The potential arsonist would have been aware of several fires in Whitechapel in 1874. Henry would surely have known of the serious fire at 15 Whitechapel Road, the premises of cabinet maker, Mr G.J. Brown, which went up in flames on 11 April 1874.[15] The fire destroyed most of the building as well as the roof of the building next door, though there were no reports of any casualties. Whether this gave Henry an idea won't ever be known, but a fire could easily have been set under the cover of darkness at Henry's business premises at number 84, and a claim for the building and a huge amount of stock.

We can't be certain who set fire to number 84, whether it was Henry himself or an unknown accomplice, but the scheme was fraught with dangers. A nice tidy fire that only burned the empty building and the stock would have been a perfect outcome. Henry may have been banking on the Fire Brigade attending and putting out the fire but without them being able to save the stock. Did he consider the Pavilion Theatre next door? Though no one was actually living there at the time, the consequences of the Pavilion catching fire while full of theatre goers was too awful to contemplate.

A postscript to the fire was another interesting piece of evidence provided by J.B. Howe in his book.[16] He described a much-changed Henry Wainwright and whisperings about the fire. Mr Howe continued his story in the smoke-filled rooms of the Royal Oak pub on the Whitechapel Road.

> I noticed a decided change in the manner and appearance of Wainwright; he was constantly in the company of Alice Day and a male companion of hers, and, whenever spoken to by others, there always appeared to be a nervous and impatient irritability about the man, which others as well as myself attributed to the loss he had sustained by the conflagration (as he received no compensation from the insurance office).
>
> I popped in to partake of a stimulant prior to departing to my home, and the subject of the fire office was discussed between us when he waxed rather warm about it, and, as there were many others present at the time, I cautioned him not to speak so loud, adding at the same time 'There are long ears and "argus eyes" near us,' when to my utter astonishment one of the bystanders who had evidently been trying to catch up every word spoken between us, exclaimed, 'Do you mean to say that I have got asses ears and asses eyes?' and in not the 'choicest Italian' began to abuse and even challenged me to fight, when, as he was about to spar up to me, Wainwright; placed himself between us and tried to explain the mistake.

This snippet of news is tantalising as it hints at a lot more of what was actually said between the pair. Henry was obviously very irritated about the fire, or, more likely irritated that the Sun Insurance company were not paying the £3,000 he'd hoped for. Had Henry becoming too vocal in the pub after a few gins, while blaming the insurers for ruining him? The fact that Howe was telling him to keep his voice down could well have been because Henry was telling him the truth about how the fire had started. Either way, the insurance claim failure had been a body blow financially and there now seemed no way to prevent his bankruptcy.

Note 1

Henry Wainwright didn't follow through with his claim against the Sun Insurance Company[17], for the simple reason that he had more pressing concerns. He was, by then, residing at Newgate Prison awaiting his trial for murder. When the case against him and Thomas concluded at the Old Bailey,

Thomas was interviewed by the Governor. He told him that the insurance claim had been falsified and exaggerated.

This statement from Thomas didn't say whether the fire was a deliberate arson or an unfortunate accident. Thomas implicates himself and his brother in a criminal attempt to defraud the Sun, and in the light of that admission, it would not be hard to imagine in all the surrounding financial difficulties that Henry faced, that setting his place alight was something he was likely to have done.

In the end, there was no civil case against the Sun, and likewise there was no criminal case for arson against the brothers, so what happened was never fully investigated, but with nothing to lose in setting number 84 ablaze, and everything to gain, it's likely Henry was the Whitechapel Road fire setter.

Note 2

At some point, Henry would have had to dispose of Harriet's body. He could have hired a boat and tied heavy weights to her body, then dropped her in the Thames, perhaps removing the head to avoid her being found and identified. Did he consider moving her body to be incinerated in the fire?

The final thought on the question of the fire was really this. Having been convicted of murdering Harriet Lane, how differently would this case have turned out if the fire had blazed out of control, causing the death of fifty theatregoers in the Pavilion? If Henry was responsible for the fire, either by his own hand or via an accomplice, and a disaster had occurred, the death of poor Harriet may not have made quite so many headlines. That night, all the innocent theatre goers out for an entertaining evening had a very narrow escape!

C. Assorted Intelligence

This chapter is a mixed bag of snippets and stories that relate to the Whitechapel Murder.

Tommy Tins: Tommy tins was the name given to British soldiers' tinned rations, c.1893, also referred to as 'Harriet Lane', due to the bad quality of the meat.[18]

The Good Ship Harriet: In 1857, an American warship, *Harriet Lane* was commanded by Captain Wainwright![19]

Trial by Jury – W.S. Gilbert: The Gilbert and Sullivan composer avoided jury service while writing his opera *Trial by Jury*, by performing one day of legal work on the Wainwright case.[20]

A Night at the Theatre (Or Not). The Whitechapel Tragedy – in Three Acts: A play was produced about the Wainwright case in Dover, but was stopped by the Lord Chamberlain due to a law which stated that, 'no living person shall be counterfeited on the stage'.[21]

What became of the Rogers' dog? Was he murdered by Wainwright as well?: Mr Rogers' dog used to scratch at the floorboards where Harriet lay buried. The dog followed Wainwright one evening and was never seen again.[22]

Waxing Lyrical?: Madame Tussauds, London; the Royal Moving Waxworks, Belfast; and MacLeod's Waxwork and Menagerie, Glasgow, all made waxwork models of the Whitechapel Mystery 'characters'.[23]

Stones End Police Station: The station was so called as it marked the end of the paved footway from the City of London to Southwark.[24]

Playing at Wainwright: Boys in Bedworth, Warwickshire, played a game called 'Wainwright', where they acted out the case. It ending when the boy, Belcher, was 'hung' on a lamp post by two belts, which broke, depositing him on the ground.[25]

Masonic Membership: Henry Wainwright was member of the Victoria Lodge of Freemasons[26] situated in Fleet Street. It's interesting to note that in the year 1874, the payments column recorded that he was 'in arrears', while by 1875 that column stated that he had, 'gone away'. He certainly had!

Though shalt not commit a Wainwright: A chapel in Camberwell held a service warning of adultery and other vices, entitled 'The Wainwright Murder and its lessons.'[27]

Looking after the jury: On the Sunday, the jury were taken on a jaunt to Richmond upon Thames to relieve the monotony. They were not allowed to read newspapers, but could play chess, cards and draughts.[28]

D. Alfred Stokes

Prior to 1875, Alf Stokes (1849–1927) probably would have gone through life unnoticed by history. He was an 'Average Alf', a very ordinary member of the labouring class, simply earning his living in mundane work making brushes in a factory. It was not a life that his ancestors would have been hugely interested in. But on 11 September 1875, 25-year-old Alf had a big decision to make. Was he going to 'look the other way' and say nothing about finding Harriet Day's corpse, or was he going to leave his mark in the history books? That decision was to change his life and, in the short term, it was to change it very much for the worse. But he knew that he had made the right decision.

Having seen the body parts in the bag, his heroic chase after the horse-drawn cab put him up front and centre of the case when it exploded in the nation's press. The state of the traffic on that day is not recorded, but his 'follow that cab' dash through the City to Borough High Street must have been physically exhausting. Stokes would have had to run the mile and a half distance dodging pedestrians and the chaotic horse drawn traffic in his attempt to keep up with Wainwright's cab. He would have taken his life in his hands in avoiding being trampled by a horse or have landed in one of the many piles of manure that carpeted London's roads.

Initially, his time was taken up by assisting the police with their enquiries and giving his statement. There then followed numerous days with the Crown's lawyers and making appearances at several court hearings. All this cost him time and wages.

His wages of '8 shillings and 4 pence per day', were replaced by a mere 2s 6d at the magistrates court and 3s 6d at the Old Bailey. The loss of 5 shillings a day for a total of 30 days, and having to wait almost 2 months for the expenses to be paid, coupled with doctor's bills for his wife and child, had pushed them over the edge. He had also lost his job. The committee of his supporters decided to make a collection for Stokes as well as asking the Home Secretary to make a further award to him.

It is interesting to note that while Stokes was pleading poverty due to loss of wages, a different newspaper article stated that his employer had been paying him his full dues: 'Mr Edmund Martin, corn merchant, of 78 and 109 New Road, Whitechapel Road, requests to be allowed to state that he paid Stokes the whole of his wages during that time the latter attended the Police court, the coroner's inquest, and the examinations at the Treasury'.[29]

Following the Wainwright trial, and after Mr Stokes had been awarded £30 by the court for his great efforts in the case, he was to be given one other memento in which to remember his actions on the fateful day in Whitechapel. This second award was reported in the Sheffield Daily Telegraph under the headline 'THE WHITECHAPEL TRAGEDY. OLD MRS LANE'S OBSERVATIONS ON HER DAUGHTER'S UNTIMELY END. The report was a touching tale of Stokes being invited to the Lanes' house for dinner.

The whole of the Lane family invited the witness Stokes to a supper at their house, for the purpose of presenting him with memorial subscribed to him by the whole of the members of the family, as a mark of their appreciation and thanks for his conduct which led to the discovery of the late terrible tragedy. Old Mrs Lane, the aged mother of the unfortunate murdered girl, was, at her express wish, brought from her bed, to which she has so long been confined, so that she might present the memorial to Stokes with her own hands.[30]

The article continued by stating that the family had obtained a large and splendid gilt framed memorial to present to Stokes for his courageous conduct. It was hoped that the item could be passed to his children one day as an incentive for them to follow the path of integrity. Harriet's mother had apparently feared for her daughter's safety and had always left her door open at night. She added that Harriet had been a good child until getting involved with 'the temptations of the world'.

Following the trial and prior to his execution, Alfred wrote to Henry Wainwright. He apologised to him, saying that he had been a good employer, but that he had to give evidence against him. A copy of the letter appeared in the newspapers.[31] This was a lengthy and heartfelt plea to Henry to not think badly of him, despite his actions having resulted in Wainwright's forthcoming demise. The words of Alfred Stokes are fascinating and illustrate the huge fall from grace that Henry had suffered:

LETTER FROM STOKES TO WAINWRIGHT

The following letter from Stokes was received by the Governor of Newgate for Henry Wainwright, 34 Baker's Row, Whitechapel, 16 Dec. Dear Sir. Will you permit me to tell you how extremely sorry I am when I think of the awful position in which you are now placed.

I trust that you will not consider that what I have done or said against you was either said or done from any personal malice towards you, or that I was lacking in friendship, because I could not bring myself to any endeavour to try and screen you. On the contrary, I, and all to whom I have spoken, who were formerly in your employment, have always esteemed you as a kind and good master, and a most generous friend.

God and yourself only know how much you were concerned in the terrible crime laid to your charge; but I do hope and trust you will consider that in giving my evidence against you I only fulfilled a national duty. Perhaps you think, that I was only I moved by a prying curiosity.

But I can assure you, that it was not that, but I was urged as it were by a strange mysterious agency for which I can scarcely account.

These unaccountable promptings began the very moment you left me with that frightful bundle while you went to fetch the cab. The very instant your back was turned I seemed to hear a supernatural voice say to me three times, as distinctly as though it were a human voice somewhere near me, 'Open that parcel. Open that parcel'. I hesitated. I seemed to hear the voice again, and then felt pressed on by an irresistible impulse to open it. I immediately rent it open.

The head and hands came up together, and as I stood for a moment aghast at the mutilated head, so grim and yet apparently so pitiable, thinking over and puzzling what I should say to you when you came back, I seemed instantly possessed and controlled by a power and agency by a cautionary prudence and energy not my own, and certainly not natural to me; and then, as I hastily closed up the parcel again, thinking that perhaps it would be best to say nothing about it, I then seemed to hear the same supernatural voice address me again, and say, 'murder, it is a murder. Will you conceal a murder?' I then said, 'No, not for my own father, oh, pray God direct me right!'

But shall I give up the very best friend I have had in my life. You then came up with the cab, took the parcels, and drove away. As I stood for a moment in utter consternation, I immediately seemed to hear the same voice again addressing me, and saying, 'Follow that cab! I at once did so; I set on to run as though I was propelled along. I ran till I nearly dropped of exhaustion, and certainly seemed sustained by a strength superior to my own. Thus, from the remembrance of that strange, inexplicable power which so suddenly overruled me, I feel convinced that I was really destined to be the humble medium by which: that mysterious and barbarous murder was to be brought to light.

Under these circumstances, I do trust that you will personally forgive me. My own personal grief is very great when I reflect upon the awful position my evidence has placed you in, and the terrible bereavement it has entailed upon your poor wife, your children, and your family.

I must now take a solemn and awful farewell of you for ever, my humble and earnest prayer is that God will he truly merciful towards you. And now, good bye for ever, both in time and eternity. 'From your grieved and obedient servant', ALFRED PHILIP STOKES.

Stokes' life was suffering a deepening financial crisis in 1876 when a public meeting had been arranged for the New Assembly Rooms, South Hackney.

The Renfrewshire Independent[32] reported on the Stokes' family plight including details of their destitute state. The newspaper headline indicated just how serious matters had become.

> **THE WITNESS STOKES STARVING.** On Saturday night a numerously attended public meeting, convened by placard, was held, for the purpose of considering the best means of assisting Stokes and his family, who for the last two months have been in absolute starvation. Stokes addressed the meeting, who stated that nothing would have induced him to come before the public under such circumstances but their destitution.

The report continued, stating that he had failed to get work due to the bad feeling towards him, and there was no money to feed his children who were crying of hunger. Due to his bankruptcy all his tools had been taken, and during this time his wife had had another baby. The £30 awarded by the court to him had not covered all his losses. Several men from the audience came forward to express their distress at hearing Stokes' story, and together collected 15 shillings which was handed over.

The 15 shillings wasn't going to go far, but at least it was a start, with the hope of further funds on the way, which couldn't come a moment too soon. Staying alive and out of the workhouse was the main priority, though having to throw himself on the mercy of the gathering was akin to having to beg on the street, which must have upset his pride.

A crank with a warped sense of justice sent Stokes two letters, threatening him with violence. Both were written in the same hand and contained poor spelling, as well as the murder of the English language. The *York Herald*[33] reported further threats thus;

THREATENING LETTERS TO STOKES.
The following letters were received by Stokes. The first says; – "May the Lord have mercy on your soul. Sir, your wife may not be surprised to find herself a widow before the execution of Henry Wainwright." On the fly sheet is drawn a coffin bearing three skulls. The second epistle is headed, "Sacred to the memory of revenge. Nothing but your blood will satisfy, ye bloodhound. We will hunt you about like a dog, until we bring you to die on a dung-hill; and you shall have not so much as a dog to look at. We swear in the name of God to have your life, and if you try for a situation, we will stop you in all ways and before Wainwright is executed, we will have your life.

In the name of God, we swear that the writer of this letter is no idle threat. We call God to witness this – May the writer of this letter be struck blind if he does not carry out his threat. – Yours revengeful, REVENGE." At the bottom of this letter is also drawn a coffin, containing a body, moderately well drawn. A post-card bears the following: – "6th Dec, 1875. – Yer wagebone, selp me Taters I'I choke yer when I cop yer agin. My sister shant speeke no more. Signed Wauewright"

Despite the passage of years, some people had not forgotten the Wainwright case, or the man that had been instrumental in getting Henry Wainwright executed. Eleven years after the Old Bailey trial a report appeared, informing readers about an assault suffered by Alfred. The report stated the following; 'THE "WAINWRIGHT MURDER CASE." A respectable looking man, named Tapling, appeared at Worship Street Police Court to a summons charging him with having assaulted Alfred Stokes'.[34]

The report added that by 1886, Stokes was running a brushmaker's business in Whitechapel but that since 1875 he had, on many occasions, been 'annoyed'

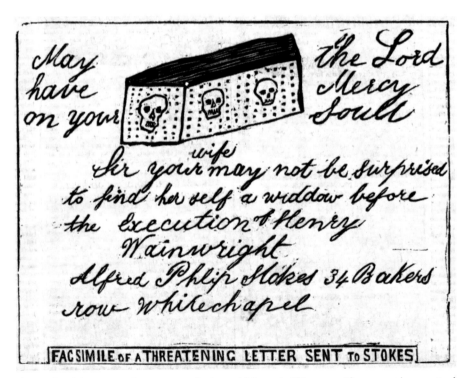

Fascimile of threatening letter sent to Stokes, which reads, 'Sir, your wife may not be surprised to find herself a widdow [sic] before the execution of Henry Wainwright'. *Illustrated Police News*, 18 December 1875. (*Copyright The British Library Board. All Rights Reserved*)

by people who had known Henry Wainwright. On this occasion Taplin had abused Stokes by saying, 'You hung Wainwright'. He then threatened to knock him down, stone dead. Taplin was later relieved of 20 shillings by the magistrate.

The occasional badgering that he suffered over the years must have been galling for Alf. He was a man who had done the right thing in reporting the body to the police, and was feted by many but abhorred by those few with a twisted sense of justice. Remaining in the brush making business in Whitechapel meant that local people were unlikely to forget him. Perhaps this may have persuaded him to leave London to try his luck in a place where he was unknown.

Some years later, prior to 1901, the Stokes family had moved to the sea air of the south coast and to Brighton where the 1911 Census recorded him at 32 Edward Street, as an 'ironmonger shop keeper.' The family had another long move when they returned to London and the bustling area of Islington, where Alfred set up as a hardware and brush dealer in the now trendy address of 17 Camden Passage. The Stokes' were surrounded by some of their children and grandchildren with daughter Henrietta helping in the shop. Alfred and his wife had an eventful life. They had survived threats and assaults as well as abject poverty, and the death of three of their ten children. Alfred and Mary died in Islington within 3 weeks of one another in 1927.

E. Criminal Trials in 1875

The case of Harriet Lane's murder has taken us from Waltham Abbey to Whitechapel and then from London Bridge to the Old Bailey. We have heard from all manner of witnesses, including written statements from both Henry and Thomas, along with a huge amount of evidence from the prosecution, but precious little from the defence. One thing of which we can be sure is that a man called Wainwright pulled the trigger. Henry Wainwright was convicted of the murder, but did he act alone in that foul deed?

The biggest deficiency in the criminal proceedings in this case was the absence of Henry and Thomas themselves in the witness box, giving their own evidence, and speaking up for themselves. What the modern reader may not know is that throughout the nineteenth century, defendants in criminal trials were not allowed to give evidence in their own defence. Indeed, it was only after the passing of the Prisoners' Counsel Act[35] in 1836 that defendants were given the right to be fully defended by a lawyer.

This nineteenth century normality amounted to a huge infringement of the prisoner's defence; It meant that they were never able to tell the court their side of the story in their own words, or be cross-examined by a relentless prosecutor, which would have tested both of their testimonies most severely. It begs the question, had Henry and Thomas been able to speak for themselves, would the outcome have been different? It's certainly possible that they could have made things worse and cemented their guilt in the eyes of the jury, but a believable explanation of innocence from the pair could have swayed the jury.

The Criminal Evidence Act,[36] 1898 finally allowed defendants to enter the witness box, making trials fairer to both the defence as well as the prosecution, just 23 years after the Wainwright case.

The moral of the story is to always keep to the straight and narrow. It's also a lesson to would be murderers: avoid schoolboy errors, and never, ever ask friends, however nice, to hold on to the dismembered parts of a corpse for you, as no good will come of it!

A Modern-day London Cab Journey in the footsteps of Henry Wainwright

On a sunny late September afternoon in 2021, I was standing in Commercial Road, Whitechapel, at the junction of Batty Street, outside the building that used to be the chemist's shop where Henry Wainwright's cab had stopped to pick up Alice Day on 11 September 1875. After a long morning walking round some notable Wainwright murder sites, I abandoned my plan to walk the route to the Hen and Chickens over London Bridge as fatigue was starting to set in. I did the next best thing, however. I hailed a cab. One of the official licenced varieties, with the obligatory black paint job.

My driver was a very nice chap called Oliver Severn, and I explained the reason for my hailing his carriage. Our journey ended in the Borough High Street and had taken longer than I had anticipated, even though the traffic, for London, was relatively light. The reason for this was that the distance was such that it would have taken me 35 minutes to have walked the route. Fortunately, the back of the cab was remarkably tidy; I was the first fare of Oliver's shift, and there were no smelly body parts to worry about. All this went to prove that Alfred Stokes should be applauded for never giving up his pursuit of Wainwright's cab, even when he must have been fit to drop. If ever there was a day when I wanted to jump in a taxi and shout, 'Follow that cab', it was today, but I resisted the temptation!

Henry's House

On the same day as the above journey, I also visited the house where Henry Wainwright lived. Arriving at Mile End Station, just round the corner from the house that the Wainwrights lived in in the early 1870s, until financial trouble forced him to leave in April 1875.

Turning into Tredegar Square off Mile End Road, I was impressed with the delightful Georgian square which came into view. The terrace of houses on the west side were beautifully presented, and the square itself looked like something out of the 1968 film *Oliver*, when little Oliver Twist gets rescued by the kindly Mr Brownlow. I could just hear them singing, *Who will Buy* in the big street scene number from the film. That scene from the film was actually recreated at Shepperton Studios in the image of Bloomsbury Square.[1]

The owner of number 40 was outside the house. He stated that after the war, the area had suffered badly from bombing, and the locality had greatly deteriorated, to the point where bulldozers were being prepared to demolish the whole square. The residents fought the plans and the area became a conservation area in 1971. The house is now Grade II listed.

The house at number 40 is a substantial property of nine rooms over three floors, plus an attic at the top, which was mainly used as servant's quarters, and also a basement, which housed the kitchen and dining room. The first room on the ground floor was the drawing room, with the first floor front room being the lounge, with bedrooms above.

The house is a gem of early nineteenth century design, and would have been an address for the well off in 1875. The house has a fine black front door with pillars either side. I can imagine the family having to leave in 1875 must have been a bitter pill to swallow. Seeing the family in reduced circumstances and closing the door for the final time must have been a day none of them would ever forget.

3 Sidney Square – Harriet's last abode

After the opulence of Tredegar Square, I next travelled on to the house where Harriet Lane spent her final night on this earth, 3 Sidney Square, London E3. It's not far from the London Hospital, which is ever-increasing in its size. The square is much smaller than Tredegar, and not nearly as grand. The early nineteenth century houses are terraced and are on three floors, plus a basement, and were plain brick built. The buildings are also within a conservation area and are Grade II listed.

The house would have been respectable by Harriet's standards in 1874, though it feels slightly down at heel now. The front door opens directly onto the narrow pavement, and there were definitely no pillars in evidence in this square. My mind went back to September 1874 when Harriet left number 3. She would have been hoping for the best that Henry Wainwright would have been able to fix things for her as well as provide some new accommodation. Little did she know that when she closed the door at Sidney Square, she would be making her last trip anywhere.

High Street, Borough – The Hen and Chickens -

My final visit of the day was to the Hen and Chickens at 54 High Street, Borough. The building is currently painted white with black windows, and has the words, 'establish 1804', fixed to the side and front. It's currently an estate

The Hen and Chickens, *Illustrated Police News*, 25 September 1875. (*Copyright The British Library Board. All Rights Reserved*)

agent business. I decided to visit, though I hadn't looked at any of the prices in the window before going in. On the left was a beautiful, large, sweeping staircase leading up to the first floor. Just behind the stairs was a small gap. I explained to the young estate agent that the building had been involved in a murder where the body was to be taken down to the basement to be buried. He didn't ask me any questions, or seem interested in what I was saying, but as I turned to leave, he said, 'Do you want to look in the basement?' Did I? Of course I did! We then made our way down the old narrow stairs to two basement rooms filled with paperwork. I could immediately feel the presence of the Wainwright brothers, as well as PCs Turner and Cox.

The Wainwright Family burial plot – Tower Hamlets Cemetery
My murder travels also took me in search of the burial site for many members of Henry Wainwright's family. I discovered the details of the plot in the Register of Burials at the City of London and Tower Hamlets Cemetery, Mile End.[22] The register stated that the plot was a private grave purchased by Henry's father, Henry William. It measured 6 feet, 6 inches long, by 2 feet 6 inches wide, and was an incredible 14 feet deep. According to the register, 7 family members had been interred. On his execution, Henry was buried at Newgate Prison so was never interred in the family plot. It is not known what became of Thomas so his space in the grave is also unoccupied.

I set off to visit the grave in the, now renamed, Tower Hamlets Cemetery Park. I knew that the graveyard, one of the 'Magnificent Seven'.[3] had been opened in 1841 and contained 350,000 bodies. It closed in 1966 when the cemetery went bankrupt. The cemetery has a fascinating history[4] and is well worth visiting.

My visit was greatly assisted by having the grave number[5] to hand and I was escorted by Heritage Officer, Claire Slack, who took me along 'Millionaires Row' past the grave of Charlie Brown,[6] the famous 'Uncrowned King of Limehouse' who ran the pub called 'The Railway Tavern' by the gates of the West India Docks.

As we reached the 'Mutiny on the Bounty' gravestone, we approached the site of a chapel which had been destroyed by bombing during the Second World War. A quick right-hand turn, and we suddenly came upon Square 58 when Claire suddenly called out to say she had found the headstone. The grave contained several family burials[7] including both of Henry Wainwright's parents.

She pointed out that the headstone had been made from sandstone, and was in quite good condition still. To the right of the stone was another memorial which had crumbled very badly. The other headstone was made of white Portland Stone, and could perhaps have been excavated by Thomas Wainwright, who spent six years at Portland Prison where he had worked on the gangs moving Portland stone.

Visiting the scene of the murder
My visit to the Hen and Chickens was exciting. To actually follow in the footsteps of Henry Wainwright and PCs Cox and Turner and seeing the

front door of Henry's former house at Tredegar Square, Mile End, was very fascinating. The most exciting prospect, however, was to actually visit the scene of the murder. But there was a problem. Whitechapel Road is a very old arterial road with many fine buildings. Over the years there has been continual redevelopment. 200-year-old properties now sit casually opposite, or next to, twenty-first century architecture all along Whitechapel Road.

And so, I attempted to find out where Henry Wainwright's warehouse (the site of Harriet's murder) would have been. I had the address and even a photograph. Unfortunately, Whitechapel Road had been renumbered since 1875, so calling at number 215 would not have been any use. In 1875, the building numbers on each side of the road were consecutive. After the number changes, the numbers then went up in twos, with odd and even sides of the road. Some premises had gone or had been enlarged and the maps of the murder site did not seem to correspond to what was there now.

The mystery was thankfully solved when it was discovered that number 215 had been renumbered[88] to number 130. The warehouse in the old photo was nothing like any of the buildings that currently sit in that part of Whitechapel Road, near to Vine Court. It was then that I also discovered that the site of Henry's warehouse, and Harriet's murder, had been demolished and rebuilt in 1900–1901, becoming the premises of Arthur Winckles Brown, a corn chandler. The murder scene is therefore no more but perhaps it's a good thing I couldn't visit. The current 120-year-old building is a very good replacement for Henry's small dilapidated premises. It has lovely pink brickwork and white stone windows, and it occupies both numbers 128 and 130.

Appendix III

Letters from Harriet Lane to her Parents

We know what Harriet looked like from the newspaper drawings that were made of her from a photograph, which appeared in several of the papers of the time. Having read this book, you may now know quite a bit about her life and her personality. We have heard other people describe her, with her attractive looks and her relationship with her close friend and confidante, Ellen Wilmore.

But we have never heard Harriet speak herself, we only have the testimony of others. Until now. The National Archives at Kew in London is a goldmine of historical records and they contain large files on the Whitechapel Tragedy murder. During one of my visits in pursuit of the truth about the case, I examined every scrap of paper in the very considerable files.

The files contained many routine papers such as the witness depositions and court documents, but it also held so many unique and amazing items, including some personal ones. These included, two pawn tickets for Harriet Lane's wedding ring and keeper. There was also a calendar for 1875, and many letters written by members of the public to the authorities.

Other fascinating gems included the following original items; a large detailed map of the Hen and Chickens as well as the murder scene; the business card of Edward Frieake; a letterheaded letter signed by Henry Wainwright; birth certificates of both of Harriet's children; photographs of Henry, as well as Alice Day; the signed petition which was submitted to the Home Office to try and spare his life; telegrams and numerous Scotland Yard documents.

The items that fascinated me the most were the two letters, which had been penned by Harriet herself, to her parents in 1874. I was holding probably the last two letters that she ever wrote in my hands. At the time of writing, although her life was no longer so comfortable and easy going as it had been when Henry was paying her £5 a month, she probably had no idea that her life was in imminent danger. It was very poignant, holding history in my hands.

The sweet little notes that she sent were not long or very detailed, but it was fascinating to actually hear her speak. Her handwriting was confident and right slanting and, as I read it, I could imagine her sitting in the window of 3 Sidney Square, at a small desk, writing that letter with the aid of candlelight after the children had gone to bed. The transcriptions of the letters are below:

Letter One: 'Sunday Night'
There are two letters[1] on the file but only one envelope. The small envelope that survives has the right-hand corner torn off, where the stamp would have been stuck. It was addressed to 'Mrs Lane, Jessamine Cottage, Alexandra Brook, Waltham Cross, Herts'. On the rear of the letter is a Waltham Cross postmark[2] which appears to be 10 September 1874, though this date cannot be confirmed, but it looks likely that the one marked 'Sunday Night' was written first.

> My Dear Mother and Father, just a note to say, I am leaving Sidney Square tonight, Tuesday, and going to Brighton for a fortnight. I will write as soon as I get there, and on my return, I will come down and see you for a day or two. I should have written before but have had no particular news to tell you. I shall defer all news when I see you, with much love, your affectionate daughter, H.King.
>
> Ps. I hope you are better, also father, I have been very unwell myself, so am ordered a change of air immediately.

Letter Two: London, Thursday.

> Dear Mother and Father, just a line to say I have returned from Brighton and shall be down on the Saturday night or Sunday. I am pleased to say I am completely settled in my new residence. I feel very anxious to see you. With much love, your affectionate daughter. L. King.
>
> Excuse this scribble, if you wish to write to me before Saturday – write to the enclosed address – Send the envelope provided.

> [The Envelope: enclosed in the letter was a very small white one, with a small flower embossed on the back. It was addressed to L. King, Post Office, 1 Whitechapel Road, London, East.]

It's interesting to note that her letters were being sent to the post office close to Henry Wainwright's premises, rather than Sidney Square. The letter suggests that Harriet was still close to her parents, but also show that she was anxious about something. Was this a concern about Henry, Mr Frieake, or her lack of funds? Who paid for her trip to Brighton? The date (10 September) is fascinating; Harriet moved into Sidney Square in May 1874 and 'left' on 11 September 1874, when she went missing.

Appendix IV

What Happened to Caroline Wainwright, Thomas' Wife, and his Children?

Astory with a happy ending is what most of us like to read. One where everything turns out all right in the end. The story of Caroline Wainwright didn't quite end like that, and next to Harriet Lane, she was the next biggest 'victim' is this whole sad affair.

Caroline was the daughter of George and Susannah Brockley, and was born at Warren Street, St Pancras on 9 February 1845. On the baptism register, her father was recorded as a 'piano forte maker'. By the time of the 1861 Census,[1] the family were living at 71 Warren Street. Her father was still making pianos, while sister Susannah was a 'piano forte singer' and sister Eliza was a 'teacher of singing'. The Brockleys were clearly a talented family.

Caroline met Thomas Wainwright and the couple got married by licence on 15 December 1866 at Holy Trinity Church,[2] Haverstock Hill, Middlesex. Thomas gave his occupation as 'ironmonger' and was living at Westminster Bridge Road. Caroline has just had her 21st birthday and was living at 1 Melverne Cottages, Hawley Road, Kentish Town.

The Wainwrights were blessed with the birth of 2 children, Herbert and Daisy, born in 1868 and 1872 respectively. One might have expected that the middle-class couple would have enjoyed a happy life together: Thomas was part of the respected Wainwright family, so what could possibly go wrong? Disaster was about to strike for both Caroline and Thomas when the case of the Whitechapel Tragedy suddenly exploded.

In October 1875, the *Illustrated Police News*[3] ran a paragraph in one of their Whitechapel articles headlined, 'THE WIFE OF THOMAS WAINWRIGHT.' It did not make for happy reading. The report stated that the unnamed Mrs. Wainwright, aged 29 was in a present state of abject poverty, and having three children aged 7, 4 and 2. to care for. (This appears to be incorrect as they couple only had 2 children). The children were suffering from scarlatina while Caroline's health was impaired due to 'anxiety and privation'.

The article then reported her much reduced financial circumstances stating that she was the daughter of a well to do tradesman from Tottenham Court Road and that she had received a 'marriage portion of £850' which had been spent long ago. She had also been 'entitled to a reversion under her grandfathers will, but this had been mortgaged nearly to its full amount'. Considerable wealth had therefore been lost, and she was under hugely reduced circumstances, now living in a small room in a small street in Kentish Town.

Caroline had been trying her best to 'eke out a living by needlework, but her health and strength were not equal to her constant labour'. Her family had been helping as much as they could, but she had finally reached the point of having to apply to the parish for relief, the ultimate shame. Being a respectable woman, the parish guardians hesitated in sending her to the Workhouse, but granted her 'outdoor relief' in the hope that her husband Thomas could be compelled to pay for her maintenance. His arrest and incarceration for being an accessory to the murder of Harriet Lane put paid to any hope of a rescue for Caroline, leaving her in a 'state of semi destitution'.

Another newspaper article, this time the *Dundee Courier*[4] explained the complicated quest that the authorities had in trying to compel Thomas to supporting his wife and children;

ANOTHER CHARGE AGAINST THOMAS WAINWRIGHT.
Thomas George Wainwright, aged 30, who was described as commission agent of the Rosamond's, Fulham, Middlesex, was brought up on a warrant at the Clerkenwell Police Court on Saturday, and charged with deserting his wife Caroline and his three children, whereby they had become chargeable to the parish of Pancras. From the evidence of Mr. Wheatley, one of the relieving officers, it appeared that this case first came under 'the notice of the authorities of the parish of St Pancras on the 19 October 1874; and on the defendant being written to, he agreed to allow his wife and family, 18s per week towards their support.

He kept his payments regularly for a short time, and he was again written to. In November, Wheatley visited the defendant at Rosamond's Villas, Parsons Green Villas, and he again agreed to allow his wife 18s per week, and on behalf of the guardians, Mr. Ricketts, solicitor, drew up an agreement binding the defendant to pay that sum, but that agreement was never executed. The defendant continued to pay some money until May 26 of the present year, when the defendant's wife again applied for relief, and was at once allowed 5s per week and two loaves. That relief had been continued ever since, and the Relief Committee renewed it monthly. Thomas Wainwright was continually written to, and invariably the next day he would send small sums of money, but nothing near sufficient to support his wife. From February to July the defendant had kept the Hen and Chickens, in the Borough, where he carried on business as furnishing ironmonger, and upon that he relied to show that he had means.

Mr. Hannay inquired if the defendant was apprehended on warrant in the first instance, and was informed that it was so. Mr. Wheatley said he believed the defendant had been travelling on commission. He had been in business at the Hen and Chickens in the Borough. The defendant said that was not his business. Mr. Mason said he told the defendant at Leman Street Police Station that his wife was chargeable, and he said that he had sent his wife as much he could. When he was taken into custody, he had over £1 in his pockets. The defendant said that was true, but he had only received the money the night before. Mr. Hannay said he could not deal with this case criminally, and he would therefore be discharged.

Money was later being collected by the public on behalf of the children left behind by the destructive murder. The *Morpeth Herald*[5] reported an unequal bias in favour of Henry's children. The figure forwarded to Mrs. Henry Wainwright later reached a huge sum. But not so the collection for Caroline and her children.

> The Wainwrights. – We understand that the sum raised by the Under-Sheriffs, Messrs. Baylis, and Crawford, for the Wilmore fund amounts about £280. These gentlemen have also collected £70 for Mrs. Henry Wainwright, and £17 for Mrs. Thomas Wainwright. The smallness of these latter sums is owing to the subscription fund opened by the Rev. Mr. Conder, of Bognor, on behalf of Mrs. Henry Wainwright. The two children of the late Harriet Lane are at present under the care of their aunt, Mrs Turner but it is contemplated buying them into an asylum, but this cannot be done at present, on account of 'the youth of the younger child.

When the Old Bailey trial had finished, Thomas was banished to Portland Gaol, leaving Caroline to fend for herself and their two young children, then aged 7 and 3. It could not have been easy, and her health would sadly suffer. With no one to help except Parish relief or the workhouse, how would she get by? Things were to take a turn for the worse two years into Thomas' sentence when Caroline succumbed to the dreaded scourge on the Victorians; tuberculosis (TB). Caroline Wainwright passed away on 7 April 1877 at Melverne Cottages, Hawley Road, Camden Town, she was only 31 years old. The death certificate[6] gave the cause of death as 'phthisis pulmonalis', which is the old-fashioned name for TB.[7] It was also commonly referred to as 'consumption'.

Herbert Brockly Wainwright

After the death of his mother in 1877, and the imprisonment of his father (from 1875 – 1881), Caroline and Thomas' son, Herbert Brockly Wainwright, had effectively become an orphan. Who would now care for him? A family member might have been prevailed upon to take him in, as often happened in those days, but one person that we can assume wasn't applying for that particular job was the wife of Henry Wainwright. Indeed, Elizabeth Wainwright had changed her identity and was now calling herself Worthington to try and distance herself from the scandal of the case. She had been well provided for by the charitable collection that had been made for her and her five children. Her charity, however, did not extend to Thomas and Caroline's offspring.

In 1881, we find Herbert living far away from the East End in Bisley near Woking, Surrey. The Census[8] entry revealed that he was an 11-year-old schoolboy from Whitechapel. His new abode was the Farm School, Bisley. In 1867 the National Refuges for Homeless and Destitute Children[9] began to look for accommodation in the countryside to house boys from London. They found a site at Bisley which became the Farm School and Country Home in 1868. The home could accommodate 150 boys, usually aged between 10 to 12 at the time of admission, and who had been homeless or destitute, but crucially, not convicted of any crime. It's not clear if Herbert's father's criminal record would have been mentioned on his application form.

The boys were taught farming skills, carpentry, tailoring and bread making. The Census of 1881 reveals that most of the boys were born in London, though not exclusively so. Some boys being born in far-away places such as Aberdeen in the north, to Weymouth on the south coast. *The Illustrated London News*[10] reported the opening of the school at Christmas 1868. The article carried a drawing of the fine early Gothic looking school building, entitled 'Home for Destitute Boys, Bisley, Surrey'.[11] The article also stated that the school was intended for the 'reformation and employment of destitute and homeless boys of London'.

After being given an education at Bisley, Herbert didn't have a 'home' to return to, so he left one institution to join another: The British Army. He joined the Royal Sussex Regiment, and in 1891 was based at the regiments home at the Chichester Barracks, later renamed the Roussillon Barracks. The Census for 1891[12] recorded that Herbert was a 20-year-old single man and a private in the Royal Sussex Regiment having been born in London. Most of the other soldiers in the barracks were Sussex men, and most were very young. The youngest in the list was a 15-year-old drummer, William Henry Ford.

After being in the Army the trail for Herbert runs cold and, frustratingly, I cannot discover what happened to him after 1881.

Daisy Louise Wainwright

Daisy was born on 22 November 1872 at Melverne Cottages, Hawley Road, Kentish Town, though she wasn't baptised until almost four years later on 27 August 1876, at Holy Trinity Church,[13] Haverstock Hill, when her father, Thomas, was in prison. Like her brother and father, her life is something of a mystery and no trace can be found of her in any of the usual public records.

The only one appearance that she did make was in the Probate Register[14] for 1909, many years after the death of her mother in 1877 and the disappearance of her father after he left prison in 1881. In 1909 she was named on two separate probate applications for both her parents. On the applications she had retained her original name, was still unmarried and gave her address as 16 Gladsmuir Road, Upper Holloway. She was referred to as the 'natural lawful daughter, and one of the next of kin'. This house still stands and is a nice looking, late Victorian three floor terraced house.

The report stated that Thomas George Wainwright, a widower, had died intestate, and gave his address as 6 Albert Square, Commercial Road, Middlesex. It added that he had died ON OR SINCE, 19 August 1881. The probate certificate gave the value of the estate as not exceeding £100 'as far as present can be ascertained'. Presumably Daisy had also lost track of her father after his release from custody.

The probate record[15] for her mother, Caroline, was registered five days after Thomas' and was also in the sum of £100. Due to the lack of information, it's hard to know what happened to any assets that Caroline and Thomas may have had. The £100 mentioned was possibly an, 'up to, but not more than £100' figure. There is no mention of Herbert Wainwright on the paperwork, suggesting that she was no longer in touch with him, or he was dead. Why did Daisy wait until 32 years after her mother's death to apply for probate? There was also a 28-year gap between her father's disappearance and her applying for his estate.

Appendix V

List of Main Characters

Allen, Sophia – Oldfield Road, Maidenhead
Harriet's sister who identified scar on her leg

Andrews, William – Pearl Street, Spitalfields
Cab driver (number 8505) who took Henry Wainwright and the body to the Borough from Whitechapel

Baylis, John – 149 Whitechapel Road
Sold an order of chloride of lime to Wainwright

Chabot Charles – Red Lion Square
Handwriting expert who compared Thomas Wainwright's writing to the Frieake letter and found them identical

Conder, Alfred – Rector of Middleton Sussex
Organised a charitable collection of money for Mrs Wainwright and her children

Day, Alice – 8 Queen's Court, Greenfield Street, Commercial Road
Ballet dancer friend of Henry Wainwright who accepted a lift in the cab containing the body of Harriet Lane

Eeles, Ernest George (aka Fowler)
Missing person enquiry officer – Charity Organisation Society, Wandsworth

Frieake, Edward William – 11 Coleman Street, City, and auction-rooms at 14 and 15, Aldgate
Auctioneer friend of Henry Wainwright who was impersonated by Thomas Wainwright

Foster, Jemima – 3 Sidney Square
Landlady of Sidney Square where Harriet lodged just before her disappearance. She met 'Mr Frieake'

Graydon, William
Rowlandson Upholsterers, 83 Whitechapel Road – Sold 2 yards of American cloth to H. Wainwright

Humphries, James
Proprietor of Princess Royal Public House 1–2 Sidney Square

Johnston, Francis – The Mount Whitechapel Road
Builder and decorator Whitechapel Road, obscured a window at 215 for Henry Wainwright in 1874

Kay, James – 7 Barchester Street, Poplar
Blacksmith at Wisemans Coachbuilders, 216 Whitechapel Road – heard 3 pistol shots

Kay, William
Wheeler at Wisemans Coachbuilders 216 Whitechapel Road – heard 3 pistol shots

King, Beatrice Wainwright
Illegitimate daughter of Harriet Lane and Henry Wainwright

King, Miriam Wainwright
Illegitimate daughter of Harriet Lane and Henry Wainwright

Lane, Harriet Louisa (AKA Mrs King)
Victim of Murder by Henry Wainwright

Lane, John
Father of victim, Harriet Lane

L'Enfant, Charles Grojean Rennie
Clerk of Bankruptcy Court – gives evidence of H. Wainwright's bankruptcy – 30 June 1875

Lloyd Jones, F.E, Reverend
Chaplain at Newgate Gaol

Martin, Edward – 78 New Road
Corn, rice and brush business owner, employer of Stokes and latterly Henry Wainwright

Marwood, Thomas
Public Executioner who hanged Henry Wainwright

Mapperson, Robert
Chief warder at Newgate who supervised the burial of Henry Wainwright

Moore
Business partner of Thomas Wainwright who absconded with £600 and who Henry wanted to blame for the murder

Payne, William John
Coroner for Southwark, conducted the inquest of both Harriet and Henry

Pettigrew, Frederick – Ironmonger, 81 Whitechapel Road
Sold spade and axe to Thomas Wainwright

Pelham, Walter John
Henry Wainwright's Solicitor

Pinnell, John Hood – Oilman, 214 Whitechapel Road
Sold a length of rope to Henry Wainwright

Rogers, George William – 11 Teddington Terrace, Tredegar Road, Bow
Delivered messages from Henry Wainwright to Mrs King

Rogers, Jane
Witnessed Henry Wainwright quarrelling with Mrs King who then was found on the floor.

Sawyer Charles – wholesale brush maker at 63 and 65, Southwark Bridge Road
Former partner of Henry Wainwright – Found bullets belonging to him in his office

Smith, Sidney – Governor of Newgate Prison
Witnessed Henry Wainwright's statement

Squires, James – Gunmaker, Newcastle Road, Whitechapel
Examined the bullets which killed Harriet Lane

Stanley, Amelie – of Bow
Relation of Mrs Foster who had seen 'Mr Frieake'

Steel, John Matthew – Foreman to William Dicker, a pawnbroker in the Commercial Road
Accepted a ring and keeper from Harriet Lane in pawn

Stokes, Alfred Philip – 34 Bakers Row, Whitechapel
Key prosecution witness who ran after the cab containing the body of Harriet Lane

Taylor, Elizabeth – 7 Clarendon Mews, Hyde Park
Sister of victim – Identified the body of Harriet

Taylor, William – 7 Clarendon Mews, Hyde Park
Brother-in-law of victim – Identified body of Harriet

Varco, Louisa
Alias name used by Harriet Lane

Wainwright, Caroline (Nee Brockley)
Wife of Thomas Wainwright who died from TB while her husband was in prison

Wainwright, Daisy Louise
Daughter of Thomas and Caroline

Wainwright, Henry (AKA Mr Percy King)
Convicted of the Murder of Harriet Lane

Wainwright, Herbert Brockley
Son of Thomas and Caroline

Wainwright, Thomas George
Brother of Henry Wainwright, convicted of being an accessory after the fact to murder

Wainwright, William
Brother of Henry and Thomas Wainwright. Committed suicide

Wells, Susan – 12 Valentine Road, South Hackney
Landlady of 44 St Peter Street – who let rooms to Mrs King – She saw 'Mr Frieake' at her premises

Wilmore, Ellen – 36 Maryland Street, Stratford
Friend of victim who looked after Harriet Lane's children

Wiseman, James – Wisemans Coachbuilders, 216 and 217 Whitechapel Road
Son of owner of Wisemans – heard 3 pistol shots

Young, Henry
Discovered a terrible smell in 215 Whitechapel Road

Metropolitan Police

Butler, John – Deputy Surveyor to the Metropolitan Police Force
Made a model of 215 Whitechapel Road and the Hen and Chickens

Cox, Arthur William Pc 290M – 'M' Division
Together with Pc Turner – Arrested Henry Wainwright and Alice Day

Forster, George William Detective Sergeant – 'H' Division
Arrested Thomas Wainwright

Fox, Matthew Insp – 'M' Division – Inspector – Stone End Police Station
Searched 215 Whitechapel Road

Garforth, Thomas – Superintendent – Stones End Police Station
Involved in the prosecution of the Wainwright's at court

McDonald, James Constantine – Chief Inspector – 'H' Division
Searched 215 Whitechapel Road – Gave Thomas Wainwright a statement form to write down his evidence

Newman, Joseph – Detective Constable – 'H' Division
Searched 215 Whitechapel Road

Turner, Henry Pc 48M – 'M' Division
Together with Pc Cox, Arrested Henry Wainwright and Alice Day

Legal Teams

The judge – Lord Chief-Justice of England
Sir Alexander James Edmund Cockburn

Counsel for the Crown – Instructed by Mr Pollard on behalf of the Treasury
Attorney General Sir John Holker Q.C.
Sir Harry Bodkin Poland
Mr Besley

Counsel for Henry Wainwright – Instructed by Mr W.J. Pelham
Mr Edward Besley
Mr Douglas Straight
Mr Tickell
Mr C.F. Gill

Counsel for Thomas Wainwright – Instructed by Mr Long
Mr George Moody

Medical Witnesses for the Crown

Bond, Thomas FRCS – 50 Parliament Street, Westminster – Surgeon Westminster Hospital
Examined the body of Harriet Lane with Dr Larkin. Vital prosecution witness

Larkin, Frederick George – Surgeon of 44 Trinity Square
Examined the body of Harriet Lane with Dr Bond. Vital prosecution witness

Representative for Alice Day at Southwark Police Court
Louis Lewis

Medical Witnesses for the Defence

Aubin, Frederick George – RCS – 519 Commercial Road
Examined the body of Harriet Lane for the defence

Meadows, Alfred FRCP – Physician and lecturer on midwifery at St. Mary's Hospital
Examined the uterus on the body of Harriet Lane for the defence

Appendix VI

Timeline of Events

13 October 1838
Henry Wainwright born

17 January 1852
Harriet Lane born

7 August 1862
Henry Wainwright marries Elizabeth Fanny Minshull

1871
Henry Wainwright meets Harriet Lane

10 February 1872
Henry Wainwright & Harriet Lane advertise a 'marriage' as Mr & Mrs King

7 August 1872
Harriet Lane gives birth to child Beatrice Wainwright King

3 December 1873
A second child is born – Miriam Wainwright King

15 March 1874
Henry Wainwright meets his creditors

May 1874
Harriet Lane moves to lodgings in Sidney Square

September 1874
Wainwright executes a mortgage on his premises in Whitechapel Road

10 September 1874
Wainwright buys chloride of lime

11 September 1874
Harriet Lane leaves her lodgings at Sidney Square to meet Henry Wainwright, and is never seen alive again

11 September 1874
Harriet Lane is murdered in Whitechapel Road

17 October 1874
'Edward Frieake' telegraphs from Dover that he has gone to the continent with Harriet Lane

November 1874
Thomas Wainwright starts an ironmongery business at the Hen & Chickens, Borough, High Street

27 November 1874
Fire at 84 Whitechapel Road. The insurance company dispute the claim from Wainwright

30 June 1875
Henry Wainwright's bankruptcy hearing

July 1875
The mortgagee takes official possession of the premises at 215 Whitechapel Road

10 September 1875
Henry & Thomas Wainwright buy American cloth, a spade and a chopper

11 September 1875
Henry Wainwright and Alice Day are both arrested

13 September 1875
Henry Wainwright and Alice Day appear at Southwark Police Court

15 September 1875
Inquest opens before the Southwark coroner

21 September 1875
Southwark Police Court second hearing. Henry Wainwright is charged with the murder of Harriet Lane. Alice Day is discharged

28 September 1875
A further remand hearing at Southwark Police Court for Henry Wainwright

1 October 1875
Coroner's inquest is resumed

2 October 1875
Thomas Wainwright is arrested and charged with being an accessory to murder

5 October 1875
Thomas and Henry Wainwright appear together for the first time at Southwark Police Court

6 October 1875
Thomas and Henry Wainwright's committal hearing continues at Southwark Police Court

12–13 October 1875
Henry and Thomas were committed to stand trial at the Central Criminal Court

14 October 1875
Coroner's jury verdict that the body is that of Harriet Lane, wilfully murdered by Henry Wainwright

19 October 1875
Funeral of Harriet Lane

27 October 1875
Thomas and Henry enter 'not guilty' pleas at the preliminary hearing at the Central Criminal Court

10 November 1875
Henry Wainwright is declared bankrupt

22 November 1875
Trial begins at the Old Bailey

1 December 1875
Henry Wainwright is convicted and sentenced to death. Thomas sentenced to seven years.

20 December 1875
The Home Secretary rejects the appeal for clemency for Henry Wainwright

21 December 1875
Henry Wainwright is executed at Newgate Prison

7 April 1877
Thomas Wainwright's wife, Caroline, dies from tuberculosis while Thomas is still in prison

1881
Thomas Wainwright is released from prison – and disappears!

1909
Thomas Wainwright's daughter, Daisy, applies for probate for the estates of both his parents

Notes

Chapter One

1. 1871 Census, RG10/561, P9 schedule 42; Mile End Old Town
2. Similar properties to this normally sell today, for around £1.5M. Rightmove c 2016
3. *Trial of the Wainwrights* by H.B. Irving
4. Principle Registry, Probate report dated 10 Nov 1863, p. 63, death occurred 27 Oct 1863
5. Will of Henry William Wainwright, in 4 pages, dated 8 April 1862, by solicitor Charles Champion. See chapter 2 for further details of the will
6. *Hobart Mercury*, 22 Nov 1875
7. Born Henry Wainwright, 13 Oct 1838 at 4 Thomas Street, Whitechapel to Henry William Wainwright and Elizabeth Wainwright formerly Rickards. Birth cert 408, Whitechapel North District
8. St Dunstan's & All Saints Parish Church, High Street, Stepney. Marriage certificate 7 Aug 1862; p. 57, cert no. 113.
9. Marriage notice, mentioned in *Aris Birmingham Gazette*, 16 Aug 1862
10. https://www.bankofengland.co.uk/monetary-policy/inflation/inflation-calculator
11. **Henry** 21 Oct 1863–25 July 1945; **Amy Elizabeth** 9 June 1865–27 Feb 1941; **Dora Rose Blanche** 19 May 1867–24 Feb 1942; **Sydney Rickards** 29 Mar 1869–22 Oct 1924; **Lillian Flora** 4 June 1871–16 Sept 1953
12. The Probate Register, dated 10 November 1863, p. 63
13. Last Will and Testament of Henry William Wainwright, 8 April 1862
14. There is no breakdown of values so we cannot be sure how much Henry's share was worth.
15. Baptism of Henry Minshull Wainwright, at St Dunstan's Church, Stepney. (P 338, Baptism register; entry no 2700.) Bapt on 31 Dec 1863 to Henry and Elizabeth Fanny Wainwright
16. *Trial of the Wainwrights*, by H.B. Irving; Page xix
17. *A Cosmopolitan Actor*, by J.B. Howe. **Mr J.B. Howe** (1828–1908) Handsome thespian with flowing locks judging by the drawing of him in his book, *A Cosmopolitan Actor*. His real name was Thomas Burdett Howe. He was known to his friends as *'Jaybe'*, as in his initials, *'J.B'*. Those initials had been printed incorrectly at the theatre as J.B. rather than T.B. and he never bothered to change it. He often appeared at the Pavilion Theatre, next to Henry Wainwright's premises at 84 Whitechapel Road. The Victoria and

Albert Museum hold 3 photographs of Mr Howe. **Sources:** The Era, 14 Mar 1908, (Page 15 & photo); Daily Telegraph, 13 Mar 1908; Middlesex Express, 16 Mar 1908; online copy of A Cosmopolitan Actor, by J.B. Howe, Chap XXIX, page 219 https://babel.hathitrust.org/cgi/pt?id=njp.32101066164185&view=1up&seq=7&skin=2021

18. *Penny Illustrated Paper*, 25 Sept 1875, p. 198
19. Harriet was christened on 15 Feb 1852 at Holy Trinity Church, Weymouth; Baptism Register, no. 175. (Birth 17 Jan 1852)
20. 1871 Census, Waltham Abbey, Reference; RG10/1347; schedule 173, p. 32
21. *The Trial of the Wainwrights.* Page 30, frame 86. https://archive.org/details/cihm_77835/page/n83/mode/2up
22. Ann Bray, nee Gater, the daughter of William Gater, was born in Cheshunt on 29 Jan 1832. In the 1861 Census she was living at Crossbrook Street, Cheshunt (*RG 9/802*; Folio: *42*; P 1.)
23. *Wolverhampton Express & Star*, 5 Oct 1875, p. 4
24. This woman was Mrs Mary Raper.
25. *South London Press*, 21 Apr 1866, p. 7

Chapter Two
1. *Lloyds Weekly London* Newspaper, 26 Sep 1875, p. 2
2. *Midland Counties Evening Express*, 21 Dec 1875, p. 3
3. *Trial of the Wainwright*s, by H.B. Irving; Page xxii
4. *Trial of the Wainwrights*, by H.B. Irving Page xxiii
5. Birth cert no. 394; Beatrice Wainwright King, 7 August 1872, Mile End district
6. Baptism Register no 807, St Dunstan's Church, Stepney; Lillian Flora Wainwright, born 11 June 1871, baptised 5 July 1871
7. *Waltham Abbey and Cheshunt Weekly Telegraph*, 10 Feb 1872. The date intimated for the wedding in the newspaper article is 22 Jan 1872
8. Distance between Henry's home and Harriet's accommodation, 1.8 miles, (Google Maps)
9. Birth cert no. 79; Miriam Wainwright King, 3 Dec 1873, Bethnal Green district
10. Reported to be £11,000 from his father's estate, shared with his brothers and sister. *The Trial of the Wainwrights*, page xix
11. *Lloyds List* newspaper, 4 Jan 1873
12. *Shipping and Mercantile Gazette*, 11 July 1874
13. *Batley Guardian*, 18 Sept 1875
14. *Trial of The Wainwrights*, edited by H.B. Irving. Page 67
15. *Trial of The Wainwrights*, edited by H.B. Irving. Page 31
16. The Dicker's pawn tickets exist in the National Archives under reference TS 18/1. The first ticket is dated May 1874, serial no. 1246. The item is described as a 'keeper' valued at 8 shillings, and is in the name of 'King, 3 Sidney Square'. The second ticket is dated May 1874, serial no. 1146. The item is described as a 'wedding ring' valued at 10 shillings, and is in the same name'.
17. *Trial of The Wainwrights*, edited by H.B. Irving. Page 41

Chapter Three

1. I walked the route that Harriet would likely have made on 11 Sept 1874. It was an easy 10-minute stroll in a busy part of Whitechapel

2. The weather for London on 11 September 1874 was 64F (18C) and cloudy according to the Royal Observatory, Greenwich readings reported in the *London Evening Standard*, 13 Sep 1875, P6

Chapter Four

1. *The Hour* newspaper, 25 Nov 1875, pp. 5–7

2. Royal Philharmonic Theatre, Islington

3. He was correct. The London Post Office Directory, business section for 1875 only lists, '*Mr Edward William Frieake, auctioneer, 11 Coleman Street and also, 14 Aldgate High Street*' on page 916. The alphabetical list contains numerous Friedlander's, Frigout's, Fripp's, and Frisby's, but only one Frieake. The Street Index section only listed one Frieake in the whole of the Metropolis. (online on Ancestry.com)

4. **Edward William Frieake** was baptised on 22 Jan 1843 at St Dunstan's Church, Stepney. During his evidence, he stated that he had not wanted the false information about '*Teddy Frieake*' going off with another woman to spoil things between him and his intended. He got married a little under 2 years later at St Mary's, Walthamstow when he married, Mary Paget on 20 Oct 1877. Tragedy struck 4 months later, Edward died, aged 35, leaving his new bride a widow for the rest of her life.

5. LETTER 'A', Sunday night, National Archives Ref TS 18/1

6. LETTER 'E', Charing Cross Hotel, Wednesday, National Archives, Ref TS 18

7. Frieake wrote to the The Weekly Dispatch who published his letter in their 26 Sep 1875, edition, p. 12. The letter stated the following: 'I most emphatically state that I never saw Harriet Lane in my life.' He added that the letter alleged to have beeen written by him was a fake

8. Edward Frieake's business card National Archives. File ref TS 18/1.

Chapter Five

1. Hen and Chickens. This building still survives at 54 Borough High Street. The premises are currently an estate-agents.

2. Trials of the Old Bailey. https://www.oldbaileyonline.org/browse.jsp?id=def1-1-18751122&div=t18751122-1#highlight

3. The '*court*' referred to is Vine Court, the dog legged lane at the rear of the building which allowed access to the rear entrance of 215 Whitechapel Road.

4. The Plumbers Arms pub on the corner of Greenfield Street is long gone. The chemist shop referred to by Stokes was Bell Edwards & Co, 100 Commercial Road, (Post Office London Directory 1875, Page 1572), and is directly opposite where the pub would have stood. Later on, Dr Frederick Blackwell, was resident at 100 Commercial Road and 1 and 1a Batty Street. In 1888 he

had been the first doctor to have been summoned by the police to the body of Jack the Ripper victim, Elizabeth Stride. (www.stgite.org.uk)

5. Trials of the Old Bailey. https://www.oldbaileyonline.org/browse.jsp?id=def1-1-18751122&div=t18751122-1#highlight
6. Why Alfred Stokes didn't simply hail his own cab and follow Wainwright? Perhaps because he was a working man without spare cash for a cab ride?
7. The City of London Police, were formed in 1832.
8. Trials of the Old Bailey. https://www.oldbaileyonline.org/browse.jsp?id=def1-1-18751122&div=t18751122-1#highlight
9. The exact spot in which the cab appears to be is at Southwark Street opposite the Hop Exchange and there is a narrow lane called 'Borough High Street', which leads down to the Hen and Chickens. There is an 'island' of buildings at this spot which then housed the Town Hall and a bank. When I visited this location in 2021, my black cab dropped me off in precisely the same spot. The Hop Exchange was a single market centre for dealers in the hop/beer trade. Southwark was an important centre for hops. (Wikipedia https://en.wikipedia.org/wiki/Hop_Exchange)
10. Trials of the Old Bailey. https://www.oldbaileyonline.org/browse.jsp?id=def1-1-18751122&div=t18751122-1#highlight
11. A check of the local papers identified the unnamed 'PC 310M' as Pc William Knight. London Evening Standard, 9 Oct 1875, p. 3
12. PC 48M Turner, correct name, Alfred Henry Turner (London evening Standard, 14 Sep 1875); Born Stockland, Devon c 1842. He and Pc Cox both received a commendation regarding the arrest. (Police Orders 27 Dec 1875
13. PC 290M Cox, Arthur William Cox, Born Sidmouth, Devon 7 Jun 1844. Warrant number 45639. He had accumulated 26 commendations during his service. (Service 27 Dec 1864–4 May 1891)

Chapter Six
1. Insp Matthew Fox, Born 3 Jun 1833, Carrick on Shannon. Died, 22 Dec 1889. (Service; 9 Apr 1860–28 Nov 1885
2. Supt Thomas Garforth, Born 3 Oct 1821, St Albans. Died 14 Oct 1888. (Service 28; Aug 1843–5 Nov 1879)
3. Trials of the Old Bailey. https://www.oldbaileyonline.org/browse.jsp?id=def1-1-18751122&div=t18751122-1#highlight
4. Dr Frederick Larkin later examined the body of Harriet Lane
5. The Primary Objects, were written by Sir Richard Mayne in 1829
6. 'The Job', is a name given by police officers to policing. Inspector Fox never married
7. Trials of the Old Bailey. https://www.oldbaileyonline.org/browse.jsp?id=def1-1-18751122&div=t18751122-1#highlight
8. The search of the house was mentioned in a report marked, 'Regina v Wainwright', a report from Inspector Fox to the Crown lawyers, from National Archives file, ref TS 18–1
9. *Penny Illustrated* Newspaper, 25 Sep 1875, P198

10. They probably got off at Higham's Park Station, the last but one stop on the Walthamstow and Chingford Branch
11. The report on the coat from Inspector Fox to the Crown lawyers, from National Archives, ref TS 18–1. The apparent lack of blood did not mean Henry was not the murderer, simply that he probably was not wearing it at the timeThe report on the coat from Inspector Fox to the Crown lawyers, from National Archives, ref TS 18–1. The apparent lack of blood did not mean Henry was *not* the murderer, simply that he probably was not wearing it at the time

Chapter Seven
1. *The Police Illustrated News*, 23 Oct 1875, Supplement edition
2. Horsemonger Lane Gaol, was completed in 1799 and was Surrey's principal prison and place of execution until its closure in 1878. It housed a capacity of around 300 inmates. 131 men and 4 women were executed there between 1800 and 1877.
3. *The London Evening Standard*, 11 Sep 1875, p. 2
4. *Weekly Dispatch*, 26 Sep 1875, p. 11
5. *Buckingham Express*, 25 Sep 1875, p. 2
6. *Weekly Dispatch*, 26 Sep 1975, p. 11
7. *Weekly Dispatch*, 25 Sep 75, p. 12
8. *London Evening Standard*, 29 Sep 1875, p. 6
9. *The York Herald*, 4 Oct 1875, p. 7
10. *London Evening Standard*, 6 Oct 1875, p. 2
11. *The Evening Standard*, 7 Oct 1875, p. 2
12. *The Morning Post,* 13 Oct 1875, p. 6
13. *The Globe*, 14 Oct 1875, p. 2
14. George Moody was born on 21 Sep 1832, Exmouth Street, Clerkenwell. (Baptism Register St Johns Church Entry 692, p. 87). He died 22 Nov 1886 in Brixton
15. Ralph Augustus Benson, Southwark Police Court Magistrate. Eldest son of Met Police magistrate, Moses George Benson. A barrister and magistrate, he inherited Lutwyche Hall, Shropshire and a large estate from his father. He died on 11 March 1886 at 3 Montague Square, Marylebone
16. 'The Big House' is a slang term used by police officers to describe a crown court
17. The names of the jury members were recorded on the National Archives case file Register no. 42722
18. *The Globe* Newspaper, 15 Sep 1875
19. *The Illustrated Police News*, 25 Sep 1875
20. Coroner, Mr William John Payne. Born 19 Oct 1822 at Aldermanbury, London, son of William Payne, (Attorney), (OPR 172 Baptism Register, 1822, St Mary's Aldermanbury). His father was the Coroner for Southwark and the City of London before him. Payne died at his residence, Font Hill, Reigate on 14 April 1884,
21. Coroner's sheets NA File TS/18/1, p. 39

Chapter Eight
1. *Evening Standard*, 21 Oct 1875, p. 6
2. *Croydon Weekly Standard*, 16 Oct 1875

Chapter Nine
1. *The Penny Illustrated Paper*, 8 Jan 1876, p. 31
2. *Belfast Telegraph*, 19 Feb 1876
3. The cost of the *Daily Telegraph* and the *Illustrated Police News* in 1875 was one penny each
4. St Mary Church, Whitechapel, Baptism Register, 27 Oct 1861, p. 44

Chapter Ten
1. The current Old Bailey, was rebuilt in 1907
2. The Great Hall was described by Stephen Fry as '*awe inspiring*' during his visit to the Old Bailey in his TV documentary; Key to the City – Exploring the Mysteries of the City of London
3. The name 'old bailey' comes from the street on which the court is located. The road marks the route of the City of London's original fortified wall, or 'bailey'
4. Picture 1, 'The Central Criminal Court during the trials of Henry & Thomas Wainwright', The Graphic, 4 Dec 1875, page 541; Picture 2, 'The Whitechapel Tragedy – Trial of the Wainwrights at the Old Bailey'. *Illustrated Police News*, 27 Nov 1875
5. *he Globe*, 23 Nov 1875, p. 2
6. *Stroud News & Gloucester Advertiser*, 5 Nov 1875
7. **John Matthew Steel**. According to all his census entries, he was a career pawnbroker who was born in Fulham in 1849, died 1908
8. Calendar of Prisoners; Old Bailey / Newgate
9. *Penny Illustrated Paper*, 27 Nov 1875
10. **John Butler** (B. 1831; London). He was the Metropolitan Police Surveyor. His son, John Dixon Butler (1860–1920) was responsible for building around 200 buildings, mostly police stations
11. *Worcestershire Chronicle*, 27 Nov 1875, p. 7
12. *Dundee Courier*, 4 Dec 1875

Chapter Eleven
1. *The Daily Telegraph*, 24 Nov 1875, p. 2
2. *Evening Standard*, 24 Nov 1875, p. 2
3. *The Evening Standard*, 24 Nov 1875, p. 2
4. *The Trial of the Wainwrights*, by H.B. Irving

Chapter Twelve
1. *The Globe*, 24 Nov 1875, p. 5
2. Frustratingly, no photograph of Harriet appears to have survived. Photos of Henry and Thomas Wainwright as well as Alice Day are all still in existence
3. *The Hour*, 25 Nov 1875, p. 5–7

4. 'Southwark Station House', was Southwark Police Court
5. Letter 'I', 5 September 1874, National Archives Ref TS 18/1
6. *The Trial of the Wainwrights* book, by B.H. Irving. A good amount of the information in this chapter has been extracted from this book. Various newspaper accounts and the text of the trial in the book regularly differ slightly on some points, so both sources have been included.

Chapter Thirteen
1. The evidence for this witness and all the others was obtained from the book, *Trial of the Wainwrights* by H.B.Irving. pp. 76–101
2. Henry's gun was never found by the police, but was more than likely either thrown in the Thames or pawned elsewhere in London
3. Both pawn tickets can be seen in the file at the National Archives. Ticket 1246 for the 'Keeper' ring, dated 22 May 1874; Ticket 1146 for 'Wedding' Ring, dated May 1874; National Archives Reference; TS 18/1
4. *Daily Telegraph*, 26 Nov 1875, p. 2

Chapter Fourteen
1. *Daily Telegraph*, 27 Nov 1875, p. 2
2. *The Hour* newspaper, 27 Nov 1875, p. 5
3. *The Hour* newspaper, 27 Nov 1875, p. 6
4. Charles Grojean Rennie L'Enfant (1831- 1904). Born in Middlesex in 1831, he became an accountant (1851 Census; HO107/1496, page 41, sch 137), before working as a clerk in the Bankruptcy Court. (1881 Census; living at 8 Sedgwick St, Hackney). His name often appeared in the newspapers giving evidence regarding bankruptcy in criminal fraud trials.
5. Charles Chabot (1815–1882). Born on 28 Jan 1815. (Born as a twin, baptised St Mary's, Battersea; Baptism Register Page 28.) He began his working life as a lithographer and later a zincographer, which are both methods of printing. (1851 Census, Lloyds Square, Finsbury, HO 107/1517, p. 23 Sch 63). He later became a hand writing expert. He later lived at 26 Albert Square, Vauxhall where he was described as an 'expert in handwriting'. (1871 Census, RG10/672, p. 23 Sch 92).
6. Chabot's 3-page letter, (National Archives, Ref TS/ 18–1)
7. *Trial of the Wainwrights*, by H.B. Irving, p. 113.

Chapter Fifteen
1. *The Trial of the Wainwrights*. Edited by H.B. Irvine
2. The chopper found *could* have been used to cut up Harriet Lanes corpse
3. Two bullets from the pistol entered Harriet's skull, though the third bullet was prevented from entering her head due to the many pins in the pad of her hair.
4. Why was Harriet's throat cut, and cut with such force? Had the murderer decided to shut her up for good and finish her off?
5. It's interesting to hear that Dr Larkin didn't mind 'taking his work home with him'.

6. The dental evidence was key in adding another element to proving that the deceased *was* Harriet Lane

7. The finding of the scar was of huge value to the identification. It was also very helpful that Dr Aubyn, (defence witness for Henry), was present at its finding to make sure that the evidence could be relied upon

8. Although he doesn't prove it's where the body what chopped up, the jury would likely have assumed that that was where the dissection had taken place

9. This is a frustrating piece of evidence. Did Dr Larkin mean to say that the exact missing teeth (minus the 2 that were never found), were the exact teeth that were found?

10. This evidence ruled out suicide as a cause of death, not that anyone but an optimistic defence counsel would have dared to offer that implausible suggestion

11. Frederick Larkin 1847–1927. His practice was at 44 Trinity Square, Southwark (Royal College of Surgeons website). Larkin's, *'Report of Post Mortem Examination of the remains of Harriet Lane in the Whitechapel Tragedy'* was published in the British Medical Journal; 1875, ii,730

12. Thomas Bond; Divisional Surgeon for 'A' Division Met Police, Wikipedia. https://en.wikipedia.org/wiki/Thomas_Bond_(British_surgeon)   He committed suicide by throwing himself out of his third floor window to his death 50 feet below (*The Penny Illustrated Paper*, 15 Jun 1901)

13. *Trial of the Wainwrights* by H.B. Irving, p. 123

14. The scar was later placed in a glass jar and was on display at the Black Museum. A drawing of the jar appears in the Illustrated Police News on 26 July 1891

15. A photograph marked "Relics of the Wainwright Case: Fragments of cigar, bullet and knife. (Black Museum) exists. (The bullet appears to be a slightly conical shape and is flat. It doesn't look particularly like a conventional bullet shape). Thanks to Lindsay Sivitar for a copy of this photograph.

16. A colour photo of the remains of Harriet Lane's ringlets of hair appears in a book called *Scotland Yard History of Crime in 100 objects* by Alan Moss and Keith Skinner (Chapter 18, 'Chignon'). A chignon is a hairstyle where hair can be built around a pin or other accessory

Chapter Sixteen
1. *Hour* newspaper, 29 Nov 1875, p. 5
2. *Hour* newspaper, 29 Nov 1875, p. 5
3. *Trial of the Wainwrights* by H.B. Irving, pp. 131–150

Chapter Seventeen
1. Dr Alfred Meadows, 1833–1887.
2. *Trial of the Wainwrights*, p. 150
3. Frederick George Aubyn, 1832–1906
4. *Trial of the Wainwrights*, p. 152
5. *Trial of the Wainwrights*, p. 228
6. *Trial of the Wainwrights*, pp. 154–7

7. *Trial of the Wainwrights*, p. 158
8. *The Hour* newspaper, 29 Nov 1875, p. 7

Chapter Eighteen
1. *London Evening Standard*, 30 Nov 1875, p. 2
2. *The Hour* newspaper, 30 Nov 1875, p. 5
3. *Trial of the Wainwrights*, by H.B. Irving, p. 165
4. *The Trial of the Wainwrights* by H.B. Irving, pp. 165–177, 180; Also see *The Hour* newspaper 30 Nov 1875, p. 5–6. Both sources combine in the section marked 'main points of Mr Moody's summing up'

Chapter Nineteen
1. *The London Evening Standard*, 1 Dec 1875, p. 2
2. Ch. Inspector Robert Alexander Tillcock, City of London Police. (1826–1888). He served for 44 years with the City of London Police, Pall Mall Gazette, 28 May 1888
3. Hour newspaper, 1 Dec 1875, p. 5
4. *Trial of the Wainwrights*, by H.B. Irving, pp. 181–205. Also used was *The London Evening Standard*, 1 Dec 1875, pp. 2–3

Chapter Twenty
1. *London Evening Standard*, 1 Dec 1875, pp. 2–3; and *Trial of the Wainwrights* by H.B. Irving, pp. 199–205; The Hour newspaper, 1 D

Chapter Twenty-One
1. Trial of the Wainwrights, by H.B. Irving; Charge to the Jury; page 206–232
2. **Circumstantial evidence:** For example, a witness could give evidence that he saw the defendant go up to the victim and say, within his hearing, 'Hey Smithy, you have been seeing my girl, I'm going to do for you, you rascal', and then punch the man on the nose causing him to fall to the ground. This witness can give 'direct evidence' of the threats and the actual assault. Circumstantial evidence is not as conclusive as direct evidence, but it can still be very useful and compelling. The was never going to be any direct evidence of Henry Wainwright killing Harriet Lane, as no one was present when it occurred. So how can we build a case against him? Circumstantial evidence is evidence which is not taken from direct observation of a fact or event, but is one that is inferred from a set of circumstances relating to an event. For example, you could give circumstantial evidence that you left a gold watch on the counter of your shop which contains only one male customer. You then go into a side room for a few moments leaving the man unsupervised. On your return you see that the watch has gone and that the man is running out of the shop. You cannot give direct evidence that he took the watch, but the circumstantial evidence points to him being guilty of stealing the it. The more circumstantial evidence the prosecution can assemble, then the better

the chance there is of a conviction. There often comes a tipping point when the weight of the circumstantial evidence become compelling to the jury. The huge amount of circumstantial evidence in the Wainwright case certainly made the charge compelling.

3. *Morning Post*, 2 Dec 1875, p. 2

Chapter Twenty-Two
1. *Illustrated Police News*, 11 Dec 1875 – p. 2 of the Supplement
2. *Evening Mail*, 3 Dec 1875, p. 3
3. *The Trial of the Wainwrights*, p. 232 Verdict and sentence
4. *Morning Post*, 2 Dec 1875, p. 2
5. *The Friend of India*, 8 Jan 1876, p. 41

Chapter Twenty-Three
1. *Penny Illustrated Paper*, 25 Sep 1875, p. 198
2. *Illustrated Police News*, 2 Oct 1875, p. 2
3. *Illustrated Police News*, 11 Dec 1875
4. *York Herald*, 13 Dec 1875
5. *Morpeth Herald*, 4 Mar 1876
6. CPI Inflation calculator
7. In 1883 John Lane's wife Elizabeth died. On 29 April 1885, John, aged 76, married 46-year-old widow Harriet Voice at South Hackney. His bride therefore became Harriet Lane! The marriage survived almost 6 years, till John's death on 22 March 1892.
8. Maryland Road is a road of dwellings and non-residential buildings and has only 4 Victorian looking properties left, having been replaced by featureless modern housing.

Chapter Twenty-Four
1. *Belfast Weekly Telegraph*, 11 Dec 1875
2. **Walter John Pelham.** (1839–1876) He was the son of solicitor Jabez Pelham He was a solicitor operating from 28A Arbour Square, Limehouse. Walter died on 4 September 1876, (Morning Post, 7 Sept 1876) only 8 months after the execution of his client Henry Wainwright.
3. *Belfast Weekly Telegraph*, 11 Dec 1875
4. *Diss Express*, 17 Dec 1875, p. 6
5. *Diss Express*, 17 Dec 1875, p. 2
6. *Bucks Herald*, 25 Mar 1876, p. 7
7. *Glasgow Herald*, 22 Dec 1875, p. 4
8. Rev Conder was the rector of Middleton, Sussex who had known Henry Wainwright as a schoolboy when he was a master at Barnet Grammar School (York Herald 8 Dec 1975)
9. Petition files under National Archives, HO144/19–48007/23
10. Richard Asheton Cross. (1823–1914); Home Secretary in Disraeli's Conservative Government from 1874 to 1880

11. John Liddle (1805–1885)
12. *North British Mail*, 22 Dec 1875, p. 5

Chapter Twenty-Five
1. Interview between – Henry and Thomas Wainwright – 8 Dec 1875. National Archives File **HO144/19/48007**; (48007/13 Document B)
2. Letter to Thomas Wainwright from Henry Wainwright. National Archives File. **HO144/19/48007**; (48007/ 13 – Document A)

Chapter Twenty-Six
1. Interview of Thomas Wainwright by visiting Magistrates, National Archives, Document 'D' – Ref HO/19/48007/13
2. The Victory Public House was situated at 167 Oxford Street, later numbered 384 in 1882. According to pub history website, London Pubs, Pubwiki.co.uk, the pub was in operation between at least 1839 to 1901.
3. Although Thomas doesn't elaborate on the possible plan for blaming Moore, it's possible that they were going pretend that as Moore also had the Hen and Chickens, they could say he hid the body of Harriet in the cellar and had absconded, hopefully blaming a man who may have fled abroad?
4. This statement has the ring of truth. If Thomas had been concerned in the murder or cutting up of the body, surely he would have assisted Henry in moving the body to the Hen and Chickens. Thomas' refusal to get involved with the movement of Harriet Lane seems to indicate that while he was happy to assist Henry with certain small activities, getting involved in moving a corpse was beyond what he was prepared to do. Why else would Henry have been forced to get help with the body from Alfred Stokes?
5. Was there another person impersonating Edward Frieake? A man called Farrant or Tarrant? Or was this another red herring?
6. I have found no documentation in the murder files at the National Archives to suggest whether Mr Arkell was approached by the Governor about Thomas Wainwright whereabouts.

Chapter Twenty-Seven
1. Transcripts from Nat Archive file; MEPO 3/191. 'Document F'. Reference 48007/13. (I have transcribed almost the whole of the record in its entirety except for a very few minor sentences in an attempt to shorten what is a long chapter. Henry's statement is so detailed and important, I felt it had to be included in full.)
2. This was the moment that Henry's life changed for good. He had given into Harriet's charms. He could not resist his newly discovered love.
3. Green Dragon Hotel, 61 Bishopsgate. The building existed from 1745 until it was demolished in the late nineteenth century.
4. Henry spares us any of the sordid details, but the Green Dragon would appear to be where the first act of adultery took place. Henry also did not try to deny that he was the father of both children

5. Of course, he is. He only wants to speak the truth now that it's too late. Talented liars often swear blind that they are telling the truth, so we cannot take his version as the gospel truth.

6. Henry seems to be trying to paint Harriet in a bad light. He mentions this mysterious, unnamed 'other man', and hints about a contagious disease. Was this an STD he was alluding to? He also fails to account for the fact that Harriet is pregnant again.

7. This was a major low point for Henry which has the ring of truth about it. He is backed into a corner. His private and business lives are both in great distress. Harriet Lane has him at her mercy. One word from her and the game would be up.

8. This last sentence of wandering the streets 'pondering his wretchedness' is convincing. He could not see which way to turn. It would be interesting to know whether he ever contemplated suicide during this period.

9. Henry's attack on Thomas could hardly have been any more venomous.

10. The Weavers Arms operated between 1839 and at least 1905. Its address was 13 Vallance Road. (London Pubology Website) www.pubology.co.uk/pubs

11. This mysterious woman was likely to have been Thomas' lady friend, Mrs Raper.

12. Henry asked for his statement to be passed to his brother William as well as his wife Elizabeth. Letters from both of them asking the authorities to send Henry's statement of 11 Dec 1875 to them were both declined. The letters still exist in the file at the National Archives.

13. Sidney Roberts Smith, (1832–1884) was the last Governor of Newgate, as after 1882, the gaol was no longer a place of punishment for convicts, and was only used to detain prisoners awaiting trial at the Old Bailey.

Chapter Twenty-Eight

1. William Thomas was 'Principle Warder' at Newgate according to the 1881 Census, RG11/374, P18, Sch 125

2. *LLOYDS WEEKLY* London newspaper, 26 Dec 75

3. *London Evening Standard*, 22 Dec 75, London was 6C and fine on 21 December 1875

4. *The Norwich Mercury*, 22 Dec 1875

5. *Lloyds Weekly* London Paper, 26 Dec 75

6. Death cert 5, City of London, St Sepulchre Registrars district, 22 Dec 1875

7. *Belfast Weekly News*, 12 Feb 1876

8. Home Office Instructions – www.capitalpunishmentuk.org/hanging1.html

9. The Closure of Newgate Prison & Auction of Creepy Lots by Neil Watson, *Whitechapel Society Journal*, April 2019 edition

10. Wikipedia https://en.wikipedia.org/wiki/William_Marwood

11. Information from Ian Eames, City of London Cemetery and Crematorium Department

12. The two-acre cemetery at Ilford is the largest in Europe and was opened in 1856. Famous burials include Sir Bobby Moore as well as Jack the Ripper victims, Catherine Eddowes and Mary Ann Nichols

Chapter Twenty-Nine

1. Petition to Home Secretary held in the National Archive, Reference HO/144/19/48007/54. **Home Secretary, Mr Richard Assheton Cross. (1823–1914). Conservative politician. He served in the post from 1874–80 under Disraeli, and also between 1885–6 under Lord Salisbury. (Wikipedia)** https://en.wikipedia.org/wiki/R._A._Cross,_1st_Viscount_Cross

2. National Archives: PCOM3, Piece number 564, Prison Registers, Home Office and Prison Commission; Male Licences

3. *Times of India*, 1 Jan 1876

4. Portland Prison Website. www.gov.uk/guidance/portland-prison

5. The huge 'Portland Breakwater', the 'Portland Breakwater Fort' and also the 'Verne Citadel' were all built by the prisoners. It was a herculean effort to collect the amount of stone that was needed to be quarried. 20 feet high Portland Stone walls surround the prison. If you look at the original entrance to the prison, built into the Portland Stone structure is a bright red pillar box. How sad that Thomas Wainwright hardly ever got to use this service. The small Grove Prison Museum is right next to the main entrance of the gaol.

6. *The North Briton* newspaper, 20 Oct 1877, p. 5

7. Richard Banner Oakley was the manager of the Co-Operative Credit Bank. He was convicted of defrauding customers out of £40,000 at the Old Bailey on 12 Aug 1876 and was sentenced to 5 years penal servitude – *Criminal Registers Old Bailey*, p. 271; he was released in July 1880, a year before Thomas Wainwright – *Stamford Mercury*, 20 Aug 1880.

8. Victorian penal discipline was very harsh. Each prisoner had a score card which was recorded on a weekly basis, and was dependant on the prisoner following all the prison rules. Any misbehaviour would lead to the loss of points. Thomas' monthly point total ranged from 201 to 279, this being mostly for the offence of talking. His Class also moved from time to time from class 1 to Class 3'

9. Then, as now, the prisons were full of hundreds of hardened criminals, many of the 'you wouldn't want to meet them in a dark alley' variety. Being a 'gentleman' in a rough prison may have been a struggle. Violence in prison was common, both on prison warders as well as on the inmates

10. *Illustrated Police News*, 8 Oct 1892; *Stamford Mercury*, 7 Oct 1892, p. 3

11. *Dundee Courier*, 4 Oct 1875

12. Caroline Wainwright died on 7 April 1877, aged 31 years. The cause of her death was Tuberculosis. Death Cert entry 218, Kentish Town, Pancras

13. Albert Square was renamed Albert Gardens, E1 in 1937 '*Ian's visits*' website www.ianvisits.co.uk/blog/2018/06/06/londons-pocket-parks-albert-square-gardens-e1

14. Probate Record, p. 124 London; T.G. Wainwright '*died on or since 19 Aug 1881*'. Died intestate dated London, 11 Nov 1909

15. Survivors Tales of Famous Crimes, edited by Walter Wood, published 1916https://archive.org/stream/survivorstalesof00wood/survivorstalesof00wood_djvu.txt

Chapter Thirty
1. www.nhs.uk/mental-health/conditions/antisocial-personality-disorder
2. *Illustrated Police News*, 18 Dec 1875, Supplement p. 2

Conclusion
1. This is exclusively my own opinion, though you may disagree!

Appendix I
1. *The Pall Mall Gazette*, 23 November 1886, P1–2.
2. George James Purkess (1832–1897) was son of a stationer / bookseller, George Purkess (1801–1859). (Yesterday's papers website The Purkess Family of Dean Street). http://john-adcock.blogspot.com/2014/04/the-purkess-family-of-dean-street.html. He took over the *IPN* in 1865.
3. Charles Peace 1832–1879, Notorious burglar and double murderer, hung at Armley Gaol 25 Feb 1879
4. *Illustrated Police News*, 18 Sep 1875
5. *Illustrated Police News* Supplement, 25 Dec 1875
6. *Illustrated Police News*, 25 Sep 1875
7. The photo taken of Alice Day was registered under the Copyright (Works of Art) Act on 23 September 1875 by Alfred Bowes of 86 Whitechapel Road. National Archive reference COPY 1/30/356
8. *The East Wind*, 4 Dec 1875, p. 5
9. This was the newspapers attempt to mimic the cockney calls of paper boys
10. *Daily Telegraph*, 28 Nov 1874
11. *Scotsman* newspaper, 2 May 1876
12. The Cosmopolitan Actor by J.B. Howe. See further details in Chapter on Henry Wainwright
13. Sun Insurance Company. In 1708 Charles Povey founded the Exchange House Fire Office. In 1710, Povey transferred his right to the Exchange House, also known as the Sun Fire Office. The name of the company was changed to the Sun Insurance Office in 1891. In 1959 it merged with Alliance to form Sun Alliance Assurance Ltd, and in 1996, Sun Alliance merged with Royal Insurance to form the Royal and Sun Alliance Insurance Group. Source; London Metropolitan Archive. https://search.lma.gov.uk/scripts/mwimain.dll/144/LMA_OPAC/web_detail/REFD+CLC~2FB~2F192?SESSIONSEARCH
14. *Morning Post*, 25 Oct 1875
15. *The Globe*, 13 April 1874, p. 4
16. The Cosmopolitan Actor by J.B. Howe. Online copy of A Cosmopolitan Actor, by J.B. Howe, Chap XXX, page 228. https://babel.hathitrust.org/cgi/pt?id=njp.32101066164185&view=1up&seq=7&skin=2021
17. The Wainwright family had long been customers of the Sun Insurance Company. Henry's father, Henry William, had been a policy holder in the late 1830–40s. In 1842, his father's insurance policy was mentioned in the Sun Alliance ledger book, number HA579, reference 1360211. The ledger

described number 84 Whitechapel Road as a dwelling with workshops. The property was mainly built of bricks and a small part of timber. The premises were insured for £500. The ledger is held at the Metropolitan London Archives.

18. *Madras Weekly News*, 10 August 1893

19. Wikipedia page entitled '*USRC Harriet Lane (1857)*'. The ship was launched in 1859 and was later abandoned at sea in 1881 https://en.wikipedia.org/wiki/USRC_Harriet_Lane_(1857)

20. *Foul Deeds and Suspicious Deaths in London's East End*, by Geoffrey Howse (Pen & Sword Books, 2005)

21. *Belfast Evening Telegraph*, 16 Oct 1876, p. 4

22. *Bradford Daily Telegraph*, 18 Oct 1875

23. *Belfast Newsletter*, 15 Jan 1876; *Greenock Herald* 1 Jan 1876; *Globe*, 12 Dec 1875

24. More behind the Blue Lamp Policing South and South East London, by David Swinden, Peter Kennison and Alan Moss, p. 252

25. *Illustrated Police News*, 29 Jan 1876

26. Victoria Lodge (1056) Masonic register, p. 184, entry no, 19; (Ancestry)

27. *York Herald*, 8 Dec 1875, p. 3

28. *Pall Mall Gazette*, 29 Nov 1875, p. 8

29. *Bury & Norwich Post*, 14 Dec 1875

30. *Sheffield Daily Telegraph*, 3 Jan 1876

31. *Reynolds Newspaper*, 26 Dec 1875

32. *The Renfrewshire Independent*, 21 Oct 1876

33. *York Herald*, 13 Dec 1875

34. *Aberdeen Evening Express*, 29 Oct 1886

35. **Prisoners' Counsel Act 1836.** The Act gave prisoners in felony trials the right to delegate the presentation of their defence to professional counsel. Prior to this alteration, prisoners could only rely on advocates to examine and cross examine witnesses and this was at the discretion of the trial judge. Should the prisoner have wished to put forward any defence to the court by way of an explanation or coherent narrative, they could only do this personally in a system labelled by John Langbein as the 'Accused speaks' trial. Such a trial relied almost exclusively upon the prisoner for an explanation of any possible defence. By forcing the prisoner to address the court, it was believed that the innocent accused was in the best position to demonstrate their innocence to the court. Theoretically, this was a genuinely truth-seeking measure but in reality, the terrified, inarticulate or mentally less adroit prisoner was rarely able to offer the court any information beyond pleading for mercy, whether they had committed the offence or not. *Law-crime-history /Journal* by Cerian Charlotte Griffiths

36. The Struggle to Make the Accused Competent in England and in Canada by Ronald D. Noble, 1970

Appendix II

1. IMDB; Oliver website

2. Register of burials at The City of London and Tower Hamlets Cemetery in Southern Grove, Mile End. p. 292

3. The Magnificent Seven. Seven huge cemeteries were built around London in the nineteenth century. The seven are; Tower Hamlets; Kensal Green; West Norwood; Highgate; Abney Park; Brompton and Nunhead
4. A short history of Tower Hamlets Cemetery has been produced. https://fothcp.org/wp-content/uploads/2019/06/THCP_LEAFLET_02.pdf
5. The grave number is 4236, and lies in Square 58
6. Charlie Brown was well known for the eclectic collection of antiques and oddities he'd acquired as payment for drink from sailors. His funeral was said to be the largest ever seen in the East End. https://londonist.com/london/secret/things-you-didn-t-know-about-tower-hamlets-cemetery
7. The plot was bought not long before the death of Henry William Wainwright and so the inscriptions relate to the person's relationship to him. The occupants of the plot are; Alfred Wainwright, son, 16 years (D. 23 Dec 1862); Henry William Wainwright, 60 years, (D. 27 Oct 1863); William Ventnor Wainwright, grandson, aged 3 months, (D. 19 Sep 1865); Martha Rickards, sister of Elizabeth, 69 years (D. 15 May 1871); James Wainwright, son, 45 years (1873); Elizabeth Wainwright, wife, 83 years (D. 2 May 1887); William George Wainwright, son, 53 years, (D. 27 Sep 1892). William George was the final interment, having shot himself at Dalston Junction in 1892
8. Survey of London Online. https://surveyoflondon.org/map/feature/874/detail/

Appendix III
1. The letters are in the National Archives File with the reference number, TS 18/1
2. The date 10 September 1874, if correct, would be an interesting one, as Harriet went missing on the following day. The postmark with the Waltham Cross postmark was clearly stamped in 1874 and on the 10th of the month. The month is the only doubt. It looks possibly like 'SP' though I cannot be sure

Appendix IV
1. 1861 Census, Reference RG9/102, Folio 71, Page 69
2. Marriage 419, Page 210, Holy Trinity Haverstock Hill Parish Church, Haverstock Hill, Middlesex
3. *Illustrated Police News*, 16 Oct 1875, P2
4. *Dundee Courier*, 4 Oct 1875
5. *Morpeth Herald*, 4 March 1876
6. Death Cert 218, Kentish Town, Middx, registered on 12 April 1877
7. TB was most commonly an infection of the lung and was a huge killer in the UK. The cause of TB was from being passed through the air from person to person through coughing, spitting, sneezing or speaking. It was also known as the 'White Death', as victims of the condition of often had an anemic pallor, while consumption was so called as the body *'wasted away'*
8. 1881 Census; Reference; RG11/770, Folio 14, Page 21

9. www.childrenshomes.org.uk/BisleySH (Children's Home Website)
10. *Illustrated London News*, 16 Jan 1869
11. The building which cost £5,757, was constructed by Carter and Son of Horseferry Road, Westminster. The frontage measured 160 feet and boasted swimming baths and its own infirmary
12. 1891 Census, reference; RG12/846, F 186, P9
13. Holy Trinity Church, Haverstock Hill; Baptism Register Page 32
14. Probate Report, London 11 Nov 1909, page 124
15. Probate Register, London 16 Nov 1909, page 124

Selected Bibliography

Murder of Harriet Lane – alias Mrs King by Henry Wainwright and Alice Day; (*National Archives Reference MEPO 3/121*). Police File, 1875.

R v Henry Wainwright and Thomas Wainwright – Murder; (*National Archives Reference TS 18/1*). Treasury File, 1875.

Wainwright, Henry; Central Criminal Court; Murder; Sentence: Death; Wainwright, Thomas G; Central Criminal Court; Accessory to Murder; Sentence: 7 years Penal Servitude. (*National Archives Reference HO 144/19/48007*). Home Office File 1875.

Trial of the Wainwrights, Edited by H.B. Irving, published 1920, price 10 shillings and sixpence. Superb record, contains 235 pages of details about the case including photos.

Memoirs of the Whitechapel Murderer, True Crime Magazine, Nov 1984 (Copy lodged in the Bishopsgate Institute)

The Murder of Harriet Lane – Pamphlet – published by Felix MacGlennon; 1930? (Copy lodged in the Bishopsgate Institute)

Illustrated Police News, the editions for September to December 1875 are an invaluable resource, especially in relation to the scores of drawings about the case. Available online at British Newspaper Archive or the British Library.

More behind the Blue Lamp, Policing South and South East London, by David Swinden, Peter Kennison & Alan Moss. (Coppermill Press, 2011). History of Stones End Police Station.

British Medical Journal, 11 Dec 1875. Report on the Post Mortem.

Old Bailey Online website, www.oldbaileyonline.org Details all the evidence.

The Good Old Days – Crime, murder and mayhem in Victorian London, by Gilda O'Neill (Viking, 2006)

A Cosmopolitan Actor, by H.B. Howe (Bedford Publishing Company, London, 1888)

Foul Deeds & Suspicious Death in London's East End, by Geoffrey Howse (Pen & Sword, 2005), Chapter 4

Survivors Tales of Famous Crimes, edited by Walter Wood, (Cassel, 1916)

Seventy-Two years at the Bar: A memoir, by Ernest Bowen-Rowlands (MacMillan, 1924), Includes a biographical memoir of Sir Harry B. Poland (Pages 379–386)

Fire – A Brief History, by Stephen J Pyne, (University of Washington Press, 2001)

Scotland Yard's History of Crime in 100 objects, by Alan Moss and Keith Skinner (The History Press, 2015)

Index